Autobiography

of a

Spiritually Incorrect Mystic

St. Martin's Griffin
New York

Autobiography of a Spiritually Incorrect Mystic

BY OSHO

Edited by Sarito Carol Neiman
Research by Ma Yoga Bhakti

www.stmartins.com

ISBN 0-312-25457-1 (hc)
ISBN 0-312-28071-8 (pbk)

10 9 8 7 6 5 4 3 2

Yes, I am the beginning of something new,
but not the beginning of a new religion.
I am the beginning of a new kind of religiousness,
which knows no adjectives, no boundaries;
which knows only freedom of the spirit,
silence of your being, growth of your potential,
and finally the experience of godliness within yourself—
not of a God outside you, but a godliness overflowing from you.

CONTENTS

Contents

PART TWO
REFLECTIONS IN AN EMPTY MIRROR: THE MANY FACES OF A MAN WHO NEVER WAS

PART THREE
THE LEGACY

APPENDIX
HIGHLIGHTS OF OSHO'S LIFE AND WORK

Contents

FOREWORD

Osho was asked many times why he didn't write an autobiography, or at least grant a series of interviews so that someone else could construct a historical account of his life. He would always dismiss these questions with a wave of his hand: timeless truths are important, he would say, not the newspaper clippings that we collect and call "history." Or, he would say, his biography is to be found in the sum of his work—in his hundreds of volumes of published talks, and in the transformed lives of the people he touched.

Nevertheless, the human mind hankers to make sense of events that happen in time. We want to grasp hold of a context within which we can persuade ourselves that we understand the meaning of the "stuff" that happens— especially when these happenings appear to be contradictory, startling, unusual. This volume is a recognition that the time has come to provide that context for understanding Osho and his work.

Ten years have passed since, in the words of his attending physician, Osho prepared for his departure from the body that had served him for fifty-nine years "as calmly as though he were packing for a weekend in the country." And in a very real sense, this autobiography could not have been assembled without that passage of time and the profound changes that have come about as a result. Since Osho packed up and went for his weekend in the country, both CNN and the Internet have been born. The utopian vision that Osho spoke of so often—of a world without the divisions of national boundaries, of race or religion, gender or creed—is now at least imaginable, even if it is not yet a reality. Meditation, which Osho insists again and again lies at the very core of his message, is not just the obscure and puzzling interest of a few eccentrics but has become increasingly recognized for its potential to benefit everybody from stressed-out business executives to cancer patients. In other words, although Osho is unquestionably still a man ahead of his time, the time has at least caught up with him enough to make it possible for more people to comprehend his unique perspective and vision.

On a more practical level, time and technology have allowed the custodians of Osho's vast body of work to digitize and make available for research nearly five thousand hours of his recorded talks in English, plus hundreds more discourses as they become available in translation from the Hindi. This means that within a matter of seconds one can know that in these talks, Osho uses variations of the word *meditation* twenty-five thousand times, and the word *love* nearly forty-two thousand times. Variations of the word *sex*, which was thought to be an unseemly topic for a mystic to speak about in the 1960s in India, appear just nine thousand three hundred times—two thousand more than references to politics and politicians.

Of course, to research the material for instances where Osho spoke directly about his own life demands more human intelligence than computer software can provide. Without three years of work dedicated specifically to that task, this book could not have happened. And finally, to construct an autobiography from the available material—one that honors Osho's understanding of the relative importance of the "truth" versus the "fact," of the timeless versus the momentary—requires a somewhat foolhardy willingness to undertake the impossible.

Example: For a number of years after graduating from the university, Osho taught philosophy. The fact-oriented mind labels him "a former philosophy professor," thereby satisfying itself that it knows something important about who he is. But as far as Osho is concerned, he might as well have been a shoemaker or a carpenter. The important thing is not what he *does*, but who he *is*. The fact-oriented mind wants to define people by what they do rather than who they are, by what possessions they acquire in life rather than what understandings they take with them when they die. But it is precisely the dimension of "being"—not the dimension of "doing" or "having"—that is Osho's central concern. To the extent that we assign significance to the outer events of his life based on our own values of "doing" and "having," we are bound to misunderstand him.

But, timeless truths aside, the fact is that Osho trained himself not to make shoes or build furniture, but to express himself in words. Both his friends and his enemies agree that he does this with uncommon eloquence, insight, and humor. To select the "right" words to represent his life might have been possible, even easy, if Osho had a consistent philosophy that he was trying to teach people. He does not. It might have been possible if he had been part of a tradition that he was trying to uphold, or declared that he was some sort of supernatural messenger or prophet who had come to found a new tradition. Nothing could be farther from the truth. On the contrary, he repeatedly emphasizes that he is not only not part of any tradition but has done everything humanly possible to prevent the creation of a tradition around him once he is gone.

So the words in this volume are not intended to be—cannot be, by the very nature of its subject—the definitive answer to the question, "Who is Osho?" They are, rather, a guide to the ongoing pursuit of that question in the context of the timeless as well as the timely, in the context of "being" as well as "doing." In the end, Osho says, we will come to know who he is only when we come to know who *we* are. In handing us that challenge, he invites us to learn from his life what we can, but to recognize that it is meaningful only to the extent that it points us in the direction of learning more about ourselves.

Sarito Carol Neiman

PREFACE

T he first thing you have to understand is the difference between the fact
and the truth. Ordinary history takes care about the facts—what actually happens in the world of matter, the incidents. It does not take care
about the truth because truth does not happen in the world of matter, it happens in consciousness. And man is not yet mature enough to take care about
the events of consciousness.

He surely takes note of events happening in time and in space; those are
the facts. But he is not mature enough, not insightful enough to take notice of
what happens beyond time and beyond space—in other words, what happens
beyond mind, what happens in consciousness. One day we will have to write
the whole of history with a totally different orientation, because the facts are
trivia—although they are material, they don't matter. And the truths are imma-
terial but they matter.

The new orientation for a future history will concern itself with what happened inside Gautam Buddha when he became enlightened, what went on happening while he was in the body for forty-two years after his enlightenment. And
what was happening in those forty-two years is not going to be discontinued just
because the body drops dead. It had no concern with the body, it was a phenomenon in consciousness—and consciousness continues. The pilgrimage of the
consciousness is endless. So what was happening in the consciousness, inside the
body, will go on happening outside the body. That is a simple understanding.

This story is a story of inner happenings.

PART ONE

Just an Ordinary Human Being: The History Behind the Legend

Q: *Who are you?*

A: I am just myself. No prophet, no messiah, no Christ. Just an ordinary human being . . . just like you.

Q: *Well, not quite!*

A: That's true . . . not quite! You are still asleep—but that is not much of a difference. One day I was also asleep; one day you will be able to awaken. You can wake up this moment, nobody is preventing it. So the difference is just meaningless.

•from an interview with Roberta Green, *Santa Ana Register,* Orange County, California

GLIMPSES OF A
GOLDEN CHILDHOOD

I have never been spiritual in the sense that you understand the word. I have never gone to the temples or the churches, or read scriptures, or followed certain practices to find truth, or worshiped God or prayed to God. That has not been my way at all. So certainly you can say that I was not doing anything spiritual. But to me, spirituality has a totally different connotation. It needs an honest individuality. It does not allow any kind of dependence. It creates a freedom for itself, whatever the cost. It is never in the crowd but alone, because the crowd has never found any truth. The truth has been found only in people's aloneness.

So my spirituality has a different meaning from your idea of spirituality. My childhood stories, if you can understand them, will point to all these qualities in some way or other. Nobody can call them spiritual. I call them spiritual because to me, they have given all that man can aspire to.

While listening to my childhood stories you should try to look for some quality—not just the story but some intrinsic quality that runs like a thin thread through all of my memoirs. And that thin thread is spiritual.

Spiritual, to me, simply means finding oneself. I never allowed anybody to do this work on my behalf—because nobody can do this work on your behalf; you have to do it yourself.

1931–1939:
KUCHWADA, MADHYA PRADESH, INDIA

I am reminded of the small village where I was born. Why existence should have chosen that small village in the first place is unexplainable. It is as it should be. The village was beautiful. I have traveled far and wide, but I have never come across that same beauty. One never comes again to the same. Things come and go, but it is never the same.

I can see that still, small village. Just a few huts near a pond, and a few tall trees where I used to play. There was no school in the village. That is of great importance, because I remained uneducated for almost nine years, and those are the most formative years. After that, even if you try, you cannot be educated. So in a way I am still uneducated, although I hold many degrees—and not just any degree, but a first-class master's degree. Any fool can do that; so many fools do it every year that it has no significance. What is significant is that for my first years I remained without education. There was no school, no road, no railway, no post office. What a blessing! That small village was a world unto itself. Even in my times away from that village I remained in that world, uneducated.

And I have come across millions of people, but the people of that village were more innocent than any, because they were very primitive. They knew nothing of the world. Not even a single newspaper had ever entered that village—you can now understand why there was no school. Not even a primary school—what a blessing! No modern child can afford it.

IN THE PAST THERE WERE CHILDREN MARRIED BEFORE THEY WERE TEN. Sometimes children were even married when they were still in their mother's womb. Just two friends would decide: "Our wives are pregnant, so if one gives birth to a boy and the other gives birth to a girl, then the marriage is settled, promised." The question of asking the boy and the girl does not arise at all; they are not even born yet! But if one is a boy and another is a girl, the marriage is settled. And people kept their word.

My own mother was married when she was seven years old. My father was not more than ten years old, and he had no understanding of what was happening. I used to ask him, "What was the most significant thing that you enjoyed in your wedding?"

He said, "Riding on the horse." Naturally! For the first time he was dressed like a king, with a knife hanging by his side, and he was sitting on the horse and everybody was walking around him. He enjoyed it tremendously. That was the thing he enjoyed most about his wedding. A honeymoon was out of the question. Where will you send a ten-year-old boy and a seven-year-old girl for a honeymoon? So in India the honeymoon never used to exist, and in the past, nowhere else in the world either.

When my father was ten years old and my mother was seven years old, my father's mother died. After the marriage, perhaps one or two years afterward, the whole responsibility fell on my mother, who was only nine years old. My father's mother had left two small daughters and two small boys. So there were four children, and the responsibility to care for them fell on a nine-year-old girl and a twelve-year-old son. My father's father never liked to live in the city where he had his shop. He loved the countryside, and when his wife died he was absolutely free. The government used to give land to people for free, because there was so much land and there were not so many people to cultivate it. So my grandfather got fifty acres of land from the government, and he left the whole shop in the hands of his children—my father and mother—who were only twelve and nine years old. He enjoyed creating a garden, creating a farm, and he loved to live there in the open air. He hated the city.

So my father never had any experience of the freedom of young people today. He never became a youth in that way. Before he could have become a youth he was already old, taking care of his younger brothers and sisters and the shop. And by the time he was twenty he had to arrange marriages for his sisters, marriages and education for his brothers.

I have never called my mother "Mother," because before I was born she was taking care of four children who used to call her *bhabhi. Bhabhi* means "brother's wife." And because four children were already calling my mother *bhabhi,* I also started calling her *bhabhi*. I learned it from the very beginning, when four other children were calling her that.

I WAS BROUGHT UP BY MY MATERNAL GRANDFATHER AND GRAND-mother. Those two old people were alone and they wanted a child who would be the joy of their last days. So my father and mother agreed: I was their eldest child, the firstborn; they sent me.

I don't remember any relationship with my father's family in the early years of my childhood. I spent my earliest years with two old men—my grandfather and his old servant, who was really a beautiful man—and my old grandmother. These three people . . . and the gap was so big, I was absolutely alone. These old people were not company, could not be company for me. And I had nobody else, because in that small village my family was the richest; and it was such a small village—not more than two hundred people in all—and so poor that my grandparents would not allow me to mix with the village children. They were dirty, and of course they were almost beggars. So there was no way to have friends. That caused a great impact. In my whole life I have never known anybody to be a friend. Yes, acquaintances I had.

In those first, early years I was so lonely that I started enjoying it—and it is really a joy. So it was not a curse to me, it proved a blessing. I started enjoying it, and I started feeling self-sufficient; I was not dependent on anybody.

I have never been interested in games for the simple reason that from my very childhood there was no way to play; there was nobody to play with. I can still see myself in those earliest years, just sitting. We had a beautiful spot where our house was, just in front of a lake. Far away for miles, the lake . . . and it was so beautiful and so silent. Only once in a while would you see a line of white cranes flying, or making love calls, and the peace would be disturbed; otherwise, it was almost the perfect place for meditation. And when a love call from a bird would disturb the peace . . . after his call the peace would deepen.

The lake was full of lotus flowers, and I would sit for hours so self-content, as if the world did not matter: the lotuses, the white cranes, and the silence . . .

And my grandparents became very aware of one thing—that I enjoyed my aloneness. They had seen that I had no desire to go to the village to meet anybody, or to talk with anybody. Even if they wanted to talk, my answers were yes or no; I was not interested in talking either. They became aware of one thing— that I enjoyed my aloneness and it was their sacred duty not to disturb me.

So for seven years continuously nobody tried to corrupt my innocence; there was nobody. Those three old people who lived in the house, the servant and my grandparents, were all protective in every possible way that nobody should disturb me. In fact I started feeling, as I grew up, a little embarrassed that because of me they could not talk, they could not be normal as everybody is.

It happens with children that you tell them, "Be silent because your father is thinking, your grandfather is resting. Be quiet, sit silently." In my childhood it happened the opposite way. Now I cannot answer why and how; it simply happened. The credit does not go to me.

All those three old people were continually making signs to each other: "Don't disturb him—he is enjoying so much." And they started loving my silence.

Silence has its vibe; it is infectious, particularly a child's silence, which is not forced, which is not because you are saying, "I will beat you if you create any nuisance or noise." No, that is not silence. That will not create the joyous vibration that I am talking about, when a child is silent on his own, enjoying for no reason; his happiness is uncaused. That creates great ripples all around.

So it was just a coincidence that for seven years I remained undisturbed—no one to nag me, to prepare me for the world of business, politics, diplomacy. My grandparents were more interested in leaving me as natural as possible—particularly my grandmother. She is one of the causes—these small things affect all your life patterns—she is one of the causes of my respect for the whole of womanhood. She was a simple woman, uneducated, but immensely sensitive. She made it clear to my grandfather and the servant: "We all have lived a certain kind of life which has not led us anywhere. We are as empty as ever, and now death is coming close." She insisted, "Let this child be uninfluenced by us. What influence can we have? We can only make him like us, and we are nothing. Give him an opportunity to be himself."

My grandfather—I heard them discussing in the night, thinking that I was asleep—used to say to her, "You are telling me to do this and I am doing it; but he is somebody else's son, and sooner or later he will have to go to his parents. What will they say? 'You have not taught him any manners, any etiquette, he is absolutely wild.' "

She said, "Don't be worried about that. In this whole world everybody is civilized, has manners, etiquette, but what is the gain? You are very civilized—what have you got out of it? At the most his parents will be angry with us. So what? Let them be angry. They can't harm us, and by that time the child will be strong enough that they cannot change his life course."

I am tremendously grateful to that old woman. My grandfather was again and again worried that sooner or later he was going to be responsible:

"They will say, 'We left our child with you and you have not taught him anything.' "

My grandmother did not even allow a tutor. There was one man in the village who could at least teach me the beginnings of language, mathematics, a little geography. He was educated only to the fourth grade—the lowest four, that is what was called primary education in India—but he was the most educated man in the town. My grandfather tried hard: "He can come and he can teach him. At least he will know the alphabet, some mathematics, so when he goes to his parents they will not say that we just wasted seven years completely."

But my grandmother said, "Let them do whatsoever they want to do after seven years. For seven years he has to be just his natural self, and we are not going to interfere." And her argument was always, "You know the alphabet, so what? You know mathematics, so what? You have earned a little money; do you want him also to earn a little money and live just like you?"

That was enough to keep that old man silent. What to do? He was in a difficulty because he could not argue—and he knew that he would be held responsible, not she, because my father would ask him, "What have you done?" And actually that would have been the case, but fortunately he died before my father could ask.

Later on my father was always saying, "That old man is responsible, he has spoiled the child." But now I was strong enough, and I made it clear to him: "In front of me, never say a single word against my maternal grandfather. He has saved me from being spoiled by you—that is your real anger. But you have other children—spoil them. And in the end you will see who is spoiled."

He had other children, and more and more children kept on coming. I used to tease him, "Please bring one child more, make it a dozen. Eleven children? People ask, 'How many children?' Eleven does not look right; one dozen is more impressive." And in later years I used to tell him, "You go on spoiling all your children; I am wild, and I will remain wild." Somehow I remained out of the grip of civilization.

MY GRANDFATHER—MY MOTHER'S FATHER—WAS A GENEROUS MAN. He was poor, but rich in his generosity. He gave to each and everyone whatsoever he had. I learned the art of giving from him; I never saw him say no to any beggar or anybody.

I called my mother's father "Nana"; that's the way the mother's father is called in India. The mother's mother is called "Nani." I used to ask my grandfather, "Nana, where did you get such a beautiful wife?" Her features were not Indian, she looked Greek, and she was a strong woman, very strong. My nana died when he was not more than fifty. My grandmother lived till eighty and she was fully healthy. Even then nobody thought she was going to die. I promised her one thing, that when she died I would come. And that was my last visit to the family—she died in 1970. I had to fulfill my promise.

For my first years I knew my nani as my mother; those are the years when one grows. My own mother came after that; I was already grown up, already made in a certain style. And my grandmother helped me immensely. My grandfather loved me, but could not help me much. He was so loving, but to be of help more is needed—a certain kind of strength. He was always afraid of my grandmother. He was, in a sense, a henpecked husband. But he loved me, he helped me . . . what can I do if he was a henpecked husband? Ninety-nine point nine percent of husbands are, so it is okay.

I CAN UNDERSTAND THE OLD MAN, MY GRANDFATHER, AND THE trouble my mischief caused him. The whole day he would sit on his gaddi, as the seat of a rich man is called in India, listening less to his customers and more to the complainers! But he used to say to them, "I am ready to pay for any damage he has done, but remember, I am not going to punish him."

Perhaps his very patience with me, a mischievous child . . . even I could not tolerate it. If a child like that were given to me for years . . . my god! Even for minutes, and I would throw the child out of the door forever. Perhaps those years worked a miracle for my grandfather; that immense patience paid. He became more and more silent. I saw it growing every day. Once in a while I would say, "Nana, you can punish me. You need not be so tolerant." And, can you believe it, he would cry! Tears would come to his eyes, and he would say, "Punish you? I cannot do that. I can punish myself but not you."

Never for a single moment have I ever seen the shadow of anger toward me in his eyes—and believe me, I did everything that one thousand children could do. In the morning, even before breakfast, I was into my mischief until late at night. Sometimes I would come home so late—three o'clock in the morning—but what a man he was! He never said, "You are too late. This is not the time for a child to come home." No, not even once. In fact, in front of me he would avoid looking at the clock on the wall.

He never took me to the temple where he used to go. I also used to go to that temple, but only when it was closed, just to steal prisms, because in that temple there were many chandeliers with beautiful prisms. I think, by and by, I stole almost all of them. When my grandfather was told about it, he said, "So what! I donated the chandeliers, so I can donate others. He is not stealing; it is his nana's property. I made that temple." The priest stopped complaining. What was the point? He was just a servant to Nana.

Nana used to go to the temple every morning, yet he never said, "Come with me." He never indoctrinated me. That is what is great . . . not to indoctrinate. It is so human to force a helpless child to follow your beliefs, but he remained untempted. Yes, I call it the greatest temptation. The moment you see someone dependent on you in any way, you start indoctrinating. He never even said to me, "You are a Jaina."

I remember perfectly—it was the time that the census was being taken. The officer had come to our house. He made many inquiries about many things. They asked about my grandfather's religion; he said, "Jainism." They then asked about my grandmother's religion. My nana said, "You can ask her yourself. Religion is a private affair. I myself have never asked her." What a man!

My grandmother answered, "I do not believe in any religion whatsoever. All religions look childish to me." The officer was shocked. Even I was taken aback. She does not believe in any religion at all! In India to find a woman who does not believe in any religion at all is impossible. But she was born in Khajuraho, perhaps into a family of Tantrikas who have never believed in any religion. They have practiced meditation, but they have never believed in any religion.

It sounds very illogical to a Western mind: meditation without religion? Yes . . . in fact, if you believe in any religion you cannot meditate. Religion is an interference in your meditation. Meditation needs no God, no heaven, no hell, no fear of punishment, and no allurement of pleasure. Meditation has nothing to do with mind; meditation is beyond it, whereas religion is only mind, it is within mind.

I know Nani never went to the temple, but she taught me one mantra that I will reveal for the first time. It is a Jain mantra, but it has nothing to do with Jainas as such. It is purely accidental that it is related to Jainism. . . .

The mantra is so beautiful; it is going to be difficult to translate it, but I will do my best . . . or my worst. First listen to the mantra in its original beauty:

Namo arihantanam namo namo / Namo siddhanam namo namo / Namo uva-jjhayanam namo namo / Namo loye savva sahunam namo namo / Aeso panch nam-mukaro / Savva pavappanano / Mangalam cha savvesam padhamam havai mangalam / Arihante saranam pavajjhami / Siddhe saranam pavajjhami / Sahu saranam pava-jjhami / Namo arihantanam namo namo / Namo siddhanam namo namo / Namo uvajjhayanam namo namo / Om, shantih, shantih, shantih. . . .

Now my effort at translation: "I go to the feet of, I bow down to, the *ari-hantas*. . . ." *Arihanta* is the name in Jainism, as *arhat* is in Buddhism, for one who has achieved the ultimate but cares nothing about anybody else. He has come home and turned his back on the world. He does not create a religion, he does not even preach, he does not even declare. Of course he has to be remembered first. The first remembrance is for all those who have known and remained silent. The first respect is not for words, but for silence. Not for serving others, but for the sheer achievement of one's self. It does not matter whether one serves others or not; that is secondary, not primary. The primary is that one has achieved one's self, and it is so difficult in this world to know one's self. . . .

The Jains call the person *arihanta* who has attained to himself and is so drowned, so drunk in the beatitude of his realization that he has forgotten the whole world. The word *arihanta* literally means "one who has killed the enemy"—and the enemy is the ego. The first part of the mantra means, "I touch the feet of the one who has attained himself."

The second part is: *Namo siddhanam namo namo*. This mantra is in Prakrit, not Sanskrit. Prakrit is the language of the Jains; it is more ancient than Sanskrit. The very word *sanskrit* means refined. You can understand by the word *refined* that there must have been something before it, otherwise what are you going to refine? *Prakrit* means unrefined, natural, raw, and the Jains are correct when they say their language is the most ancient in the world. Their religion, too, is the most ancient. The mantra is in Prakrit, raw and unrefined. The second line is: *Namo siddhanam namo namo*—"I touch the feet of the one who has become his being." So, what is the difference between the first and the second? The *arihanta* never looks back, never both-ers about any kind of service, Christian or otherwise. The *siddha* once in a while holds out his hand to drowning humanity—but only once in awhile, not always. It is not a necessity, it is not compulsory; it is his choice. He may or he may not.

Hence the third: *Namo uvajjhayanam namo namo*—"I touch the feet of the masters, the *uvajjhaya*." They have achieved the same, but they face the world, they serve the world. They are in the world and not of it . . . but still in it.

The fourth: *Namo loye savva sahunam namo namo*—"I touch the feet of the teachers." You know the subtle difference between a master and a teacher. The master has known, and imparts what he has known. The teacher has received from one who has known, and delivers it intact to the world, but he himself has not known. The composers of this mantra are really beautiful; they even touch the feet of those who have not known themselves, but at least are carrying the message of the masters to the masses.

Number five is one of the most significant sentences I have ever come across in my whole life. It is strange that it was given to me by my grand-mother when I was a small child. When I explain it to you, you too will see the beauty of it. Only she was capable of giving it to me. I don't know any-body else who had the guts to really proclaim it, although all Jainas repeat it in their temples. But to repeat is one thing; to impart it to one you love is totally another.

"I touch the feet of all those who have known themselves" . . . without any distinction, whether they are Hindus, Jainas, Buddhists, Christians, Mohammedans. The mantra says, "I touch the feet of all those who have known themselves." This is the only mantra, as far as I know, that is absolutely nonsectarian.

The other four parts are not different from the fifth; they are all contained in it, but it has a vastness that those others do not have. The fifth line ought to be written on all the temples, all the churches, irrespective of to whom they belong, because it says, "I touch the feet of all those who have known it." It does not say, "who have known God." Even the "it" can be dropped: I am only putting "it" in the translation. The original simply means, "touching the feet of those who have known"—no "it." I am putting "it" in just to fulfill the demands of your language; otherwise someone is bound to ask, "Known? Known what? What is the object of knowledge?" There is no object of knowl-edge; there is nothing to know, only the knower.

This mantra was the only religious thing, if you can call it religious, given to me by my grandmother—not by my grandfather but by my grandmother.

One night she said, "You look awake. Can't you sleep? Are you planning tomorrow's mischief?"

I said, "No, but somehow a question is arising in me. Everybody has a religion, and when people ask me, 'To what religion do you belong?' I shrug my shoulders. Now, certainly shrugging your shoulders is not a religion, so I want to ask you, what should I say?"

She said, "I myself don't belong to any religion, but I love this mantra, and this is all I can give you—not because it is traditionally Jaina, but only because I have known its beauty. I have repeated it millions of times and always I have found tremendous peace . . . just the feeling of touching the feet of all those who have known. I can give you this mantra; more than that is not possible for me."

Now I can say that woman was really great, because as far as religion is concerned, everybody is lying. Christians, Jews, Jainas, Mohammedans—everybody is lying. They all talk of God, heaven and hell, angels and all kinds of nonsense, without knowing anything at all. She was great, not because she knew but because she was unable to lie to a child.

Nobody should lie—to a child, at least, it is unforgivable. Children have been exploited for centuries just because they are willing to trust. You can lie to them very easily and they will trust you. If you are a father, a mother, they will think you are bound to be true. That's how the whole of humanity lives in corruption, in a very slippery, thick mud of lies told to children for centuries. If we can do just one thing, a simple thing—not lie to children and to confess to them our ignorance—then we will be religious and we will put them on the path of religion. Children are only innocence; leave them not your so-called knowledge. But you yourself must first be innocent, unlying, true.

JAINISM IS THE MOST ASCETIC RELIGION IN THE WORLD, OR IN OTHER words the most masochistic and sadistic. Jaina monks torture themselves so much that one wonders if they are insane. They are not. They are businessmen, and the followers of the Jaina monks are all businessmen. It is strange, the whole Jaina community consists only of businessmen—but not really strange because the religion itself is basically motivated for profit in the other world. The Jaina tortures himself in order to gain something in the other world that he knows he cannot attain in this.

I must have been about four or five years old when I saw the first naked Jaina monk being invited into my grandmother's house. I could not resist laughing. My grandfather told me, "Keep quiet! I know you are a nuisance. I can forgive you when you are a pain in the neck to the neighbors, but I cannot forgive you if you try to be mischievous with my guru. He is my master; he initiated me into the inner secrets of religion."

I said, "I am not concerned about the inner secrets, I am concerned about the outer secrets that he is showing so clearly. Why is he naked? Can't he at least wear short pants?"

Even my grandfather laughed. He said, "You don't understand."

I said, "Okay, I will ask him myself."

All the villagers had assembled for the darshan of the Jaina monk. In the middle of the so-called sermon I stood up. That was forty or so years ago, and since then I have been fighting these idiots continuously. That day a war began that is only going to end when I am no more. Perhaps it may not end even then; my people may continue it.

I asked simple questions that he could not answer. I was puzzled. My grandfather was ashamed. My grandmother patted me on the back and said, "Great! You did it! I knew you were able to."

What had I asked? Just simple questions. I had asked, "Why don't you want to be born again?" That's a very simple question in Jainism, because Jainism is nothing but an effort not to be born again. It is the whole science of preventing rebirth. So I asked him the basic question, "Don't you ever want to be born again?"

He said, "No, never."

Then I asked, "Why don't you commit suicide? Why are you still breathing? Why eat? Why drink water? Just disappear, commit suicide. Why make so much fuss over a simple thing?" He was not more than forty years of age. . . . I said to him, "If you continue in this way, you may have to continue for another forty years or even more." It is a scientific fact that people who eat less live longer. . . .

So I said to the monk—I did not know these facts then—"If you don't want to be born again, why are you living? Just to die? Then why not commit suicide?" I don't think anybody had ever asked him such a question. In polite society nobody ever asks a real question, and the question of suicide is the most real of all.

Marcel says: Suicide is the only real philosophical question. I had no idea of Marcel then. Perhaps at that time there was no Marcel, and his book had not been written yet. But this is what I said to the Jaina monk: "If you don't want to be born again, which you say is your desire, then why do you live? For what? Commit suicide! I can show you a way. Although I don't know much about the ways of the world, as far as suicide is concerned I can give you some advice. You can jump off the hill at the side of the village, or you can jump into the river."

I told the Jaina monk, "In the rainy season you can jump into the river with me. We can keep company for a little while, then you can die, and I will reach the other shore. I can swim well enough."

He looked at me so fiercely, so full of anger, that I had to tell him, "Remember, you will have to be born again because you are still full of anger. This is not the way to get rid of the world of worries. Why are you looking at me so angrily? Answer my question in a peaceful and silent way. Answer joyously! If you cannot answer, simply say, 'I don't know.' But don't be angry."

The man said, "Suicide is a sin. I cannot commit suicide. But I want never to be born again. I will achieve that state by slowly renouncing everything that I possess."

I said, "Please show me something that you possess—because, as far as I can see, you are naked and you don't possess anything. What possessions do you have?"

My grandfather tried to stop me. I pointed toward my grandmother and then said to him, "Remember, I asked permission of Nani, and now nobody can prevent me, not even you. I spoke to her about you because I was worried that if I interrupted your guru and his rubbishy, so-called sermon, you would be angry with me. She said, 'Just point toward me, that's all. Don't be worried: just a look from me and he will become silent.'" And strange . . . it was true! He became silent, even without a look from my nani.

Later on my nani and I both laughed. I said to her, "He did not even look at you."

She said, "He could not, because he must have been afraid that I would say, 'Shut up! Don't interfere with the child.' So he avoided me. The only way to avoid me was to not interfere with you."

In fact he closed his eyes as if he was meditating. I said to him, "Nana, great! You are angry, boiling, there is fire within you, yet you sit with closed eyes as if you are meditating. Your guru is angry because my questions are annoying him. You are angry because your guru is not capable of answering. But I say, this man who is sermonizing here is just an imbecile." And I was not more than four or five years old.

From that time on that has remained my language. I immediately recognize the idiot wherever he is, whoever he is. Nobody can escape my X-ray eyes.

I DON'T REMEMBER THE NAME OF THE JAINA MONK, PERHAPS HIS name was Shanti Sagar, meaning "ocean of bliss." He certainly was not that. That is why I have forgotten even his name. He was just a dirty puddle, not an ocean of bliss or peace. And he was certainly not a man of silence, because he became very angry.

Shanti can mean many things. It may mean peace, it may mean silence; those are the two basic meanings. Both were missing in him. He was neither peaceful nor silent, not at all. Nor could you say that he was without any turmoil in him because he became so angry that he shouted at me to sit down.

I said, "Nobody can tell me to sit down in my own house. I can tell you to get out, but you cannot tell me to sit down. But I will not tell you to get out because I have a few more questions. Please don't be angry. Remember your name, Shanti Sagar—ocean of peace and silence. You could at least be a little pool. And don't be disturbed by a little child."

Without bothering whether he was silent or not, I asked my grandmother, who was by now all laughter, "What do you say, Nani? Should I ask him more questions, or tell him to get out of our house?"

I did not ask my grandfather, of course, because this man was his guru. My nani said, "You can ask whatsoever you want to, and if he cannot answer, the door is open, he can get out."

That was the woman I loved. That was the woman who made me a rebel. Even my grandfather was shocked that she supported me in such a way. That so-called Shanti Sagar immediately became silent the moment he saw that my grandmother supported me. Not only her, the villagers were immediately on my side. The poor Jaina monk was left absolutely alone.

I asked him a few more questions. I asked, "You have said, 'Don't believe anything unless you have experienced it yourself.' I see the truth in that, hence this question. . . ."

Jainas believe there are seven hells. Up to the sixth there is a possibility of coming back, but the seventh is eternal. Perhaps the seventh is the Christian hell, because there too, once you are in it you are in it forever. I continued, "You referred to seven hells, so the question arises, have you visited the seventh? If you have, then you could not be here. If you have not, on what authority do you say that it exists? You should say that there are only six hells, not seven. Now please be correct: Say that there are only six hells, or if you want to insist on seven, then prove to me that at least one man, Shanti Sagar, has come back from the seventh hell."

He was dumbfounded. He could not believe that a child could ask such a question. Today, I too cannot believe it! How could I ask such a question? The only answer I can give is that I was uneducated, and utterly without any knowledge. Knowledge makes you very cunning. I was not cunning. I simply asked the question that any child could have asked if he were not educated. Education is the greatest crime man has committed against poor children. Perhaps the last liberation in the world will be the liberation of children.

I was innocent, utterly unknowledgeable. I could not read or write, not even count beyond my fingers. Even today, when I have to count anything I start with my fingers, and if I miss a finger I get mixed up. He could not answer. My grandmother stood up and said, "You have to answer the question. Don't think that only a child is asking; I am also asking and I am your hostess."

Now again I have to introduce you to a Jaina convention. When a Jaina monk comes to a family to receive his food, after taking his meal, as a blessing to the family, he gives a sermon. The sermon is addressed to the hostess. My grandmother said, "I am your hostess today, and I also am asking the same question. Have you visited the seventh hell? If not, say truthfully that you have not, but then you cannot say there are seven hells."

The monk became so puzzled and confused—more so by being confronted by a beautiful woman—that he started to leave. My nani shouted, "Stop! Don't leave! Who is going to answer my child's question? And he still has a few more to ask. What kind of man are you, escaping from a child's questions!"

The man stopped. I said to him, "I drop the second question, because the monk cannot answer it. He has not answered the first question either, so I will ask him the third; perhaps he may be able to answer that."

He looked at me. I said, "If you want to look at me, look into my eyes." There was great silence, nobody said a word. The monk lowered his eyes, and I then said, "Then I don't want to ask. My first two questions are unanswered, and the third is not asked because I don't want a guest of the house to be ashamed. I withdraw." And I really withdrew from the gathering, and I was so happy when my grandmother followed me.

The monk was given his farewell by my grandfather, but as soon as he had left, my grandfather rushed back into the house and asked my grandmother, "Are you mad? First you supported this boy who is a born troublemaker, then you went with him without even saying good-bye to my master."

My grandmother said, "He is not my master, so I don't care a bit. Moreover, what you think to be a born troublemaker is the seed. Nobody knows what will come out of it."

I know now what has come out of it. Unless one is a born troublemaker one cannot become a buddha. And I am not just a buddha as Gautam the Buddha is; that is too traditional. I am Zorba the Buddha. I am a meeting of the East and the West. In fact, I do not divide East and West, higher and lower, man and woman, good and bad, God and the devil. No, a thousand times no—I don't divide. I join together all that has been divided up to now. That is my work.

That day is immensely significant in order to understand what happened during my whole life, because unless you understand the seed, you will miss the tree and the flowering, and perhaps the moon through the branches.

From that very day I have always been against everything masochistic. Of course I came to know the word much later, but the word does not matter. I have been against all that is ascetic; even that word was not known to me in those days, but I could smell something foul. You know I am allergic to all kinds of self-torture. I want every human being to live to the fullest; minimum is not my way. Live to the maximum, or if you can go beyond the maximum, then fantastic. Go! Don't wait! And don't waste time waiting for Godot. . . .

. . . I am not against the idea of ending life. If one decides to end it, then of course it is his right. But I am certainly against making it a long torture. When this Shanti Sagar died, he took one hundred and ten days of not eating. A man is capable, if he is ordinarily healthy, of easily lasting ninety days without food. If he is extraordinarily healthy then he can survive longer.

So remember, I was not rude to the man. In that context my question was absolutely correct, perhaps more so because he could not answer it. And, strange to tell you today, that was the beginning not only of my questioning, but also the beginning of people not answering. I have met many so-called spiritual people, but nobody has ever answered any of my questions. In a way that day determined my whole flavor, my whole life.

Shanti Sagar left very annoyed, but I was immensely happy, and I did not hide it from my grandfather. I told him, "Nana, he may have left annoyed, but I am feeling absolutely correct. Your guru was just mediocre. You should choose someone of a little more worth."

Even he laughed and said, "Perhaps you are right, but now at my age to change my guru will not be very practical." He asked my nani, "What do you think?"

My nani, as ever true to her spirit, said, "It is never too late to change. If you see what you have chosen is not right, change it. In fact, be quick, because you are getting old. Don't say, 'I am old, so I cannot change.' A young man can afford not to change but not an old man—and you are old enough."

And only a few years later he died, but he could not gather the courage to change his guru. He continued in the same old pattern. My grandmother used to poke him, saying, "When are you going to change your guru and your methods?"

He would say, "Yes, I will, I will."

One day my grandmother said, "Stop all this nonsense! Nobody ever changes unless one changes right now. Don't say 'I will, I will.' Either change or don't change, but be clear."

That woman could have become a tremendously powerful force. She was not meant to be just a housewife. She was not meant to live in that small village. The whole world should have known about her. Perhaps I am her vehicle; perhaps she has poured herself into me. She loved me so deeply that I have never considered my real mother to be my real mother. I always consider my nani to be my real mother.

Whenever I had to confess anything, any wrong that I had done to somebody, I could confess it only to her, nobody else. She was my trust. I could confide anything to her because I had come to realize one thing, and that was that she was capable of understanding.

. . . That moment in my life, asking the Jaina monk strange, irritating, annoying questions, I don't consider that I did anything wrong. Perhaps I helped him. Perhaps one day he will understand. If he had had courage he would have understood even that day, but he was a coward—he escaped. And since then, this has been my experience: The so-called mahatmas and saints are all cowards. I have never come across a single mahatma—Hindu, Mohammedan, Christian, Buddhist—who can be said to be really a rebellious spirit. Unless one is rebellious, one is not religious. Rebellion is the very foundation of religion.

NANA WAS NOT JUST A MATERNAL GRANDFATHER. IT IS VERY DIFFI-cult for me to define what he was to me. He used to call me Rajah—*rajah* means "the king"—and for those seven years he managed to have me live like a king. On my birthday he used to bring an elephant from a nearby town. . . . Elephants in India, in those days, were kept either by kings—because it is very costly, the maintenance, the food, and the service that the elephant requires—or by saints. Two types of people used to have them. The saints could have elephants because they had so many followers. Just as the followers looked after the saint, they looked after the elephant. Nearby there was a saint who had an elephant, so for my birthday my maternal grandfather used to put me on the elephant with two bags, one on either side, full of silver coins.

In my childhood, notes had not appeared in India; silver was still used for the rupee. My grandfather would fill two big bags, hanging on either side, with silver coins, and I would go around the village throwing the silver coins. That's how he used to celebrate my birthday. Once I started, he would come in his bullock cart behind me with more rupees, and he would go on telling me, "Don't be miserly—I am keeping enough. You cannot throw more than I have. Go on throwing!"

He managed in every possible way to give me the idea that I belonged to some royal family.

SEPARATION HAS ITS OWN POETRY, ONE JUST HAS TO LEARN ITS language, and one has to live it in its depth. Then out of sadness itself comes a new kind of joy . . . which looks almost impossible, but it happens. I have known it because of the death of my nana. It was a total separation. We will not meet again, yet there was a beauty in it. He was old, and dying, perhaps from a severe heart attack. We were not aware of it because the village had no doctor, not even a pharmacist, no medicine, so we didn't know the cause of his death, but I think it was a severe heart attack.

I asked him in his ear, "Nana, have you something to say to me before you depart? Any last words? Or do you want to give me something to remember you by forever?" He took off his ring and put it in my hand. That ring is with some sannyasin* now; I gave it to someone. But that ring was always a mystery. His whole life he would not allow anybody to see what was in it, yet again and again he used to look into it. That ring had a glass window on both sides that you could look through. On top was a diamond; on each of its sides there was a glass window.

He had not allowed anybody to see what it was that he used to look at through the window. Inside there was a statue of Mahavira, the Jaina tirthankara; a really beautiful image, and very small. It was a small picture of Mahavira inside, and those two windows were magnifying glasses. They magnified it and it looked really huge.

With tears in his eyes my grandfather said, "I don't have anything else to give you because all that I have will be taken away from you too, just as it has been taken away from me. I can only give you my love for the one who has known himself."

Although I did not keep his ring, I have fulfilled his desire. I have known the one, and I have known it in myself. In a ring what does it matter? But the poor old man, he loved his master, Mahavira, and he gave his love to me. I respect his love for his master, and for me. The last words on his lips were, "Don't be worried, because I am not dying."

We all waited to see if he was going to say something else, but that was all. His eyes closed and he was no more.

I still remember that silence. The bullock cart was passing through a riverbed. I exactly remember each detail. I didn't say anything because I didn't want to disturb my grandmother. She did not say a thing. A few moments passed, then I became a little worried about her and said, "Say something; don't be so quiet, it is unbearable."

Can you believe it, she sang a song! That's how I learned that death has to be celebrated. She sang the same song she had sung when she was in love with my grandfather for the first time.

This too is worth noting: that ninety years ago, in India, she had had

*Traditionally, a sannyasin is a spiritual seeker who renounces the world. As Osho uses the term, it is a seeker, or disciple, who remains in the world but tries to bring meditation and awareness to everything he or she does.

courage to fall in love. She remained unmarried up till the age of twenty-four. That was very rare. I asked her once why she had remained unmarried for so long. She was such a beautiful woman. . . . I just jokingly told her that even the king of Chhattarpur, the state where Khajuraho is, might have fallen in love with her.

She said, "It is strange that you should mention it, because he did. I refused him, and not only him but many others too." In those days in India, girls were married when they were seven, or at the most nine years of age. Just the fear of love . . . if they are older they may fall in love. But my grandmother's father was a poet; his songs are still sung in Khajuraho and nearby villages. He insisted that unless she agreed, he was not going to marry his daughter to anybody. As chance would have it, she fell in love with my grandfather.

I asked her, "That is even stranger; you refused the king of Chhattarpur, and yet you fell in love with this poor man. For what? He was certainly not a very handsome man, nor extraordinary in any other way. Why did you fall in love with him?"

She said, "You are asking the wrong question. Falling has no 'why' to it. I just saw him, and that was it. I saw his eyes, and a trust arose in me that has never wavered."

I had also asked my grandfather, "Nani says she fell in love with you. That's okay on her part, but why did you allow the marriage to happen?"

He said, "I am not a poet or a thinker, but I can recognize beauty when I see it."

I never saw a more beautiful woman than my nani. I myself was in love with her, and loved her throughout her whole life. When she died at the age of eighty, I rushed home and found her lying there, dead. They were all just waiting for me because she had told them that they should not put her body on the funeral pyre until I arrived. She had insisted that I set light to her funeral pyre, so they were waiting for me. I went in, uncovered her face . . . and she was still beautiful! In fact, more beautiful than ever because all was quiet; even the turmoil of her breathing, the turmoil of living was not there. She was just a presence.

To put the fire to her body was the most difficult task I have ever done in my life. It was as if I was putting fire to one of the most beautiful paintings of Leonardo, or Vincent van Gogh. Of course to me she was more valuable than the *Mona Lisa,* more beautiful to me than Cleopatra. It is not an exaggeration. All that is beautiful in my vision somehow comes through her. She helped me in every way to be the way I am. Without her I may have been a shopkeeper or perhaps a doctor or an engineer, because when I passed my matriculation my father was so poor, it was difficult for him to send me to university. But he was even ready to borrow money in order to do it. He was utterly insistent that I go to university. I was willing, but not to go to medical college, and I was not willing to go to engineering college either. I flatly refused to be a doctor or an engineer. I told him, "If you want to know the truth, I want to be a sannyasin, a hobo."

He said, "What!? A hobo!"

I said, "Yes. I want to go to university to study philosophy so that I can be a philosophical hobo."

He refused, saying, "In that case I am not going to borrow money and take all that trouble."

My grandmother said, "Don't you worry, son; you go and do whatsoever you want to do. I am alive, and I will sell everything I have just to help you to be yourself. I will not ask where you want to go and what you want to study."

She never asked, and she sent me money continually, even when I became a professor. I had to tell her that I was now earning for myself, and I should rather send her money.

She said, "Don't worry, I have no use for this money, and you must be using it well."

People used to wonder where I got all the money to purchase my books, because I had thousands of books. Even when I was just a student in high school I had thousands of books in my house. My whole house was full of books, and everybody wondered where I got all the money from. My grandmother had told me, "Never tell anyone that you get money from me, because if your father and mother come to know they will start asking me for money, and it will be difficult for me to refuse."

She went on giving money to me. You will be surprised to know that even the month she died she had sent the usual money to me. On the morning of the day she died she had signed the check. You will also be amazed to know that was the last money she had in the bank. Perhaps somehow she knew that there was not going to be any tomorrow.

I am fortunate in many ways, but I was most fortunate in having my maternal grandparents . . . and those early golden years.

THE REBELLIOUS SPIRIT

As far back as I can remember, I loved only one game, to argue—to argue about *everything*. So very few grown-up people could even *stand* me—*understanding* was out of the question.

I was never interested in going to school. That was the worst place. I was forced finally to go, but I resisted as much as I could, because there were only children who were not interested in things I was interested in, and I was not interested in things they all were interested in. So I was an outsider.

My interest has remained the same: to know what is the ultimate truth, what is the meaning of life, why I am here and not anyone else. And I was determined that unless I find the answer, I am not going to rest and I am not going to let anybody around me rest, either.

1939–1951:
GADARWADA, MADHYA PRADESH, INDIA

My grandfather's death was my first encounter with death. Yes, an encounter and something more; not just an encounter, otherwise I would have missed the real meaning of it. I saw the death, and something more that was not dying, that was floating above it, escaping from the body . . . the elements. That encounter determined my whole course of life. It gave me a direction, or rather a dimension, that was not known to me before.

I had heard of other people's deaths, but only heard. I had not seen, and even if I had seen, they did not mean anything to me. Unless you love someone and he then dies, you cannot really encounter death. Let that be underlined:

<u>Death can only be encountered in the death of the loved one.</u>

When love plus death surrounds you, there is a transformation, an immense mutation, as if a new being is born. You are never the same again. But people do not love, and because they do not love they can't experience death the way I experienced it. Without love, death does not give you the keys to existence. With love, it hands over to you the keys to all that is.

My first experience of death was not a simple encounter. It was complex in many ways. The man I had loved was dying. I had known him as my father. He had raised me with absolute freedom, no inhibitions, no suppressions, and no commandments. . . .

Love with freedom—if you have it, you are a king or a queen. That is the real kingdom of God—love with freedom. Love gives you the roots into the earth, and freedom gives you the wings.

My grandfather gave me both. He gave his love to me, more than he ever had given to either my mother or even my grandmother; and he gave me freedom, which is the greatest gift. As he was dying he gave me his ring, and with a tear in his eye told me, "I don't have anything else to give you."

I said, "Nana, you have already given me the most precious gift."

He opened his eyes and said, "What is that?"

I laughed and said, "Have you forgotten? You have given me your love and you have given me freedom. I think no child ever had such freedom as you gave to me. What more do I need? What more can you give? I am thankful. You can die peacefully."

THAT WAS MY FIRST ENCOUNTER WITH DEATH, AND IT WAS A BEAU- tiful encounter. It was not in any way ugly, as it more or less happens for almost every child around the world. Fortunately I was together with my dying grandfather for hours, and he died slowly. By and by, I could feel death happening to him, and I could see the great silence of it

I was also fortunate that my nani was present. Perhaps without her I may have missed the beauty of death, because love and death are so similar, perhaps the same. She loved me. She showered her love upon me, and death was there, slowly happening. A bullock cart—I can still hear its sound—the rattling of its wheels on the stones, the driver continuously shouting to the bullocks, the sound of his whip hitting them. . . . I can hear it all, still. It is so deeply rooted in my experience that I don't think even my death will erase it. Even while dying I may again hear the sound of that bullock cart.

My nani was holding my hand and I was completely dazed, not knowing what was happening, utterly in the moment. My grandfather's head was in my lap. I held my hands on his chest and slowly, slowly the breathing disappeared. When I felt that he was no longer breathing I said to my grandmother, "I'm sorry, Nani, but it seems that he is no longer breathing."

She said, "That's perfectly okay. You need not be worried. He has lived enough, there is no need to ask for more." She also told me, "Remember, because these are the moments not to be forgotten: never ask for more. What is, is enough."

THE FIRST SEVEN YEARS ARE THE MOST IMPORTANT IN LIFE, NEVER again will you have that much opportunity. Those seven years decide your seventy years, all the foundation stones are laid in those seven years. So by a strange coincidence I was saved from my parents—and by the time I reached them, I was almost on my own, I was already flying. I knew I had wings. I knew that I didn't need anybody's help to make me fly. I knew that the whole sky is mine.

I never asked for their guidance, and if any guidance was given to me I always retorted, "This is insulting. Do you think I cannot manage it myself? I do understand that there is no bad intention in giving guidance—for that I am thankful—but you do not understand one thing, that I am capable of doing it on my own. Just give me a chance to prove my mettle. Don't interfere."

In those seven years I became really a strong individualist, hard-core. Now it was impossible to put any trip on me.

My father's shop was in front of the house where the family lived. That's how it happens in India: house and shop are together so it is easily manageable. I used to pass through my father's shop with closed eyes.

He asked me, "This is strange. Whenever you pass through the shop into the house, or from the house"—it was just a twelve-foot space to pass—"you always keep your eyes closed. What ritual are you practicing?"

I said, "I am simply practicing so that this shop does not destroy me as it has destroyed you. I don't want to see it at all; I am absolutely uninterested, totally uninterested." And it was one of the most beautiful cloth shops in that city—the best materials were available there—but I never looked to either side, I simply closed my eyes and passed by.

He said, "But in opening your eyes there is no harm."

I said, "One never knows—one can be distracted. I don't want to be distracted by anything."

Naturally—I was his eldest son—he wanted me to help him. He wanted me, after my education, to come and take charge of the shop. He had managed well; the shop had become a big place, slowly, slowly. He said, "Of course, who else is going to look after it? I will be getting old; do you want me to be here forever?"

I said, "No, I don't, but you can retire. You have your younger brothers who are interested in the shop, in fact too interested—even afraid that you may give the shop to me. I have told them, 'Don't be afraid of me; I am no one's competitor.' Give this shop to your younger brothers."

But in India the tradition is that the eldest son inherits everything. My father was the eldest son of his father; he inherited everything. All that he had now was supposed to be mine to take care of. Naturally he was worried . . . but there was no way. He tried in every possible way, to somehow get me interested.

He would say to me, "Even if you become a doctor you cannot earn as much in the whole month as I can earn in a day. If you become an engineer, what salary are you going to get? If you become a professor—I can hire your professors, no problem. And you know there are so many thousands of graduates, postgraduates, Ph.D.'s, unemployed."

First he tried to persuade me not to go to the university because he was very much afraid that it would make me absolutely independent for six years—going far away. Then he would not even be able to keep an eye on me. He had already been regretting that for seven years he left me with my mother's parents. I told him, "Don't be afraid. What you are afraid of has already happened: I have already graduated! Those seven years . . . No university is needed to corrupt me; I am corrupted completely—out of your hands. These means of persuasion—salaries, respect, money—I don't give any value to them. And I am not going to become a doctor or an engineer, so don't be worried. In fact, I am going to remain a vagabond my whole life."

He said, "That is even worse! It is better you become an engineer or a doctor, but a vagabond? That is a new profession. You have got some mind to think of such things—you want to become a vagabond! Even those who are vagabonds feel humiliated if you say, 'You are a vagabond,' but you are telling your own father that all your life you want to be just a vagabond!"

I said, "That is what is going to happen."

Then he started saying, "Then why do you want to go to the university?"

I said, "I want to be an educated vagabond, not a vagabond out of weakness. I don't want to do anything in my life out of weakness—because I could not be anything else, that's why I am a vagabond—that is not my way. First I want to prove to the world that I can be anything that I want to be, still I choose to be a vagabond—out of strength. Then there is respectability even if you are a vagabond, because respectability has nothing to do with your vocation, your profession; respectability has something to do with acting out of strength, clarity, intelligence.

"So be perfectly aware that I am not going to the university to be able to find some good job. I am not born to do such stupid things, and there are so many to do those things. But a very cultured, sophisticated, educated vagabond is very much needed because you don't see any around. There are vagabonds but they are just third-rate people, they are failures. I want first to be absolutely successful and then to kick all that success and just be a vagabond."

He said, "I cannot understand your logic, but if you have decided to be a vagabond I know there is no way to change you."

Those seven years . . . he reminded me again and again, "That was our basic fault. That was the time we could have managed to make you something of worth. But your nana and your nani, those two old fellows destroyed you completely."

And after my nana's death, my nani never went back to the village; she was so heartbroken. I have seen thousands of couples very intimately because I have been staying with so many families, wandering around India, but I could never find anybody who could be compared with those two old people: They really loved each other.

She stayed in my father's town, but she was a very independent woman. She did not like the big joint family; my father's brothers, their wives, their children—it was a huge caravan. She said, "This is not the place for me. I have lived my whole life with my husband, in silence. Only for seven years were you there, otherwise there has not been much conversation either, because there was nothing to say. We had talked about all those things before, so there was nothing to say—we just sat silently." She said, "I would like to live alone." So a house was found for her near the river where she would find some similarity to the place she had lived with my grandfather; in this town we had no lake but we had a beautiful river.

The whole day I was in school or roaming around the town or doing a thousand and one things, and at night I always stayed with my nani. Many times she said, "Your parents may feel bad. We took you from them for seven years, for which they cannot forgive us. We thought that we should return you as clean as we had got you, not trying to impose anything on you. But they are angry; they don't say so but I can feel it and I hear from other people that we spoiled you. And now you don't go to sleep with your father and mother and your family; you come here every night. They will think that the spoiling is continuing—the old man is gone but the old woman is still here."

I said to her, "But if I don't come, can you really sleep? For whom do you prepare the second bed every night before I come? Because I do not tell you that tomorrow I will be coming. About tomorrow, from the very beginning I have been uncertain because who knows what will happen tomorrow? Why do you prepare the second bed? And not only the second bed . . ."

I had a long habit, which my physician somehow had to manage to finish; it took him almost two or three years. From my very childhood, as long as I remember, I needed sweets before going to bed; otherwise I could not sleep. So she was not only preparing my bed, she used to go out and buy the sweets that I liked. And she would keep the sweets by my bed so that I could eat—even in the middle of the night if I felt like it again, I could eat them.

I asked her, "For whom do you bring these sweets? You don't eat them; since nana died you have not tasted sweets." My nana loved sweets. In fact, it seems he gave me this idea of sweets; he also used to eat before going to sleep. That is not done in any Jaina family. Jainas don't eat in the night; they don't even drink water or milk or anything. But he lived in a village where he was the only Jaina, so there was no problem. It is perhaps from him that I got the habit; it must have been he, eating and calling me also to join him. I must have joined him, and by and by it became a routine thing. For seven years he trained me!

So I could not go to my house for two reasons. One reason was those sweets—because in my mother's place it was not possible: there were so many children that if you allowed one child, then all the children would ask. And anyway it was against the religion, you simply could not even ask. But my difficulty was that I could not go to sleep without them.

Secondly, I felt, "My nani must be feeling alone—and here in this house it is difficult to be alone, so many people, it is always a marketplace. Nobody will be missing me if I am not here." Nobody ever missed me; they just made certain that I was sleeping with my nani, then there was no problem.

So even after those seven years I was not under the influence of my parents. It was just accidental that from the very beginning I was on my own. Doing right or wrong—that was not the important thing, but doing on my own. And slowly, slowly, that became my style of life, about everything—for example, about clothes.

In my town I was the only non-Mohammedan dressed liked a Mohammedan. My father said, "You can do anything but at least don't do this, because I have to live in the society, I have to think of the other children. And from where did you get this idea?"

Mohammedans in my town used, instead of the dhoti that Indians use, a certain kind of pajama that is called a *salvar*. That is used by Pakhtoons in Afghanistan and Pakhtoonistan—those faraway places near the Himalayas, beyond the Himalayas. But it is a beautiful pajama, and not made in a miserly way like a regular pajama; it has so many folds. If you have a real *salvar* you can make at least ten pajamas out of it, it has so many folds. Those folds give it its beauty, when they all become gathered. And I wore a long Pakhtoon *kurtha*, not an Indian *kurtha*. The Indian *kurtha* is short and the sleeves are not very loose. The Pakhtoon *kurtha* sleeves are very loose and the *kurtha* is very long; it goes below the knees. And I had a Turkish cap.

My father used to tell me, "You enter the shop anyway with closed eyes, and with closed eyes you go out. Why don't you use the back door?" He said, "You can come in from the back door, you can go out from the back door; you can have the key to yourself because nobody uses the back door. At least we will be saved the trouble of answering every customer, 'Who is the Mohammedan going inside with closed eyes?' And you get these strange ideas. We have a cloth shop—all kinds of cloth is there, ready-made clothes are there, you can have any style, but . . . Mohammedan?"

In India, a Mohammedan style is thought to be the worst thing. I said, "This is why, because all you people think that the Mohammedan style is the worst thing. I am protesting against you all, that the dress of the Mohammedan is the best. And you can see it; wherever I go only I am noticed, nobody else is noticed. Whenever I enter the classroom I am noticed; anywhere I go I am immediately noticed."

And the way I was using that dress . . . It was a really graceful dress, and with a Turkish cap. The Turkish cap is long and has a tassel of hair hanging by the side; very rich Turkish people use it. I was so small, but that dress helped me in many ways.

I might go to meet the town commissioner, and the man guarding the gate would just look at me and he would tell me, "Come on." Seeing that dress . . . He would not have allowed me, a small boy, to enter, but, "With this dress he must be a sheik or somebody very important." And even the commissioner would stand up, seeing my dress. "Sheik" is used for very respectable people, and he would say, "Sheikji, *betye*—Sheikji, please sit down."

I told my father, "This dress helps me in so many ways. Just the other day I went to see a minister, and he also thought that I was a sheik belonging to some rich Arabian or Persian family. And you want me to drop this dress and just use a dhoti and *kurtha,* which nobody is going to notice?"

I continued to wear that dress up to my matriculation. They tried hard to stop me, but the harder they tried . . . I said, "If you stop trying perhaps I may drop it; while you continue to try I am the last person to drop it."

One day my father put all my *salvars* and my *kurthas* and my three Turkish caps in a bundle and went into the godown, the basement, and put them there somewhere, where many kinds of things were broken, useless. I could not find anything, so when I came out of the bathroom I simply went naked, with my eyes closed, into the shop. As I was going out my father said, "Wait! Just come back. Put on your clothes."

I said, "You bring them, wherever they are."

He said, "I had never thought you would do this. I thought you would look around and search for the clothes and you would not find them, because I had put them in such a place that you wouldn't find them. Then naturally you would wear the normal clothes that you are supposed to wear. I never thought that you would do this!"

I said, "I take direct action. I don't believe in unnecessary talk."

I didn't even ask anybody where my clothes were. Why should I ask? My nakedness will serve the same purpose. He said, "You can have your clothes back, and nobody is going to bother you about them anymore. But please, don't start walking naked because that will create more trouble—that a cloth merchant's son has no clothes to wear. You are notorious and you will make us notorious also: 'Look at the poor child!' Everybody will think that we are not giving you clothes."

It went on—I never missed a single opportunity to sharpen my intelligence. I turned every possible opportunity toward sharpening my intelligence, individuality. You can understand now, looking at the whole picture, but in fragments . . . The people who came in contact with me of course were unable to understand what kind of man I am—crazy, nuts—but I was going about it very methodically.

I SAID TO MY FATHER, "NO." THAT WAS MY FIRST WORD BEFORE ENTER- ing primary school. I said to my father, "No, I don't want to enter this gate. This is not a school, it's a prison." The very gate, and the color of the building . . . It is strange, particularly in India, the jails and the schools are painted the same color and they are both made of red brick. It is very difficult to know whether the building is a prison or a school. Perhaps once a practical joker had managed to play a trick, but he did it perfectly.

I said, "Look at this school—you call it a school? Look at this gate! And you are here to force me to enter for at least four years."

My father said, "I was always afraid . . ." and we were standing at the gate, on the outside of course, because I had not yet allowed him to take me in. He went on, ". . . I was always afraid that your grandfather, and particularly this woman, your grandmother, were going to spoil you."

I said, "Your fear was right, but the work has been done and nobody can undo it now, so please let us go home."

He said, "What! You have to be educated."

I said, "What kind of a beginning is this? I am not even free to say yes or no. You call it education? But if you want it, please don't ask me: Here is my hand, drag me in. At least I will have the satisfaction that I never entered this ugly institution on my own. Please, at least do me this favor."

Of course, my father was getting very upset, so he dragged me in. Although he was a very simple man, he immediately understood that it was not right. He said to me, "Although I am your father it does not feel right for me to drag you in."

I said, "Don't feel guilty at all. What you have done is perfectly right, because unless someone drags me in I am not going to go of my own decision. My decision is 'no.' You can impose your decision on me because I have to depend on you for food, clothes, shelter, and everything. Naturally you are in a privileged position."

The entry into school was the beginning of a new life. For years I had lived just like a wild animal. Yes, I cannot say a wild human being, because there are no wild human beings.

Only once in a while a man becomes a wild human being. I am now; Buddha was, Zarathustra was, Jesus was—but at that time it was perfectly true to say that for years I had lived like a wild animal.

I never went to school willingly. And I am happy that I was dragged in, that I never went on my own, willingly. The school was really ugly—all schools are ugly. In fact, it is good to create a situation where children learn, but it is not good to educate them. Education is bound to be ugly.

And what did I see as the first thing in the school? The first thing was an encounter with the teacher of my first class. I have seen beautiful people and ugly people, but I have never seen something like that again! He was the master, and he was going to teach me. I could not even look at the man. God must have created his face in a tremendous hurry. Perhaps his bladder was full, and just to finish the job he did this man and then rushed to the bathroom. What a man he created! He had only one eye, and a crooked nose. That one eye was enough, but the crooked nose really added great ugliness to the face. And he was huge! He must have weighed at least four hundred pounds, not less than that.

He was my first master—I mean teacher, because in India schoolteachers are called "masters." Even now if I saw that man I would certainly start trembling. He was not a man at all; he was a horse!

That first teacher—I don't know his real name, and nobody in the school knew it either, particularly the children; they just called him Kantar Master. *Kantar* means "one-eyed"; that was enough for the children, and also it was a condemnation of the man. In Hindi *kantar* not only means "one-eyed," it is also used as a curse. It cannot be translated in that way because the nuance is lost in the translation. So we all called him Kantar Master in his presence, and when he was not there we called him just Kantar—that one-eyed fellow.

He was not only ugly; everything he did was ugly. And of course on my very first day something was bound to happen. He used to punish the children mercilessly. I have never seen or heard of anybody else doing such things to children.

He was teaching arithmetic. I knew a little because my grandmother used to teach me at home; particularly a little language and some arithmetic. So I was looking out of the window at the beautiful pipal tree shining in the sun. There is no other tree that shines so beautifully in the sun, because each leaf dances separately, and the whole tree becomes almost a chorus—thousands of shining dancers and singers together, but also independent. I looked at the tree with its leaves dancing in the breeze, and the sun shining on each leaf, and hundreds of parrots just jumping from one branch to another, enjoying, for no reason. Alas, they didn't have to go to school.

I was looking out of the window and Kantar Master jumped on me.

He said, "It is better to get things right from the very beginning."

I said, "I absolutely agree about that. I also want to put everything as it should be from the very beginning."

He said, "Why were you looking out of the window when I was teaching arithmetic?"

I said, "Arithmetic has to be heard, not seen. I don't have to see your beautiful face, I was looking out of the window to avoid it. As far as the arithmetic is concerned, you can ask me; I heard it and I know it."

He asked me, and that was the beginning of a very long trouble—not for me but for him. The trouble was that I answered correctly. He could not believe it and said, "Whether you are right or wrong I am still going to punish you, because it is not right to look out of the window when the teacher is teaching."

I was called in front of him. From his desk he took out a box of pencils. I had heard of these famous pencils. He used to put one of those pencils between each of your fingers, and then squeeze your hands tight, asking, "Do you want a little more? Do you need more?" to small children!

I looked at the pencils and said, "I have heard of these pencils, but before you put them between my fingers, remember it will cost you very dearly, perhaps even your job."

He laughed. I can tell you it was like a monster in a nightmare laughing at you. He said, "Who can prevent me?"

I said, "That is not the point. I want to ask: is it illegal to look out of the window when arithmetic is being taught? And if I am able to answer the questions on what was being taught and am ready to repeat it word for word, then is it wrong in any way to look out of the window? Then why has the window been created in this classroom? For what purpose? Because for the whole day somebody is teaching something, and a window is not needed during the night when there is nobody to look out of it."

He said, "You are a troublemaker."

I said, "That's exactly true, and I am going to the headmaster to find out whether it is legitimate for you to punish me when I have answered you correctly."

He became a little more mellow. I was surprised because I had heard that he was not a man who could be subdued in any way.

I then said, "And then I am going to the president of the municipal committee who runs this school. Tomorrow I will come with a police commissioner so that he can see with his own eyes what kind of practices are going on here."

He trembled. It was not visible to others, but I can see such things, which other people may miss. I may not see walls, but I cannot miss small things, almost microscopic. I told him, "You are trembling, although you will not be able to admit it. But we will see. First let me go to the headmaster."

I went and the headmaster said, "I know this man tortures children. It is illegal, but I cannot say anything about it because he is the oldest schoolteacher in the town, and almost everybody's father and grandfather has been his pupil once at least. So no one can raise a finger against him."

I said, "I don't care. My father has been his student and also my grandfather. I don't care about either my father or my grandfather; in fact I don't really belong to that family. I have been living away from them. I am a foreigner here."

The headmaster said, "I could see immediately that you must be a stranger but, my boy, don't get into unnecessary trouble. He will torture you."

I said, "It is not easy. Let this be the beginning of my struggle against all torture. I will fight."

And I hit with my fist—of course just a small child's fist—on his table, and told him, "I don't care about education or anything, but I must care about my freedom. Nobody can harass me unnecessarily. You have to show me the educational code. I cannot read, and you will have to show me whether it is unlawful to look out of the window even though I could answer all the questions correctly."

He said, "If you answered correctly then there is no question at all about where you were looking."

I said, "Come along with me."

He came with his educational code, an ancient book that he always carried. I don't think anybody had ever read it. The headmaster told Kantar Master, "It is better not to harass this child because it seems that it may bounce back on you. He won't give up easily."

But Kantar Master was not that type of man. Afraid, he became even more aggressive and violent. He said, "I will show this child—you need not worry. And who cares about that code? I have been a teacher here my whole life and is this child going to teach me the code?"

I said, "Tomorrow, either I will be in this building or you, but we cannot both exist here together. Just wait until tomorrow."

I rushed home and told my father. He said, "I was worried whether I had entered you in school just to bring trouble upon others and upon yourself, and also to drag me into it."

I said, "No, I am simply reporting so that later you don't say you were kept in the dark."

I went to the police commissioner. He was a lovely man; I had not expected that a policeman could be so nice. He said, "I have heard about this man. In fact my own son has been tortured by him. But nobody complained. It is illegal to torture, but unless you complain nothing can be done, and I cannot complain myself because I am worried that he may fail my child. So it is better to let him go on torturing. It is only a question of a few months, then my child will go into another class."

I said, "I am here to complain, and I am not concerned about going into another class at all. I am ready to stay in this class my whole life."

He looked at me, patted me on the back and said, "I appreciate what you are doing. I will come tomorrow."

I then rushed to see the president of the municipal committee, who proved to be just cow dung. He said to me, "I know. Nothing can be done about it. You have to live with it, you will have to learn how to tolerate it."

I said to him, and I remember my words exactly, "I am not going to tolerate anything that is wrong to my conscience."

He said, "If that is the case, I cannot take it in hand. Go to the vice president, perhaps he may be more helpful." And for that I must thank that cow dung, because the vice-president of that village, Shambhu Dube, proved to be the only man of any worth in that whole village, in my experience. When I knocked on his door—I was only eight or nine years old, and he was the vice president—he called, "Yes, come in." He was expecting to see some gentleman, and on seeing me he looked a little embarrassed.

I said, "I am sorry that I am not a little older—please excuse me. Moreover, I am not educated at all, but I have to complain about this man, Kantar Master."

The moment he heard my story—that this man tortures little children in the first grade by putting pencils between their fingers and then squeezing, and that he has pins which he forces under the nails—he could not believe it.

He said, "I have heard rumors, but why has nobody complained?"

I said, "People are afraid that their children will be tortured even more."

He said, "Are you not afraid?"

I said, "No, because I am ready to fail. That's all he can do." I said I was ready to fail and I was not insisting on success, but I would fight to the last: "It is either this man or me—we both cannot be there in the same building."

Shambhu Dube called me close to him. Holding my hand he said, "I always love rebellious people, but I never thought a child of your age could be a rebel. I congratulate you."

We became friends, and this friendship lasted until he died. That village had a population of twenty thousand people, but in India it is still a village. In India, unless the town has one hundred thousand people it is not considered a town. When there are more than fifteen hundred thousand people, then it is a city. In my whole life I never came across another in that village of the same caliber, quality, or talent as Shambhu Dube. If you ask me, it will look like an exaggeration, but in fact, in the whole of India I never found another Shambhu Dube. He was just rare.

When I was traveling all over India he would wait for months for me to come and visit the village just for one day. He was the only person who ever came to see me when my train would pass through the village. Of course I am not including my father or my mother; they had to come. But Shambhu Dube was not my relative; he just loved me. And this love started at that meeting, on that day when I had gone to protest against Kantar Master.

Shambhu Dube was the vice president of the municipal committee, and he said to me, "Don't be worried. That fellow should be punished; in fact, his service is finished. He has applied for an extension but we will not give it to him. From tomorrow you will not see him in that school again."

I said, "Is that a promise?"

We looked into each other's eyes. He laughed and said, "Yes, it is a promise."

The next day Kantar Master was gone. He was never able to look at me after that. I tried to contact him, knocked at his door many times just to say good-bye, but he was really a coward, a sheep under a lion's skin. But that first day in school turned out to be the beginning of many, many things. . . .

THE FIRST THING MY OWN FATHER TAUGHT ME—AND THE ONLY thing that he ever taught me—was a love for the small river that flows by the side of my town. He taught me just this—swimming in the river. That's all that he ever taught me, but I am tremendously grateful to him because that brought so many changes in my life. Exactly like Siddhartha, I fell in love with the river.

It was my daily routine to be with the river for at least five to eight hours. From three o'clock in the morning I would be with the river; the sky would be full of stars and the stars reflecting in the water. And it is a beautiful river; its water is so sweet that people have named it Shakkar—*shakkar* means "sugar." It is a beautiful phenomenon.

I have seen it in the darkness of the night with the stars, dancing its course toward the ocean. I have seen it with the early rising sun. I have seen it in the full moon. I have seen it with the sunset. I have seen it sitting by its bank alone or with friends, playing on the flute, dancing on its bank, meditating on its bank, rowing a boat in it or swimming across it. In the rains, in the winter, in the summer . . .

I can understand Hermann Hesse's Siddhartha and his experience with the river. It happened with me: so much transpired, because slowly slowly, the whole existence became a river to me. It lost its solidity; it became liquid, fluid.

And I am immensely grateful to my father. He never taught me mathematics, language, grammar, geography, history. He was never much concerned about my education. He had ten other children . . . and I had seen it happen many times where people would ask, "In what class is your son studying?" And he would have to ask somebody because he would not know. He was never concerned with any other education. The only education that he gave to me was a communion with the river. He himself was in deep love with the river.

Whenever you are in love with flowing things, moving things, you have a different vision of life. Modern man lives with asphalt roads, cement and concrete buildings. These are nouns, remember, these are not verbs. The skyscrapers don't go on growing; the road remains the same whether it is night or day, whether it is a full-moon night or a night absolutely dark. It doesn't matter to the asphalt road, it does not matter to the cement and concrete buildings.

Man has created a world of nouns and he has become encaged in his own world. He has forgotten the world of the trees, the world of the rivers, the world of the mountains and the stars. There they don't know of any nouns, they have not heard about nouns; they know only verbs. Everything is a process. God is not a thing but a process.

IN MY TOWN THERE WAS ONLY ONE CHURCH. THERE WERE VERY FEW Christians, perhaps four or five families, and I was the only non-Christian who used to visit the church. But that was not special; I used to visit the mosques, the *gurudwara,* Hindu temples, Jaina temples. I always had the idea that everything belongs to me. I don't belong to any church, I don't belong to any temple, but any temple and any church that exists on the earth belongs to me.

Seeing a non-Christian boy coming every Sunday, the priest became interested in me. He said to me, "You seem to be very interested. In fact, in my whole congregation—it is such a small congregation—you seem to be the most interested. Others are sleeping, snoring, but you are so alert and listening and watching everything. Would you like to become like Jesus Christ?" and he showed me Jesus Christ's picture, of course of him hanging on the cross.

I said, "No, absolutely no! I have no desire to be crucified. And a man who is crucified must have something wrong with him; otherwise who cares to crucify anybody? If his whole country, his people, decided to crucify him, then that man must have something wrong with him. He may be a nice man, he may be a good man, but something must have led him to crucifixion. Perhaps he had a suicidal instinct.

"The people who have suicidal instincts are not generally so courageous as to commit suicide, but they can manage to get others to murder them. And then you will never find that they had a suicidal instinct, that they prompted you to kill them so that the responsibility falls on you."

I said, "I don't have any suicidal instinct in me. Perhaps he was not a suicidal man, but certainly he was some kind of masochist. Just looking at his face—and I have seen many of his pictures—I see him looking so miserable, so deadly miserable, that I have tried standing before a mirror and looking as miserable as he looks, but I have failed. I have tried hard, but I cannot even make his face; how can I become Jesus Christ? That seems to be impossible. And why should I become Jesus Christ?"

He was shocked. He said, "I thought you were interested in Jesus."

I said, "I am certainly interested, more interested than you are, because you are a mere preacher, salaried. If you don't get a salary for three months you will be gone, and all your teaching will disappear." And that's what finally happened, because those Christian families were not permanent residents of the town—they were all railway employees, so sooner or later they got transferred. He was left alone with a small church that they had made. Now there was nobody to give money, to support him, nobody to listen to him except me.

On Sundays he used to say, "Dear friends—"

I would say, "Wait! Don't use the plural. There are no friends, just 'dear friend' will do. It is almost like two lovers talking; it is not a congregation. You can sit down—nobody is there. We can have a good chitchat. Why unnecessarily go on standing for one hour, and shout and . . . ?"

And that's how it happened. Within three months he was gone, because if you don't pay him . . . Although Jesus says, "Man cannot live by bread alone," man cannot live without bread either. He needs the bread. It may not be enough, he needs many more things, but many more things come only later on; first comes the bread. Man certainly can live by bread alone. He will not be much of a man—but who *is* much of a man? But nobody can live without bread, not even Jesus.

I was going into the mosque, and they allowed me. Christians, Mohammedans—these are converting religions; they want people from other folds to come to their fold. They were very happy seeing me there—but the same question: "Would you like to become like Hazrat Muhammad?" I was surprised to know that nobody was interested in my just being myself, helping me to be myself.

Everybody was interested in somebody else, the ideal, their ideal, and I have only to be a carbon copy? God has not given me any original face? I have to live with a borrowed face, with a mask, knowing that I don't have any face at all? Then how can life be a joy? Even your face is not yours.

If you are not yourself, how can you be happy?

The whole existence is blissful because the rock is rock, the tree is tree, the river is river, the ocean is ocean. Nobody is bothering to become somebody else; otherwise they would all go nuts. And that's what has happened to man.

You are being taught from the very childhood not to be yourself, but the way it is said is very clever, cunning. They say, "You have to become like Krishna, like Buddha," and they paint Buddha and Krishna in such a way that a great desire arises in you to be a Buddha, to be a Jesus, to be a Krishna. This desire is the root cause of your misery.

I was also told the same things that you have been told, but from my very childhood I made it a point that whatsoever the consequence I was not going to be deviated from myself. Right or wrong I am going to remain myself. Even if I end up in hell I will have at least the satisfaction that I followed my own course of life. If it leads to hell, then it leads to hell. Following others' advice and ideals and disciplines, even if I end up in paradise I will not be happy there, because I will have been forced against my will.

Try to understand the point. If it is against your will, even in paradise you will be in hell. But following your natural course of being, even in hell you will be in paradise.

Paradise is where your real being flowers.

Hell is where you are crushed and something else is imposed on you.

IN MY VILLAGE, AS HAPPENS ALL OVER THE EAST, EVERY YEAR *RAM-leela* was played—the life of Rama. The man who used to play the part of Ravana, the enemy of Rama who steals Rama's wife, was a great wrestler. He was the champion of the whole district, and the next year he was going to stand for the championship of the whole state. We used to take a bath in the river almost simultaneously in the morning, so we became friends. I told him, "Every year you become Ravana, and every year you are being deceived. Just the moment that you are going to break Shiva's bow so that you can get married to Sita, the daughter of Janaka, a messenger comes running in and informs you that your capital of Sri Lanka is on fire. So you have to go, rush back to your country. And meanwhile, Rama manages to break the bow and marry the girl. Don't you get bored every year with the same thing?"

He said, "But this is how the story goes."

I said, "The story is in our hands if you listen to my suggestion. You must have seen that most of the people are asleep because they have seen the same thing year after year, generation after generation—make it a little juicy."

He said, "What do you mean?"

I said, "This time you do one thing I say . . ." And he did it!

When the messenger came with the message: "Your capital, the golden Sri Lanka, is on fire, you have to get there soon," he said, "You shut up, idiot"—he spoke in English!

That's what I had told him! All the people who were asleep woke up: "Who is speaking English in the *Ramleela*?"

And Ravana said, "You go away. I don't care. You have deceived me every year. This time I am going to marry Sita."

And he went and broke the bow of Shiva to pieces and threw it into the mountains—it was just a bamboo bow. And he asked Janaka, "Where is your daughter? Bring her! My jumbo jet is waiting!"

It was so hilarious. Even after forty years, whenever I meet somebody from my village, they remember that *Ramleela*. They said, "Nothing like that has ever happened."

The manager had to drop the curtains. And the man was a great wrestler, at least twelve people had to carry him out.

That day the *Ramleela* could not be played. And next day they had to change Ravana; they found another person.

By the river, Ravana met me. He said, "You disturbed my whole thing."

I said, "But did you see the people clapping, enjoying, laughing? For years you have been playing the part and nobody has clapped, nobody has laughed. It was worth it!"

Religion needs a religious quality. A few qualities are missing. One of the most important is a sense of humor.

They stopped me from meeting their actors. They made it clear to every actor that if anybody listened to me or met me, he would not be allowed to act. But they forgot to tell one man, who was not an actor. . . .

He was a carpenter. He used to come to do some work in my house also. So I said to him, "I cannot approach the actors this year. Last year was enough!

Although I did no harm to anybody—everybody loved it, the whole city appreciated it. But now they are guarding every actor and they don't allow me close to them. But you are not an actor, your function is some other work. You can help me."

He said, "Whatever I can do, I will do, because last year it was really great. Can I be of some help?"

I said, "Certainly." And he did it!

In the war, Lakshmana, Rama's younger brother, gets wounded by a poisonous arrow. It is fatal. The physicians say that unless a certain herbal plant from the mountain Arunachal is brought, he cannot be saved, by the morning he will be dead. He is lying down on the stage unconscious. Rama is crying.

Hanuman, his most devoted follower, says, "Don't be worried. I will go immediately to Arunachal, find the herb, bring it before the morning. I just want some indications from the physician how to find it, how it looks. There may be so many herbs on the Arunachal, and the time is short, soon it is night."

The physician said, "There is no difficulty. That special herb has a unique quality. In the night it radiates and is full of light so you can see it. So anywhere you see a luminous herb you can bring it."

Hanuman goes to Arunachal, but he is puzzled because the whole of Arunachal is full of luminous herbs. It is not only one herb that has that special quality. There are many other herbs that have the same quality of being luminous in the night.

Now the poor Hanuman—he is just a monkey—is at a loss what to do. So he decides to take the whole mountain, and put the mountain there in front of the physician to find the herb.

The carpenter was on top of the roof. He had to pull the rope on which Hanuman comes with a cardboard mountain with lighted candles. And I had told him, "Stop exactly in the middle. Let him hang there, with the mountain and everything." And he managed it!

The manager rushed out. The whole crowd was agog with excitement at what was happening. And Hanuman was perspiring, because he was hanging onto the ropes with the mountain also, in the other hand. The manager rushed up. He asked the carpenter, and the carpenter said, "I don't know what has gone wrong. The rope has got stuck somewhere."

In a hurry, finding nothing, the manager cut the ropes and Hanuman with his mountain fell on the stage. And naturally he was angry. But the thousands of people were immensely happy. That made him even more angry.

Rama continued repeating the lines he had been told to say. He said, "Hanuman, my devoted friend . . ."

And Hanuman said, "To hell with your friends! Perhaps I have fractures."

Rama went on saying, "My brother is dying."

Hanuman said, "He can die anytime! What I want to know is, who cut the rope? I will kill him!"

Again the curtain had to be dropped, the *Ramleela* postponed. And the manager and the people who were organizing it, all approached my father saying, "Your son is destroying everything. He's making a mockery of our religion."

I said, "I'm not making a mockery of your religion. I'm simply giving it a little sense of humor."

I would like people to laugh. What is the point of repeating an old story every year? Then everybody is asleep because they know the story, they know every word of it. It is absolutely pointless.

But it is very difficult for the old traditionalists, the orthodox people, to accept laughter. You cannot laugh in a church.

MY FATHER'S FATHER LOVED ME VERY MUCH, JUST BECAUSE OF MY mischiefs. Even in his old age he was mischievous. He never liked my father or my uncles because they were all against this old man's mischievousness. They all said to him, "You are now seventy and you should behave. Now your sons are fifty, fifty-five, your daughters are fifty, their children are married, their children's children are there—and you go on doing such things that we feel ashamed."

I was the only one with whom he was intimate, and I loved the old man for the simple reason that he had not lost his childhood. Even at the age of seventy, he was as mischievous as any child. And he would play his mischief even on his own sons and daughters and sons-in-law, and they would be just shocked.

I was his only confidant because we conspired together. Of course many things he could not do—I had to do them. For example, his son-in-law was sleeping in the room and my grandfather could not go up onto the roof, but I could go. So we conspired together; he would help me, he would become a ladder for me to go onto the roof and remove a tile. And with just a bamboo and a brush attached to it, in the night, touching the face of the son-in-law . . . He would scream, and the whole house would run there . . . "What is the matter?" But by that time we had disappeared, and he would say, "There was some ghost or somebody just touching my face. I tried to catch him but I could not; it was dark."

My grandfather remained utterly innocent, and I saw the great freedom that he had. In my whole family he was the eldest. He should have been the most serious and most burdened with so many problems and so many anxieties, but nothing affected him. Everybody was serious and worried when there were problems; only he was not worried. But one thing I never liked—and that was sleeping with him. He had the habit of sleeping with his face covered and I would have to sleep with my face also covered, and that was suffocating.

I told him clearly, "About everything I agree, but this I cannot tolerate. You cannot sleep with your face uncovered; I cannot sleep with my face covered—it suffocates me. You do it lovingly"—he would keep me close to his heart and cover me completely—"that's perfectly good, but in the morning my heart will not be beating! Your intention is good, but you will be alive in the morning and I will be gone. So our friendship is out of the bed."

He wanted me there because he loved me and he had said, "Why don't you come and sleep with me?"

I said, "You know perfectly well that I don't want to be suffocated by anybody, even if his intention is good." Also, we used to go for a long walk in the mornings and sometimes, when there was a moon, in the night. But I never allowed him to hold my hand. And he would say, "But why? You may fall, you may stumble upon a stone or anything."

I said, "That's better. Let me stumble, it is not going to kill me. It will teach me how not to stumble, how to be alert, how to remember where the rocks are. But you holding my hand—how long can you hold my hand? How long are you going to be with me? If you can guarantee that you will always be with me, then of course I am willing."

He was a very sincere man. He said, "That I cannot guarantee; I cannot even say about tomorrow. And one thing is certain, you will live long and I will be dead, so I will not be here forever to hold your hand."

"Then," I said, "it is better for me to learn from now, because one day you will leave me in the middle, helpless. So you leave me alone, let me fall. I will try to get up. You wait; you just watch, and that will be more compassionate toward me than holding my hand."

And he understood it. He said, "You are right—one day I will not be there."

It is good to fall a few times, get hurt, stand up again—to go astray a few times. There is no harm. The moment you find you have gone astray, come back. Life has to be learned through trial and error.

I used to tell my father, "Don't give me any advice, even if I ask you. You have to be very straightforward about it. You have simply to say, 'Find out your own way.' Don't give me advice." Because when some cheap advice is available, who bothers to find one's own way?

I had been consistently telling my teachers, "Please remember one thing: I don't want your wisdom—simply teach your subject. You are a teacher of geography and you are trying to teach me morality? What relationship has morality with geography?"

I remember the poor man who was my geography teacher. He was in trouble because I had taken something from the pocket of the student who was sitting by my side. I had taken his money from his pocket, and this teacher was telling me, "Don't do that."

I said, "That's not your business. You are a geography teacher and this is a question of morality. If you want, I am ready to go to the principal; you come with me. Nowhere in the geography syllabus . . . I have read it, and nowhere is it said that you cannot take somebody else's money. And money is simply money; whoever has it, it is his. Right now it is mine. A few moments before it may have been his, but he has lost it. He should be more alert. If you want to give advice, give advice to him.

"In the first place, what is the need to bring so much money to the geography class? There is nothing to buy, nothing to purchase; there is not going to be any shopping. Why did he bring his money here? Then if he has brought the money, he should be alert. It is not my fault, it is his fault, and I have simply taken advantage of it, which is my right. To take advantage of situations is everybody's right."

I remember that poor man. He was always in difficulty, and always in difficulty with me. He would see me outside of class and he would say, "You can do whatsoever you want to do, just don't bring so much philosophy into poor geography. And I don't know anything about philosophy—I simply know about geography. And you turn the question in such a way that even in the night I go on thinking whether it was geographical or religious or philosophical."

Just in front of my school there were two beautiful kadamba trees. The kadamba is a very fragrant flower, and I used to sit in those trees whenever I could escape from the classes. That was the best place, because teachers would be passing underneath and the principal would be passing and nobody would be thinking that I may be hiding in the tree; and the trees were thick. But whenever this teacher of geography would pass by there, I could not resist dropping at least one or two stones on his head. And he would look up, and he would say, "What are you doing there?"

One day I said, "This is not geography class. You disturbed my meditation."

And he said, "What about those two stones that fell on my head?"

I said, "That is simply coincidence. I dropped the stones; it's strange how you appeared exactly at the right time. Now I will be wondering about it. You also wonder about it, how it happened exactly."

He used to come to tell my father, "Things are going too far." He was a bald-headed man; and in Hindi the word for bald-headed is *munde*. His name was Chotelal, but he was known as Chotelal Munde. Chotelal was rarely used, just Munde was enough because he was the only completely bald-headed person. When just in front of his house, I would knock on the door and his wife or somebody else would open the door, and they would say, "Why do you torture him? You torture him in the school, you torture him in the market, you torture him in the river when he goes to take his bath."

One day his wife opened the door and she said, "Will you stop torturing Munde or not?" and he was just there, behind her.

He grabbed his wife and he said, "You also call me Munde! This boy has spread around the whole city the idea that my name is Chotelal Munde—and now my own wife is converted by him. I can forgive everybody else but my own wife, in my own house . . ."

But I was insistent with my teachers: "Please keep on your track and don't give me any advice that does not belong to your subject, so that I can explore my life in my own way. Yes, I will commit many mistakes, many errors. I am willing to commit mistakes, errors, because that is the only way to learn."

MY GRANDFATHER WAS NOT A RELIGIOUS MAN, NOT AT ALL. HE WAS closer to Zorba the Greek: eat, drink, and be merry; there is no other world, it is all nonsense. My father was a very religious man; perhaps it was because of my grandfather—the reaction, the generation gap. But it was just upside down in my family: My grandfather was an atheist and perhaps because of his atheism my father turned out to be a theist. And whenever my father would go to the temple, my grandfather would laugh and he would say, "Again! Go on, waste your life in front of those stupid statues!"

I love Zorba for many reasons; one of the reasons was that in Zorba I found my grandfather again. He loved food so much that he used to not trust anybody; he would prepare it himself. In my life I have been a guest in thousands of families in India, but I have never tasted anything so delicious as my grandfather's cooking. And he loved it so much that every week it was a feast for all his friends—and he would prepare the whole day.

My mother and my aunts and the servants and cooks—everybody was thrown out of the kitchen. When my grandfather was cooking, nobody was to disturb him. But he was very friendly to me; he allowed me to watch and he said, "Learn, don't depend on other people. Only you know your taste. Who else can know it?"

I said, "That is beyond me; I am too lazy, but I can watch. The whole day cooking? I cannot do it." So I have not learned anything, but just watching was a joy—the way he worked, almost like a sculptor or a musician or a painter. Cooking was not just cooking, it was art to him. And if anything went just a little below his standard, he would throw it away immediately. He would cook it again, and I would say, "It is perfectly okay."

He would say, "You know it is not perfectly okay, it is just okay; but I am a perfectionist. Until it comes up to my standard, I am not going to offer it to anybody. I love my food."

He used to make many kinds of drinks . . . and whatsoever he did the whole family was against him: They said that he was just a nuisance. He wouldn't allow anybody in the kitchen, and in the evening he gathered all the atheists of the town. And just to defy Jainism, he would wait till the sun set. He would not eat before because Jainism says: eat before sunset; after sunset eating is not allowed. He used to send me again and again to see whether the sun had set or not.

He annoyed the whole family. And they could not be angry with him—he was the head of the family, the oldest man—but they were angry at me. That was easier. They said, "Why do you go on coming again and again to see whether the sun has set or not? That old man is getting you also lost, utterly lost."

I was very sad because I came across the book *Zorba the Greek* only when my grandfather was dying. The only thing that I felt at his funeral pyre was that he would have loved it if I had translated it for him and read it for him. I had read many books to him. He was uneducated. He could write only his signature, that was all. He could neither read nor write—but he was very proud of it.

He used to say, "It is good that my father did not force me to go to school, otherwise he would have spoiled me. These books spoil people so much." He would say to me, "Remember, your father is spoiled, your uncles are spoiled; they are continually reading religious books, scriptures, and it is all rubbish. While they are reading, I am living; and it is good to know through living."

He used to tell me, "They will send you to the university—they won't listen to me. And I cannot be much help, because if your father and your mother insist, they will send you to the university. But beware: Don't get lost in books."

He enjoyed small things. I asked him, "Everybody believes in God, why don't you believe, Baba?" I called him baba; that is a word for grandfather in India.

He said, "Because I am not afraid."

A very simple answer: "Why should I be afraid? There is no need to be afraid; I have not done any wrong, I have not harmed anybody. I have just lived my life joyously. If there is any God, and I meet him sometime, he cannot be angry at me. I will be angry at him: 'Why have you created this kind of world?' I am not afraid."

When he was dying I asked him again, because the doctors were saying that it was a question of only a few minutes. His pulse was getting faint, his heart was sinking, but he was fully conscious. I asked him, "Baba, one question . . ."

He opened his eyes and said, "I know your question: Why don't you believe in God? I knew that you were going to ask this question when I was dying. Do you think death will make me afraid? I have lived so joyously and so completely, there is no regret that I am dying.

"What else am I going to do tomorrow? I have done it all, there is nothing left. And if my pulse is slowing down and my heartbeat is slowing down, I think everything is going to be perfectly okay, because I am feeling very peaceful, very calm, very silent. Whether I die completely or live, I cannot say right now. But one thing you should remember: I am not afraid."

WHEN I PASSED MY MATRICULATION EXAMS, MY WHOLE FAMILY WAS in a great turmoil, because they all wanted something. Somebody wanted me to be a doctor, somebody wanted me to be a scientist, somebody wanted me to be an engineer—because in India these are respectable jobs, paying jobs. You become rich, you become well known, you are honored. But I said, "I am going to study philosophy."

They all said, "This is nonsense! No man of sense will go and study philosophy. What will you do after that? Six years wasted in the university studying things that are of no use. They don't have any value, you will not even get a small service, a small job."

And they were right. In India, if you apply for the smallest job, like a clerk in the post office, which needs only matriculation as qualification, and you have a master's degree in philosophy, you top the university, you have a gold medal—you will be refused. Only because of these things! These are *dis*qualifications, you are a difficult person! A clerk should not be a philosopher; otherwise there are bound to be difficulties.

So they said, "You will suffer your whole life. Think it over."

I said, "I never think, you know that. I simply see. And there is no question of choice, I know what I am going to study. It is not a question of weighing which job will be more profitable. Even if I become a beggar, I am going to study philosophy."

They were at a loss. They all asked me, "But what is the reason that you want to study philosophy?"

I said, "The reason is that my whole life I am going to fight against philosophers. I have to know everything about them."

They said, "My God! This is your idea? We have never imagined that a man should study philosophy because he is going to fight philosophers his whole life." But they knew that I was crazy. They said, "Something like this was expected." Still they persisted: "There is time, you can still think about it. The universities will be opening in one month; you can still change your mind."

I said, "One month, one year, one life makes no difference, because I don't have any choice. It is my choiceless responsibility."

One of my uncles, who was a graduate from the university, said, "It is absolutely impossible to talk with him—he uses words that don't seem to carry any meaning. Choicelessness . . . responsibility . . . what do these things have to do with life? You will need money, you will need a house, you will need to support a family."

I said, "I am not going to have a family. I am not going to have a house and I am not going to support anybody!" And I have not supported anybody and I have not made any house. I am the poorest man in the world!

They could not manage to force me to become a doctor, engineer, scientist, but they all were angry. And when I became a wandering teacher around the country, doing the job for which I had studied logic and philosophy because I wanted to be perfectly acquainted with the enemy, soon there was not a single man who was ready to accept my challenge. Then my family started feeling guilty, feeling that it was good that they were not able to make me a doctor, engineer, scientist. I had proved that they were wrong. They started asking me, "Forgive us."

I said, "There is no problem, because I never took all your advice seriously. I never bothered! Whatever I was going to do, I was going to do in spite of everything going against me. So don't feel guilty. I have never taken your advice seriously; I was hearing you but not listening. I had a decision in me, a decisiveness."

IN SEARCH
OF THE DEATHLESS

Q: *You know that you will live in some form beyond this life?*
A: Not in any form. I will live without form.
Q: *Eternally?*
A: Eternally. I have been here eternally and I am going to be here eternally.
Q: *Will you have consciousness beyond death?*
A: Yes, because death has nothing to do with consciousness.
Q: *Will you have identity beyond death?*
A: No identity.

•from an interview with John McCall,
Seattle Post-Intelligencer

In the East we have been watching the death experience of people. How you die reflects your whole life, how you lived. If I can see just your death, I can write your whole biography—because in that one moment your whole life becomes condensed. In that one moment, like a lightning bolt, you show everything.

A miserly person will die with clenched fists—still holding and clinging, still trying not to die, still trying not to relax. A loving person will die with open hands, sharing . . . even sharing his death, as he shared his life. You can see everything written on the face—whether this man has lived his life fully alert, aware. If he has, then on his face there will be a light shining; around his body there will be an aura. You come close to him and you will feel silent—not sad, but silent. It even happens that if a person has died blissfully you will feel suddenly happy near him.

It happened in my childhood. A very saintly person in my village died. I had a certain attachment to him. He was a priest in a small temple, a very poor man, and whenever I would pass—and I used to pass at least twice a day; when going to the school near the temple, I would pass—he would call me and he would always give me some fruit, some sweet.

When he died, I was the only child who went to see him. The whole town gathered. Suddenly I could not believe what happened—I started laughing. My father was there; he tried to stop me because he felt embarrassed. A death is not a time to laugh. He tried to shut me up. He told me again and again, "You keep quiet!"

But I have never felt that urge again. Since then I have never felt it; never before had I ever felt it—to laugh so loudly, as if something beautiful has happened. And I could not hold myself. I laughed loudly, everybody was angry, I was sent back, and my father told me, "Never again are you to be allowed in any serious situation! Because of you, even I was feeling very embarrassed. Why were you laughing? What was happening there? What is there in death to laugh about? Everybody was crying and weeping and you were laughing."

And I told him, "Something happened. That old man released something and it was tremendously beautiful. He died an orgasmic death." Not exactly these words, but I told him that I felt he was very happy dying, very blissful dying, and I wanted to participate in his laughter. He was laughing, his energy was laughing.

I was thought mad. How can a man die laughing? Since then I have been watching many deaths, but I have not seen that type of death again. When you die, you release your energy and with that energy, your whole life's experience. Whatsoever you have been—sad, happy, loving, angry, passionate, compassionate—whatsoever you have been, that energy carries the vibrations of your whole life. Whenever a saint is dying, just being near him is a great gift; just to be showered with his energy is a great inspiration. You will be put in a totally different dimension. You will be drugged by his energy, you will feel drunk. Death can be a total fulfillment, but that is possible only if life has been lived.

IT WAS ONE OF MY PASTIMES IN MY CHILDHOOD TO FOLLOW EVERY funeral procession. My parents were continually worried: "You don't know the man who has died, you have no relationship, no friendship with him. Why should you bother and waste your time?" Because the Indian funeral takes three, four, or five hours.

First, going out of the city, the procession walking, taking the dead body, and then burning the body on the funeral pyre . . . And you know Indians, they can't do anything efficiently. The funeral pyre won't catch fire, it will just live halfheartedly and the man will not burn, and everybody is making all kinds of effort because they want to get away from there as quickly as possible. But the dead people are also tricky. They will try their hardest to keep you there as long as possible.

I told my parents, "It is not a question of being related to somebody. I am certainly related with death, that you cannot deny. It does not matter who dies—it is symbolic to me. One day I will be dying. I have to know how people behave with the dead, how the dead behave with the living people; otherwise, how am I going to learn?"

They said, "You bring strange arguments."

"But," I said, "you have to convince me that death is not related to me, that I am not going to die. If you can convince me of that, I will stop going; otherwise let me explore." They could not say to me that I would not be dying, so I said, "Then just keep quiet. I am not telling you to go. And I enjoy everything that happens there."

The first thing I have observed is that nobody talks about death, even there. The funeral pyre is burning somebody's father, somebody's brother, somebody's uncle, somebody's friend, somebody's enemy: he was related to many people in many ways. He is dead—and they are all engaged in trivia.

They would be talking about the movies, they would be talking about politics, they would be talking about the market. They would be talking about all kinds of things—except death. They would gather into small cliques and sit around the funeral pyre. I would go from one clique to another: Nobody was talking about death. And I know for certain that they were talking about other things to keep themselves occupied, so that they didn't see the burning body—because it was their body too.

They could see, if they had a little insight into things, that they are burning there on the funeral pyre—nobody else. It is only a question of time. Tomorrow somebody else from among these people will be there on the funeral pyre; the day after tomorrow somebody else will be—every day people are being brought to the funeral pyre. One day I am going to be brought to the funeral pyre, and this is the treatment that these people will be giving to me. This is their last farewell: they are talking about prices going up, the rupee devaluating—in front of death. And they are all sitting with their backs toward the funeral pyre.

They had to come, so they have come—but they never wanted to come. So they want to be there almost absently present, just to fulfill a social conformity, just to show that they were present. And that too is to make sure that when they die, they will not be just taken away by the municipal corporation truck. Because they have participated in so many people's deaths, naturally it becomes obligatory for other people to give them a send-off. They know why they are there—they are there because they want people to be there when they are on the funeral pyre.

But what are these people doing? I asked people whom I knew. Sometimes one of my teachers was there, talking about stupid things—that somebody is flirting with somebody's wife . . . I said, "Is this the time to talk about somebody's wife and what she is doing? Think about the wife of this man who has died. Nobody is worried about that, nobody is talking about that.

"Think of your wife when you will be dead. With whom will she be flirting? What will she do? Have you made any arrangements for that? And can't you see the stupidity? Death is present and you are trying to avoid it in every possible way." But all the religions have done that, and these people were simply representing certain traditions of certain religions.

MY MOTHER'S FATHER USED TO TELL ME THAT WHEN I WAS BORN HE consulted one of the best known astrologers of those days. The astrologer was to make my birth chart, but he studied it and he said, "If this child survives after seven years, only then will I make the chart. It seems impossible that he can survive for more than seven years, so if the child is going to die it is useless to make the chart; it will be of no use. And it has been my habit," the astrologer said, "that unless I am certain that the chart will be useful I never make it."

He died before he had done it, so his son had to prepare the chart. But he was also puzzled; he said, "It is almost certain that this child is going to die at the age of twenty-one. Every seven years he will have to face death." So my parents, my family, were always worried about my death. Whenever I would come to the end of a seven-year cycle, they would become afraid. And he was right. At the age of seven I survived, but I had a deep experience of death—not of my own, but of the death of my maternal grandfather. And I was so much attached to him that his death appeared to be my own death.

In my own childish way I imitated his death. I would not eat for three days, would not drink water, because I felt that if I did so it would be a betrayal. He was part and parcel of me. I had grown with his presence, his love.

When he died I felt that it would be a betrayal to eat. I didn't want to live. It was childish, but through it something very deep happened. For three days I remained lying down; I would not come out of the bed. I said, "Now that he is dead, I do not want to live." I survived, but those three days became a death experience. I died in a way, and I came to realize—now I can tell you about it, though at that time it was just a vague experience—I came to feel that death is impossible. This was a feeling. When I reached the age of fourteen, my family again became disturbed that I would die. I survived, but then I again tried it consciously. I said to them, "If death is going to occur as the astrologer has said, then it is better to be prepared. And why give a chance to death? Why should I not go and meet it halfway? If I am going to die, then it is better to die consciously."

So I took leave from my school for seven days. I went to my principal and I told him, "I am going to die."

He said, "What nonsense you are talking! Are you committing suicide? What do you mean you are going to die?"

I told him about the astrologer's prediction that the possibility of death would confront me every seven years. I told him, "I am going into retreat for seven days to wait for death. If death comes, it is good to meet it consciously so that it becomes an experience."

I went to a temple just outside of my village. I arranged with the priest that he should not disturb me. It was a very lonely, unvisited temple—old, in ruins. No one ever came to it. So I told him, "I will remain in the temple. You just give me something to eat and something to drink once a day, and the whole day I will be lying there waiting for death."

For seven days I waited. Those seven days became a beautiful experience. Death never came, but on my part I tried in every way to be dead. Strange, weird feelings happened. Many things happened, but the basic note was this—that if you are feeling you are going to die, you become calm and silent. Nothing creates any worry then, because all worries are concerned with life. Life is the basis of all worries. When you are going to die anyway one day, why worry?

I was lying there. On the third or fourth day a snake entered the temple. It was in view, I was seeing the snake, but there was no fear. Suddenly I felt very strange. The snake was coming nearer and nearer, and I felt very strange. There was no fear, so I thought, "When death is coming, it may be coming through this snake, so why be afraid? Wait!"

The snake crossed over me and went away. Fear had disappeared. If you accept death, there is no fear. If you cling to life, then every fear is there.

Many times flies came around me. They would fly around, they would creep over me, on my face. Sometimes I felt irritated and would have liked to throw them off, but then I thought, "What is the use? Sooner or later I am going to die, and then no one will be here to protect the body. So let them have their way."

The moment I decided to let them have their way, the irritation disappeared. They were still on the body, but it was as if I was not concerned. They were as if moving, as if creeping on someone else's body. There was a distance immediately. If you accept death, a distance is created. Life moves far away with all its worries, irritations, everything. I died in a way, but I came to know that something deathless is there. Once you accept death totally, you become aware of it.

Then again at the age of twenty-one, my family was waiting. So I told them, "Why do you go on waiting? Do not wait. Now I am not going to die."

Physically, someday I will die, of course. However, this prediction of the astrologer helped me very much because he made me aware very early on about death. I could meditate and could accept that it was coming.

ENLIGHTENMENT:
A DISCONTINUITY
WITH THE PAST

T here is a beautiful Buddhist story:

In a certain town a very beautiful young woman suddenly arrived out of the blue. Nobody knew from where she came; her whereabouts were completely unknown. But she was so beautiful, so enchantingly beautiful, that nobody even thought about where she had come from. People gathered together, the whole town gathered—and all the young men, almost three hundred young men, wanted to get married to the woman.

The woman said, "Look, I am one and you are three hundred. I can be married only to one, so you do one thing. I will come again tomorrow; I give you twenty-four hours. If one of you can repeat Buddha's Lotus Sutra, I will marry him."

All the young men rushed to their homes; they didn't eat, they didn't sleep, they recited the sutra the whole night, they tried to cram it in. Ten succeeded. The next morning the woman came and those ten people offered to recite. The woman listened. They had succeeded.

She said, "Right, but I am one. How can I marry ten? I will give you twenty-four hours again. The one who can also explain the meaning of the Lotus Sutra I will marry. So you try to understand—because reciting is a simple thing, you are mechanically repeating something and you don't understand its meaning."

There was no time at all—only one night!—and the Lotus Sutra is a long sutra. But when you are infatuated you can do anything. They rushed back, they tried hard. The next day three persons appeared. They had understood the meaning.

And the woman said, "Again the trouble remains. The number is reduced, but the trouble remains. From three hundred to three is a great improvement, but again, I cannot marry three persons—I can marry only one. So, twenty-four hours more . . . The one who has not only understood it but tasted it too, that person I will marry. So in twenty-four hours try to taste the meaning of it. You are explaining, but this explanation is intellectual. Good, better than yesterday—you have some comprehension—but the comprehension is intellectual. I would like to see some meditative taste, some fragrance. I would like to see that the lotus has entered into your presence, that you have become something of the lotus. I would like to smell the fragrance of it. So tomorrow I come again."

Only one person came, and certainly he had achieved. The woman took him to her house outside the town. The man had never seen the house; it was very beautiful, almost a dreamland. And the parents of the woman were standing at the gate. They received the young man and said, "We are very happy."

The woman went inside, and the man chitchatted a little with the parents. Then the parents said, "You go. She must be waiting for you. This is her room." They showed him. He went, he opened the door, but there was nobody there. It was an empty room. But there was a door entering into the garden. So he looked—maybe she has gone into the garden. Yes, she must have gone because on the path there were footprints. So he followed the footprints. He walked almost a mile. The garden ended and now he was standing on the bank of a beautiful river—but the woman was not there. The footprints also disappeared. There were only two shoes, golden shoes, belonging to the woman.

Now he was puzzled. What has happened? He looked back—there was no garden, no house, no parents, nothing. All had disappeared. He looked again. The shoes were gone, the river was gone. All that there was, was emptiness—and a great laughter.

And he laughed too. He got married.

This is a beautiful Buddhist story. He got married to emptiness, got married to nothingness. This is the marriage for which all the great saints have been searching. This is the moment when you become a "bride of Christ" or a *gopi* of Krishna. But everything disappears—the path, the garden, the house, the woman, even the footprints. Everything disappears. There is just a laughter, a laughter that arises from the very belly of the universe.

I WAS FROM MY VERY CHILDHOOD IN LOVE WITH SILENCE. AS LONG AS I could manage I would just sit silently. Naturally my family used to think that I was going to be good for nothing—and they were right! I certainly proved good for nothing, but I don't regret it.

It came to such a point that sometimes I would be sitting and my mother would come to me and say something like, "There seems to be nobody in the whole house. I need somebody to go to the market to fetch some vegetables." I was sitting in front of her, and I would say, "If I see somebody I will tell them."

It was accepted that my presence meant nothing; whether I was there or not, it did not matter. Once or twice they tried, and then they found that "it is better to leave him out, and not take any notice of him." In the morning they would send me to fetch vegetables. And in the evening I would come to ask, "I have forgotten for what you had sent me, and now the market is closed. . . ."

My mother said, "It is not your fault, it is our fault. The whole day we have been waiting, but in the first place we should not have asked you. Where have you been?"

I said, "As I went out of the house, just close by there was a very beautiful bodhi tree"—the kind of tree under which Gautam Buddha became awakened. The tree got the name bodhi tree because of Gautam Buddha. One does not know what it used to be called before Gautam Buddha; it must have had some name, but after Buddha it became associated with his name.

There was a beautiful bodhi tree, and it was so tempting for me. There used to be always such silence, such coolness underneath it, nobody to disturb me, that I could not pass it without sitting under it for some time. And those moments of peace, I think sometimes may have stretched the whole day.

After just a few disappointments they thought, "It is better not to bother him." And I was immensely happy that they had accepted the fact that I was almost nonexistent. It gave me tremendous freedom. Nobody expected anything from me. When nobody expects anything from you, you fall into a silence. The world has accepted you; now there is no expectation from you.

When sometimes I was late coming home, they used to search for me in two places. One was my nani's house, and the other was the bodhi tree—and because they started searching for me under the bodhi tree, I started climbing the tree and sitting in the top of it. They would come and they would look around and say, "He does not seem to be here."

And I myself would nod: I said, "Yes, that's true. I'm not here."

MY FIRST EXPERIENCE OUT OF THE BODY WAS FALLING FROM A TREE. I used to meditate just behind the university, where there was a beautiful hillock and three tall trees, very silent, and nobody used to go there. I used to sit in one of the trees and meditate. One day suddenly I saw that I was sitting in the tree, and at the same time my body had fallen down and was lying on the ground. For a moment I could not figure out how to enter into it again. It was just a coincidence that a woman who used to bring milk to the university from the nearby village had seen my body falling down, so she came close. She must have heard that in situations when the inner body becomes separated from the outer body, if you rub between the eyes, the third eye, that is the door. The spirit that has left will be able to enter.

So she rubbed my third eye. I could see her rubbing my forehead, and the next moment I opened my eyes and thanked her and asked her how she knew to do that.

She had simply heard about it. It was a primitive village, but she had heard the traditional idea that the third eye is the place from where one leaves and where one can come back.

I HAVE BEEN LOOKING FOR THE DOOR TO ENLIGHTENMENT AS LONG as I remember—from my very childhood. I must have carried that idea from my past life, because I don't remember a single day in my childhood in this life that I was not looking for it. Naturally, I was thought crazy by everybody. I never played with any children. I never could find any way to communicate with the children of my own age. To me they looked stupid, doing all kinds of idiotic things. I never joined any football team, volleyball team, hockey team.

Of course, they all thought me crazy. And as far as I was concerned, as I grew I started looking at the whole world as crazy.

In the last year, when I was twenty-one, it was a time of nervous breakdown and breakthrough. Naturally, those who loved me—my family, my friends, my professors—could understand a little bit what was going on in me. Why I was so different from other children, why I would go on sitting for hours with closed eyes, why I sat by the bank of the river and went on looking at the sky for hours, sometimes for the whole night. Naturally, the people who could not understand such things—and I did not expect them to understand—thought me mad.

In my own home I had become almost absent. By and by they stopped asking me anything, and slowly, slowly they started feeling as if I were not there. And I loved it, the way I had become a nothingness, a nobody, an absence.

That one year was tremendous. I was surrounded with nothingness, emptiness. I had lost all contact with the world. If somebody reminded me to take a bath, I would go on taking the bath for hours. Then they had to knock on the door: "Now come out of the bathroom. You have taken enough bath for one month! Just come out." If they reminded me to eat, I ate; otherwise, days would pass and I would not eat. Not that I was fasting—I had no idea about eating or fasting. My whole concern was to go deeper and deeper into myself. And the door was so magnetic, the pull was so immense—like what physicists now call black holes.

They say there are black holes in existence. If a star comes by chance to a black hole, it is pulled into it; there is no way to resist that pull, and to go into the black hole is to go into destruction. We don't know what happens on the other side. My idea, for which some physicist has to find evidence, is that the black hole on this side is a white hole on the other side. The hole cannot be just one side; it is a tunnel. I have experienced it in myself. Perhaps on a bigger scale the same happens in the universe. The star dies; as far as we can see, it disappears. But every moment new stars are being born. From where? Where is their womb? It is simple arithmetic that the black hole is just a womb—the old disappears into it and the new is born.

This I have experienced in myself—I am not a physicist. That one year of tremendous pull drew me farther and farther away from people, so much so that I would not recognize my own mother, I might not recognize my own father; there were times I forgot my own name. I tried hard, but there was no way to find what my name used to be. Naturally, to everybody else during that one year I was mad. But to me that madness became meditation, and the peak of that madness opened the door.

I WAS TAKEN TO A *VAIDYA*, TO AN AYURVEDIC PHYSICIAN. IN FACT, I was taken to many doctors and to many physicians but only one *vaidya* told my father, "He is not ill. Don't waste your time." Of course, they were dragging me from one place to another. And many people would give me medicines and I would tell my father, "Why are you worried? I am perfectly okay." But nobody would believe what I was saying. They would say, "You keep quiet. You just take the medicine, what harm can it do?" So I used to take all sorts of medicines.

There was only one *vaidya* who was a man of insight—his name was Pundit Bhaghirath Prasad. That old man has gone, but he was a rare man of insight. He looked at me and he said, "He is not ill." And he started crying and said, "I have been searching for this state myself. He is fortunate. In this life I have missed this state. Don't take him to anybody. He is reaching home." And he cried tears of happiness.

He was a seeker. He had been searching all over the country from this end to that. His whole life was a search and enquiry. He had some idea of what it was about. He became my protector—my protector against the doctors and other physicians. He said to my father, "You leave it to me. I will take care." He never gave me any medicine. When my father insisted, he just gave me sugar pills and told me, "These are sugar pills. Just to console them you can take them. They will not harm, they will not help. In fact, there is no help possible."

WHEN YOU FIRST ENTER INTO THE WORLD OF NO-MIND IT LOOKS LIKE madness—the "dark night of the soul," the mad night of the soul. All the religions have noted the fact; hence all the religions insist on finding a master before you start entering into the world of no-mind—because he will be there to help you, to support you. You will be falling apart but he will be there to encourage you, to give you hope. He will be there to interpret the new to you. That is the meaning of a master: to interpret that which cannot be interpreted, to indicate that which cannot be said, to show that which is inexpressible. He will be there, he will devise methods and ways for you to continue on the path—otherwise you might start escaping from it.

And remember, there is no escape. If you start escaping you will simply go berserk. Sufis call such people the *mastas*. In India they are known as mad *paramahansas*. You cannot go back because it is no longer there, and you cannot go ahead because it is all dark. You are stuck. That's why Buddha says, "Fortunate is the man who has found a master."

I myself was working without a master. I searched and I could not find one. It was not that I had not searched; I had searched long enough, but I could not find one. It is very rare to find a master, rare to find a being who has become a nonbeing, rare to find a presence who is almost an absence. Rare to find a man who is simply a door to the divine, an open door to the divine that will not hinder you, through which you can pass. It is very difficult.

The Sikhs call their temple the *guruduwara*, the door of the master. That is exactly what the master is—the door. Jesus says again and again, "I am the gate, I am the way, I am the truth. Come follow me, pass through me. And unless you pass through me you will not be able to reach."

Yes, sometimes it happens that a person has to work without a master. If the master is not available then one has to work without a master, but then the journey is very hazardous.

For one year I was in such a state that it was almost impossible to know what was happening. For one year continuously it was even difficult to keep myself alive. Just to keep myself alive was a very difficult thing—because all appetite disappeared. Days would pass and I would not feel any hunger; days would pass and I would not feel any thirst. I had to force myself to eat, force myself to drink. The body was so nonexistential that I had to hurt myself to feel that I was still in the body. I had to knock my head against the wall to feel whether my head was still there or not. Only when it hurt would I be a little in the body.

Every morning and every evening I would run for five to eight miles. People used to think that I was mad. Why was I running so much? Sixteen miles a day! It was just to feel myself, to feel that I still existed, not to lose contact with myself—just to wait until my eyes became attuned to the new that was happening.

And I had to keep myself close to myself. I would not talk to anybody because everything had become so inconsistent that even to formulate one sentence was difficult. In the middle of the sentence I would forget what I was saying. In the middle of the road I would forget where I was going. Then I would have to come back. I would read a book—I would read fifty pages and then suddenly I would realize, "What am I reading? I don't remember at all." My situation was such . . .

The door of the psychiatrist's office burst open and a man rushed in. "Doctor!" he cried. "You've got to help me. I'm sure I'm losing my mind. I can't remember anything—what happened a year ago, or even what happened yesterday. I must be going crazy!"

"Hmm," pondered the shrink. "Just when did you first become aware of this problem?"

The man looked puzzled. "What problem?"

This was my situation! Even to complete a full sentence was difficult. I had to keep myself shut in my room. I made it a point not to talk, not to say anything, because to say anything was to say that I was mad. For one year it persisted. I would simply lie on the floor and look at the ceiling and count from one to a hundred then back from a hundred to one. Just to remain capable of counting was at least something. Again and again I would forget. It took one year for me to gain a focus again, to have a perspective.

It happened. It was a miracle. But it was difficult. There was nobody to support me, there was nobody to say where I was going and what was happening. In fact, everybody was against it—my teachers, my friends, my well-wishers. All were against it. But they could not do anything, they could only condemn, they could only ask what I was doing.

I was not doing anything! Now it was beyond me; it was happening. I had done something; unknowingly I had knocked at the door, now the door had opened. I had been meditating for many years, just sitting silently doing nothing, and by and by I started getting into that space where you *are*, and you are not doing anything; you are simply there, a presence, a watcher.

You are not even a watcher because you are not watching—you are just a presence. Words are not adequate because whatsoever word is used, it seems as if it is being done.

No, I was not doing it. I was simply lying, sitting, walking—deep down there was no doer. I had lost all ambition; there was no desire to be anybody, no desire to reach. I was simply thrown into myself. It was an emptiness, and emptiness drives one crazy. But emptiness is the only door to God. That means that only those who are ready to go mad ever attain, nobody else.

YOU ASK ME, WHAT HAPPENED WHEN YOU BECAME ENLIGHTENED?

I laughed, a real uproarious laugh, seeing the whole absurdity of trying to be enlightened. The whole thing is ridiculous because we are born enlightened, and to try for something that is already the case is the most absurd thing. If you already have it, you cannot achieve it; only those things can be achieved which you don't have, which are not intrinsic parts of your being. But enlightenment is your very nature.

I had struggled for it for many lives—it had been the only target for many, many lives. And I had done everything that is possible to do to attain it but I had always failed. It was bound to be so—because it cannot be an attainment. It is your nature, so how can it be your attainment? It cannot be made an ambition.

Mind is ambitious—ambitious for money, for power, for prestige. And then one day, when it gets fed up with all these extrovert activities, it becomes ambitious for enlightenment, for liberation, for nirvana, for God. But the same ambition has come back; only the object has changed. First the object was outside, now the object is inside. But your attitude, your approach has not changed; you are the same person in the same rut, in the same routine.

"The day I became enlightened" simply means the day I realized that there is nothing to achieve, there is nowhere to go, there is nothing to be done. We are already divine and we are already perfect—as we are. No improvement is needed, no improvement at all. God never creates anybody imperfect. Even if you come across an imperfect man, you will see that his imperfection is perfect. God never creates any imperfect thing.

I have heard about a Zen master, Bokuju, who was telling this truth to his disciples, that all is perfect. A man stood up—very old, a hunchback—and he said, "What about me? I am a hunchback. What do you say about me?" Bokuju said, "I have never seen such a perfect hunchback in my life."

When I say "the day I achieved enlightenment," I am using wrong language—because there is no other language, because our language is created by us. It consists of words like *achievement, attainment, goals, improvement, progress, evolution.* Our languages are not created by enlightened people; and in fact they cannot create language even if they want to, because enlightenment happens in silence. How can you bring that silence into words? And whatsoever you do, the words are going to destroy something of that silence.

Lao Tzu says: The moment truth is asserted, it becomes false. There is no way to communicate truth. But language has to be used; there is no other way. So we always have to use the language with the condition that it cannot be adequate to the experience. Hence I say "the day I achieved my enlightenment." It is neither an achievement nor mine.

I laughed that day because of all my stupid, ridiculous efforts to attain it. I laughed on that day at myself, and I laughed on that day at the whole of humanity, because everybody is trying to achieve, everybody is trying to reach, everybody is trying to improve.

To me it happened in a state of total relaxation—it always happens in that state. I had tried everything. And then, seeing the futility of all effort, I dropped the whole project. I forgot all about it. For seven days I lived as ordinarily as possible.

The people I used to live with were very much surprised, because this was the first time they had seen me live just an ordinary life. Otherwise my whole life was a perfect discipline.

For two years I had lived with that family, and they had known that I would get up at three o'clock in the morning, then I would go for a long four- or five-mile walk or run, and then I would take a bath in the river. Everything was absolutely routine. Even if I had a fever or I was ill, there was no difference: I would simply go on in the same way.

They had known me to sit in meditation for hours. Up to that day I had not eaten many things. I would not drink tea, coffee; I had a strict discipline about what to eat, what not to eat. When I relaxed for seven days, when I dropped the whole thing and when on the first day I woke up at nine o'clock in the morning and drank tea, the family was puzzled. They said, "What has happened? Have you fallen?" They used to think of me as a great yogi.

One picture of those days still exists. I used to use only one single piece of cloth and that was all. In the day I would cover my body with it, in the night I would use it as a blanket to cover myself. I slept on a bamboo mat. That was my whole comfort—that blanket, that bamboo mat. I had nothing—no other possessions. They were puzzled when I woke up at nine. They said, "Something is wrong. Are you very ill, seriously ill?"

I said, "No, I am not seriously ill. I have been ill for many years; now I am perfectly healthy. Now I will wake up only when sleep leaves me, and I will go to sleep only when sleep comes to me. I am no longer going to be a slave to the clock. I will eat whatsoever my body feels like eating, and I will drink whatsoever I feel like drinking." I said, "Enough is enough." And in seven days I completely forgot the whole project, and I forgot it forever.

And the seventh day it happened—it happened just out of nowhere. And when I laughed, the gardener heard the laughter. He used to think that I was a little bit crazy, but he had never seen me laugh in that way. He came running. He said, "What is the matter?"

I said, "Don't be worried. You know I am crazy—now I have gone completely crazy! I am laughing at myself. Don't feel offended. Just go back to sleep."

FOR MANY LIVES I HAD BEEN WORKING—WORKING UPON MYSELF, struggling, doing whatsoever can be done—and nothing was happening. Now I understand why nothing was happening. The very effort was the barrier, the very ladder was preventing, the very urge to seek was the obstacle. Not that one can reach without seeking—seeking is needed—but then comes a point when seeking has to be dropped. The boat is needed to cross the river, but then comes a moment when you have to get out of the boat and forget all about it and leave it behind. Effort is needed, without effort nothing is possible. And also with *only* effort, nothing is possible.

Just before the twenty-first of March, 1953, seven days before, I stopped working on myself. A moment comes when you see the whole futility of effort. You have done all that you can do and nothing is happening. You have done all that is humanly possible. Then what else can you do? In sheer helplessness one drops all search. And the day the search stopped, the day I was not seeking for something, the day I was not expecting something to happen, it started happening. A new energy arose—out of nowhere. It was not coming from any source. It was coming from nowhere and everywhere. It was in the trees and in the rocks and the sky and the sun and the air—it was everywhere.

I had been seeking so hard and thinking it was very far away—and it was so near and so close! The eyes had become focused on the faraway, the horizon, and they had lost the ability to see that which is just close.

The day effort ceased, I also ceased—because you cannot exist without effort, and you cannot exist without desire, and you cannot exist without striving. The phenomenon of the ego, of the self, is not a thing—it is a process. It is not a substance sitting there inside you; you have to create it each moment. It is like pedaling a bicycle: if you pedal it goes on and on; if you don't pedal it stops. It may go on a little because of the momentum, but the moment you stop pedaling, in fact, the bicycle starts stopping. It has no more energy, no more power to go anywhere. It is going to fall and collapse.

The ego exists because we go on pedaling desire, because we go on striving to get something, because we go on jumping ahead of ourselves. That is the very phenomenon of the ego—the jump ahead of yourself, the jump into the future, the jump into the tomorrow. The jump into the nonexistential creates the ego. Because it comes out of the nonexistential it is like a mirage. It consists only of desire and nothing else. It consists only of thirst and nothing else.

The ego is not in the present, it is in the future. If you are in the future, then ego seems to be very substantial. If you are in the present, the ego is a mirage; it starts disappearing.

The day I stopped seeking . . . and it is not right to say that I stopped seeking; better will be to say the day seeking stopped. Let me repeat it: The better way to say it is the day the seeking stopped. Because if I stop it, then "I" am there again. Now stopping becomes my effort, now stopping becomes my desire, and desire goes on existing in a very subtle way.

You cannot stop desire, you can only understand it. In the very understanding is the stopping of it. Remember, nobody can stop desiring—and the reality happens only when desire stops.

So this is the dilemma. What to do? Desire is there, and buddhas go on saying desire has to be stopped, and they go on saying in the next breath that you cannot stop desire. So what to do? You put people in a dilemma. They are in desire, certainly. You say it has to be stopped—okay. And then you say it cannot be stopped. Then what is to be done?

The desire has to be understood. You can understand it, you can just see the futility of it. A direct perception is needed, an immediate penetration is needed.

The day desiring stopped, I felt very hopeless and helpless. No hope because no future. Nothing to hope because all hoping has proved futile, it leads nowhere. You go in rounds. It goes on dangling in front of you, it goes on creating new mirages, it goes on calling you, "Come on, run fast, you will reach." But howsoever fast you run, you never reach. It is like the horizon that you see around the earth. It appears, but it is not there. If you go toward it, it goes on running from you. The faster you run, the faster it moves away. The slower you go, the slower it moves away. But one thing is certain—the distance between you and the horizon remains absolutely the same. Not even a single inch can you reduce the distance between you and the horizon.

You cannot reduce the distance between you and your hope. Hope is the horizon. You try to bridge yourself with the horizon, with the hope, with a projected desire. The desire is a bridge—a dream bridge, because the horizon does not exist. So you cannot make a bridge to it, you can only dream about the bridge. You cannot be joined with the nonexistential.

The day the desire stopped, the day I looked into it and realized it was simply futile, I was helpless and hopeless. But that very moment something started happening. The same started happening for which I had been working for many lives and it was not happening. In your hopelessness is the only hope, and in your desirelessness is your only fulfillment, and in your tremendous helplessness suddenly the whole existence starts helping you.

Existence is waiting. When it sees that you are working on your own, it does not interfere. It waits. It can wait infinitely because there is no hurry for existence. It is eternity. The moment you are not on your own—the moment you drop, the moment you disappear—the whole existence rushes toward you, enters you. And for the first time things start happening.

Seven days I lived in a very hopeless and helpless state, but at the same time something was arising. When I say "hopeless" I don't mean what you mean by the word. I simply mean there was no hope in me. Hope was absent. I am not saying that I was hopeless and sad. I was happy, in fact; I was very tranquil, calm and collected and centered. Hopeless, but in a totally new meaning. There was no hope, so how could there be hopelessness? Both had disappeared.

The hopelessness was absolute and total. Hope had disappeared and with it, its counterpart hopelessness had also disappeared. It was a totally new experience—of being without hope. It was not a negative state. I have to use words, but it was not a negative state. It was absolutely positive. It was not just absence, a presence was felt. Something was overflowing in me, over-flooding me.

And when I say I was helpless, I don't mean the word in the dictionary sense. I simply say I was selfless. That's what I mean when I say helpless. I had recognized the fact that I am not—so I cannot depend on myself, so I cannot stand on my own ground. There was no ground underneath, I was in an abyss . . . a bottomless abyss. But there was no fear because there was nothing to protect. There was no fear because there was nobody to be afraid.

Those seven days were of tremendous transformation, total transforma-tion. And the last day the presence of a totally new energy, a new light and new delight, became so intense that it was almost unbearable—as if I was exploding, as if I was going mad with blissfulness. The younger generation in the West has the right expression for it—I was blissed out, stoned.

It was impossible to make any sense out of it, what was happening. It was a nonsense world—difficult to figure it out, difficult to manage in categories, difficult to use words, language, explanations. All scriptures appeared dead, and all the words that have been used for this experience looked very pale, anemic. This was so alive. It was like a tidal wave of bliss.

The whole day was strange, stunning, and it was a shattering experience. The past was disappearing as if it had never belonged to me, as if I had read about it somewhere. As if I had dreamed about it, as if it were somebody else's story I had heard. I was becoming loose from my past, I was being uprooted from my history. I was losing my autobiography. I was becoming a nonbeing, what Bud-dha calls *anatta*. Boundaries were disappearing, distinctions were disappearing.

Mind was disappearing; it was millions of miles away. It was difficult to catch hold of it, it was rushing farther and farther away and there was no urge to keep it close. I was simply indifferent about it all. It was okay. There was no urge to remain continuous with the past. By the evening it became so difficult to bear it—it was hurting, it was painful. It was like when a woman goes into labor, when a child is to be born and the woman suffers tremendous pain—the birth pangs.

I used to go to sleep in those days nearabout twelve or one in the night, but that day it was impossible to remain awake. My eyes were closing, it was diffi-cult to keep them open. Something was imminent, something was going to happen. It was difficult to say what it was—maybe it was going to be my death—but there was no fear. I was ready for it. Those seven days had been so beautiful that I was ready to die; nothing more was needed. They had been so tremendously blissful, I was so contented, that if death was coming, it was welcome.

But something was going to happen—something like death, something very drastic, something that would be either a death or a new birth, a crucifixion or a resurrection—something of tremendous import was just around the corner. And it was impossible to keep my eyes open, I was drugged.

I went to sleep nearabout eight. It was not like sleep. Now I can understand what Patanjali means when he says that sleep and samadhi are similar. Only with one difference—that in samadhi you are fully awake and asleep also—asleep and awake together. The whole body relaxed, every cell of the body totally relaxed, all functioning relaxed and yet a light of awareness burns within you . . . clear, smokeless. You remain alert and yet relaxed, loose but fully awake. The body is in the deepest sleep possible and your consciousness is at its peak. The peak of consciousness and the valley of the body meet.

I went to sleep. It was a very strange sleep. The body was asleep, I was awake. It was so strange—as if one is torn apart into two directions, two dimensions; as if the polarity has become completely focused, as if I were both the polarities together . . . the positive and negative were meeting, sleep and awareness were meeting, death and life were meeting. That is the moment when you can say the creator and the creation meet.

It was weird. For the first time it shocks you to the very roots, it shakes your foundations. You can never be the same after that experience; it brings a new vision to your life, a new quality.

Nearabout twelve my eyes suddenly opened—I had not opened them. The sleep was broken by something else. I felt a great presence around me in the room. It was a very small room. I felt a throbbing life all around me, a great vibration—almost like a hurricane, a great storm of light, joy, ecstasy. I was drowning in it.

It was so tremendously real that everything else became unreal. The walls of the room became unreal, the house became unreal, my own body became unreal. Everything was unreal because now there was for the first time reality.

That's why when Buddha and Shankara say the world is maya, a mirage, it is difficult for us to understand. Because we know only this world, we don't have any comparison. This is the only reality we know. What are these people talking about—this is maya, illusion? This is the only reality. Unless you come to know the really real, their words cannot be understood. Their words remain theoretical, they look like hypotheses: Maybe this man is propounding a philosophy—"The world is unreal."

When Berkeley in the West said that the world is unreal, he was walking with one of his friends, a very logical man; the friend was almost a skeptic. He took a stone from the road and hit Berkeley's feet hard. Berkeley screamed, blood rushed out, and the skeptic said, "Now, the world is unreal? You say the world is unreal? Then why did you scream? This stone is unreal? Then why did you scream? Then why are you holding your leg and why are you showing so much pain and anguish on your face? It is all unreal."

Now this type of man cannot understand what Buddha means when he says the world is a mirage. He does not mean that you can pass through the wall. He is not saying this—that you can eat stones and it will make no difference whether you eat bread or stones. He is not saying that.

He is saying that there is a reality: once you come to know it, *this* so-called reality simply pales, simply becomes unreal. With a higher reality in your vision the comparison arises, not otherwise.

In the dream, the dream is real. You dream every night, and every morning you say it was unreal, and again in the night when you dream, the dream becomes real. In a dream it is so difficult to remember that it is a dream, but in the morning it is so easy. What happens? You are the same person. In the dream there is only one reality. How to compare? How to say it is unreal? Compared to what? It is the only reality. Everything is as unreal as everything else, so there is no comparison. In the morning when you open your eyes another reality is there. Now you can say the dream was all unreal. Compared to this reality, the dream becomes unreal.

There is an awakening—compared to the reality of that awakening, this whole reality becomes unreal.

That night for the first time I understood the meaning of the word *maya*. Not that I had not known the word before, not that I was not aware of the meaning of the word. As you are aware, I was also aware of the meaning—but I had never understood it before. How can you understand without experience? That night another reality opened its door, another dimension became available. Suddenly it was there, the other reality, the separate reality—the really real, or whatsoever you want to call it. Call it God, call it truth, call it *dhamma*, call it Tao, or whatsoever you will. It was nameless. But it was there—so transparent and yet so solid one could have touched it. It was almost suffocating me in that room. It was too much and I was not yet capable of absorbing it.

A deep urge arose in me to rush out of the room, to go under the sky—it was suffocating me. It was too much! It will kill me! If I had remained a few moments more, it would have suffocated me—it looked like that. I rushed out of the room, came out into the street. A great urge was there just to be under the sky with the stars, with the trees, with the earth . . . to be with nature. And immediately as I came out, the feeling of being suffocated disappeared. It was too small a place for such a big phenomenon. Even the sky is a small place for that big phenomenon. It is bigger than the sky. Even the sky is not the limit for it. But then I felt more at ease.

I walked toward the nearest garden. It was a totally new walk, as if gravitation had disappeared. I was walking, or I was running, or I was simply flying; it was difficult to decide. There was no gravitation, I was feeling weightless—as if some energy was taking me. I was in the hands of some other energy.

For the first time I was not alone, for the first time I was no more an individual, for the first time the drop had fallen into the ocean. Now the whole ocean was mine, I was the ocean. There was no limitation. A tremendous power arose as if I could do anything whatsoever. I was not there, only the power was there.

I reached the garden where I used to go every day. The garden was closed, closed for the night. It was too late, it was almost one o'clock in the night. The gardeners were fast asleep. I had to enter like a thief, I had to climb the gate. But something was pulling me toward the garden. It was not within my capacity to prevent myself. I was just floating.

That's what I mean when I say again and again, "Float with the river, don't push the river." I was relaxed, I was in a let-go. I was not there, *it* was there, call it God—God was there. I would like to call it *it*, because God is too human a word and has become too dirty by too much use, has become too polluted by so many people. Christians, Hindus, Mohammedans, priests and politicians— they all have corrupted the beauty of the word. So let me call it *it*. It was there and I was just carried away . . . carried by a tidal wave.

The moment I entered the garden everything became luminous, it was all over the place—the benediction, the blessedness. I could see the trees for the first time—their green, their life, their very sap running. The whole garden was asleep, the trees were asleep. But I could see the whole garden alive, even the small grass leaves were so beautiful.

I looked around. One tree was tremendously luminous—the maulshree tree. It attracted me, it pulled me toward itself. I had not chosen it, God himself had chosen it. I went to the tree, I sat under the tree. As I sat there things started settling. The whole universe became a benediction.

It is difficult to say how long I was in that state. When I went back home it was four o'clock in the morning, so I must have been there by clock time at least three hours, but it was infinity. It had nothing to do with clock time. It was timeless.

Those three hours became the whole eternity, endless eternity. There was no time, there was no passage of time; it was the virgin reality—uncorrupted, untouchable, unmeasurable.

And that day something happened that has continued—not as a continuity, but it has still continued as an undercurrent. Not as a permanency—each moment it has been happening again and again. It has been a miracle each moment.

And since that night I have never been in the body. I am hovering around it. I became tremendously powerful and at the same time very fragile. I became very strong, but that strength is not the strength of a Muhammad Ali. That strength is not the strength of a rock; that strength is the strength of a rose flower—so fragile in his strength, so sensitive, so delicate.

The rock will be there, the flower can go any moment. But still the flower is stronger than the rock because it is more alive. Or the strength of a dewdrop on a leaf of grass just shining in the morning sun—so beautiful, so precious, and yet it can slip any moment. So incomparable in its grace, but a small breeze can come and the dewdrop can slip and be lost forever.

Buddhas have a strength that is not of this world. Their strength is totally of love . . . like a rose flower or a dewdrop. Their strength is very fragile, vulnerable. Their strength is the strength of life, not of death. Their power is not of that which kills; their power is of that which creates. Their power is not of violence, aggression; their power is that of compassion.

But I have never been in the body again, I am just hovering around the body. And that's why I say it has been a tremendous miracle. Each moment I am surprised I am still here, I should not be. I should have left any moment, still

I am here. Every morning I open my eyes and I say, "So, again I am still here?" Because it seems almost impossible. The miracle has been a continuity.

Just the other day somebody asked a question. "Osho, you are getting so fragile and delicate and so sensitive to the smells of hair oils and shampoos that it seems we will not be able to see you unless we all go bald." By the way, nothing is wrong with being bald—bald is beautiful! Just as black is beautiful, so bald is beautiful. But that is true and you have to be careful about it.

I am fragile, delicate, and sensitive. That is my strength. If you throw a rock at a flower nothing will happen to the rock, but the flower will be gone. But still you cannot say that the rock is more powerful than the flower. The flower will be gone because the flower was alive. And the rock—nothing will happen to it because it is dead. The flower will be gone because the flower has no strength to destroy. The flower will simply disappear and give way to the rock. The rock has a power to destroy because the rock is dead.

Remember, since that day I have never been in the body really; just a delicate thread joins me with the body. And I am continuously surprised that somehow the whole must be willing me to be here—because I am no longer here with my own strength, I am no longer here on my own. It must be the will of the whole to keep me here, to allow me to linger a little more on this shore. Maybe the whole wants to share something with you through me.

Since that day the world is unreal. Another world has been revealed. When I say the world is unreal I don't mean that these trees are unreal. These trees are absolutely real—but the way you see these trees is unreal. These trees are not unreal in themselves—they exist in God, they exist in absolute reality—but the way you see them, you never see them. You are seeing something else, a mirage.

You create your own dream around you, and unless you become awake you will continue to dream. The world is unreal because the world that you know is the world of your dreams. When dreams drop and you simply encounter the world that is there, then the real world appears.

There are not two things, God and the world. God *is* the world if you have eyes, clear eyes, without any dust of dreams, without any haze of sleep. If you have clear eyes, clarity, perceptiveness, there is only God.

Then somewhere God is a green tree, and somewhere else God is a shining star, and somewhere else God is a cuckoo, and somewhere else God is a flower, and somewhere else a child and somewhere else a river—then *only* God is. The moment you start seeing, only God is.

But right now whatsoever you see is not the truth, it is a projected lie. That is the meaning of a mirage. And once you see—even for a single split second, if you can see, if you can allow yourself to see—you will find immense benediction present all over, everywhere, in the clouds, in the sun, on the earth.

This is a beautiful world. But I am not talking about your world, I am talking about my world. Your world is very ugly, your world is your world created by a self, your world is a projected world. You are using the real world as a screen and projecting your own ideas on it.

When I say the world is real, the world is tremendously beautiful, the world is luminous with infinity, the world is light and delight, it is a celebration, I mean my world—or your world if you drop your dreams.

That night I became empty and became full. I became nonexistential and became existence. That night I died and was reborn. But the one that was reborn has nothing to do with the one that died, it is a discontinuous thing. On the surface it looks continuous, but it is discontinuous. The one who died, died totally; nothing of him has remained.

I have known many other deaths, but they were nothing compared to it, they were partial deaths.

Sometimes the body died, sometimes a part of the mind died, sometimes a part of the ego died, but as far as the person was concerned, it remained. Renovated many times, decorated many times, changed a little bit here and there, but it remained, the continuity remained.

That night the death was total. It was a date with death and with God simultaneously.

ENLIGHTENMENT IS A VERY INDIVIDUAL PROCESS. BECAUSE OF ITS individuality, it has created many problems. First, there are no fixed stages through which a person necessarily passes. Every person passes through different phases, because every person in many lives has gathered different kinds of conditionings.

So it is not a question of enlightenment, it is a question of the conditionings—that will shape your way. And everybody has different conditions, so no two persons' paths are going to be the same. That's why I insist again and again: There is no superhighway, there are only footpaths—and that too, not ready-made. Not that you find them already there and you have just to walk on them—no. As you walk, you make them. Your very walking makes them.

It is said that the path of enlightenment is like a bird flying in the sky: It leaves no footprints behind; nobody can follow the footprints of the bird. Every bird will have to make its own footprints, but they disappear immediately as the bird goes on flying. Similar is the situation, that's why there is no possibility of a leader and a follower. That's why I say these people like Jesus, Moses, Mohammed, Krishna—who say, "You just believe me and follow me"—don't know anything about enlightenment.

If they had known, then this statement would be impossible. Anybody who has become enlightened knows that he has not left any footprints behind; now saying to people, "Come and follow me," is just absurd.

So what happened to me is not necessary for anybody else to pass through. It is possible that one may remain normal and suddenly become enlightened.

If there are fifty people in the same room, and if we all go to sleep, everybody will have his own dream. You can't have a common dream, that is an impossibility. There is no way to create a common dream. Your dream will be yours, my dream will be mine, and we will be in different places, in different dreams. And when we wake up, I may wake up at a certain stage in my dream, you may wake up at a certain stage in your dream. How can they be the same?

Enlightenment is nothing but awakening. For the enlightened person, all our lives are just dreams. They may be good dreams, they may be bad dreams; they may be nightmares, they may be very nice and beautiful dreams, but all the same they are dreams.

You can wake up any moment. That is always your potentiality. Sometimes you may make an effort to wake up and you find that it is difficult. You may have had dreams in which you are trying to shout but you cannot shout. You want to wake up and get out of the bed but you cannot, your whole body is as if paralyzed.

In the morning you wake up and you simply laugh at the whole thing, but at the moment when it was happening, it was not anything to laugh at. It was really serious. Your whole body was almost dead, you could not move your hands, you could not speak, you could not open your eyes. You knew that now you were finished! But in the morning you simply don't pay any attention to it; you don't even reconsider it, what it was. Just knowing that it was a dream, it becomes meaningless. You are awake—whether the dreams were good or bad does not matter.

The same is the situation with enlightenment. All the methods that are used are simply somehow to create a situation in which your dream is broken. How much you are attached to the dream will be different, individual to individual. How deep is your sleep will be different, individual to individual. But all methods are just to shake you so that you can wake up. At what point you will wake up does not matter at all.

So my "breakdown and breakthrough" is not going to be for everybody. It happened that way to me. There were reasons why it happened that way. I was working alone on myself with no friends, no fellow travelers, no commune. To work alone, one is bound to get into many troubles, because there are moments that can only be called dark nights of the soul. So dark and so dangerous, it seems as if you have come to the last breath of your life, this is death, nothing else. That experience is a nervous breakdown.

Facing death, with nobody to support and encourage you . . . nobody to say not to be worried, that this will pass away. Or, "This is only a nightmare, and the morning is very close. The darker the night, the closer is the sunrise. Don't be worried." Nobody around whom you trust, who trusts you—that was the reason for the nervous breakdown. But it was not harmful. It looked harmful at the moment, but soon the dark night was gone and the sunrise was there, the breakdown had become the breakthrough.

To each individual it will happen differently. And the same is true after enlightenment: The expression of enlightenment will be different. That has also created a great difficulty.

The first has created a great difficulty—for example, if I were to make a religion, then this would be a basic thing in it: that anybody who becomes enlightened first will have to go through a nervous breakdown, only then he will have a breakthrough. That is how all the religions are created: individuals imposing their experience on the whole of humanity, without taking into consideration the uniqueness of every individual. And then after enlightenment, the same problem is there. Mahavira remained naked; hence the followers of Mahavira for twenty-five centuries, who have gone to the ultimate stage of following him, have remained naked. To be naked became absolutely necessary. Jainas don't think that Buddha is enlightened because he is not naked! A personal phenomenon becomes now a universal criterion—that too is false.

What happened to Mahavira was his individual flowering in that way. He was really one of the most beautiful men ever, and it would have been a shame if he had used clothes. His body was just worth seeing.

He was the son of a king, and his father was immensely interested in the art of Indian wrestling, and he prepared Mahavira for Indian wrestling. He wanted him to be the champion of the whole country—and he could have been a champion, his body was solid steel. He had been brought up so that twenty-four hours a day were devoted to a single theme, that he was to become the champion wrestler of the whole country. Naturally, his body was prepared. It had the proportion, every inch was taken care of. Great wrestlers were giving him training, people were massaging him, experts were giving him herbs and medicines—in every possible way he was being prepared.

And then he renounced the world. Rather than becoming a wrestler, he became a meditator. And when he became enlightened, he dropped the clothes. He had only one cloth that he used to cover his body, and after his enlightenment, as he was coming down the hill, a beggar asked him for something because it was so cold and he had nothing. And Mahavira looked at himself: He had only one shawl, so he made two pieces out of one shawl and gave half to the beggar. Half he kept himself—it was not enough to cover the body now, and just as he was descending from the hill into the valley, a rosebush caught hold of that piece of the shawl in its thorns. He looked back and he laughed, and he said, "This is too much! I have never refused anything to anybody, so you can take this half also. Anyway it is of no use. I unnecessarily saved it from that beggar, because what will he do with the half? It won't cover him if it does not cover me. You can take it. Perhaps that beggar will be passing this way, and he will get this other half also." That's how he became naked.

But he enjoyed the morning sun and the cool air in the hot country, the hottest part of India, Bihar. And it felt so light that he thought, "What is the need?" And he never asked for anything from anybody. He gave anything that anybody asked, but he never asked anything from anybody. He remained naked. But this is not necessarily a stage that every enlightened person has to go through. Buddha never became naked, Lao Tzu never became naked, Kabir never became naked.

So it has been a very significant problem for religions. They cannot accept other enlightened people for small reasons, because they don't suit their ideas. They have to fit with a certain concept, and that concept is derived from their own founder. And nobody can fit with that, so everybody else is denounced as unenlightened.

Enlightenment is a very individual song—always unknown, always new, always unique. It never comes as a repetition. So never compare two enlightened persons; otherwise you are bound to do injustice to one or the other, or both. And don't have any fixed idea. Just very liquid qualities should be remembered. I say liquid qualities, not very set qualifications.

For example, every enlightened person will have a deep silence—almost tangible. In his presence, those who are open, receptive, will become silent. He will have a tremendous contentment, whatever happens makes no difference to his contentment.

He will not have any question left, all questions have dissolved—not that he knows all answers, but all questions have dissolved. And in that state of utter silence, no-mind, he is capable of answering any question with tremendous profundity. It needs no preparation. He himself does not know what he is going to say, it comes spontaneously; sometimes he himself is surprised. But that does not mean that he has answers inside himself, ready-made. He has no answers at all. He has no questions at all. He has just a clarity, a light that can be focused on any question, and all the implications of the question and all the possibilities of its being answered suddenly become clear.

So you may find that sometimes you ask something, and the enlightened man answers something else. That happens because you are not aware of the implications of your own question. He does not answer only your words. He answers *you*. He answers the mind that has produced the question. So many times the question and the answer may look not fitting, but they certainly meet. It is just that you will have to dig a little deeper into the question, and you will find that it was exactly *the* question. It will happen many times that you will understand your question for the first time when it has been answered, because you were not aware of that dimension, you were not aware of your own mind, your own unconscious, from where those words have come.

But the enlightened man has no answers, no scriptures, no quotation marks. He is simply available; just like a mirror he responds, and he responds with intensity and totality.

So these are liquid qualities, not qualifications. Don't look at small things—what he eats, what he wears, where he lives—those are all irrelevant. Just watch for his love, for his compassion, for his trust. Even if you take advantage of his trust, that does not change his trust. Even if you misuse his compassion, cheat his love, that does not make any difference. That is your problem. His trust, his compassion, his love remain just the same.

His only effort in life will be how to make people awake. Whatever he does, this is the only purpose behind every act: how to make more and more people awake, because through awakening he has come to know the ultimate bliss of life.

SHARPENING THE SWORD

From my very childhood I have loved to tell stories, real, unreal. I was not at all aware that this telling of stories would give me an articulateness and that it would be of tremendous help after enlightenment.

Many people become enlightened, but not all of them become masters—for the simple reason that they are not articulate, they cannot convey what they feel, they cannot communicate what they have experienced. Now it was just accidental with me, and I think it must have been accidental with those few people who became masters, because there is no training course for it. And I can say it with certainty only about myself.

When enlightenment came, I could not speak for seven days; the silence was so profound that even the idea of saying anything about it did not arise. But after seven days, slowly, as I became accustomed to the silence, to the beatitude, to the bliss, the desire to share it—a great longing to share it with those whom I loved—was very natural.

I started talking with the people with whom I was in some way concerned, friends. I had been talking to these people for years, talking about all kinds of things. I had enjoyed only one exercise, and that was talking, so it was not very difficult to start talking about the enlightenment—although it took years to refine and bring into words something of my silence, something of my joy.

1953–1956:
THE UNIVERSITY STUDENT

The scholars are so clever in destroying all that is beautiful with their commentaries, their interpretations, their so-called learning. They make everything so heavy that with them, even poetry becomes nonpoetic. I myself never attended any poetry class in the university. I was called again and again by the head of the department, asking, "You attend other classes, why don't you come to the poetry classes?"

I said, "Because I want to keep my interest in poetry alive. I love poetry, that's why. And I know perfectly well that your professors are absolutely unpoetic; they have never known any poetry in their lives. I know them perfectly well. The man who teaches poetry in the university goes for a morning walk with me every day. I have never seen him looking at the trees, listening to the birds, watching the beautiful sunrise."

And in the university where I was, the sunrise and the sunset were something tremendously beautiful. The university was on a hill surrounded by smaller hillocks all around. I have traveled all over India and I have never seen more beautiful sunsets and sunrises anywhere. For some unknown, mysterious reason Sagar University seems to have a certain situation where clouds become so colorful at the time of sunrise and sunset that even a blind man will become aware that something tremendously beautiful is happening.

But I never saw the professor who was teaching poetry at the university looking at the sunset, or stopping even for a single moment. And whenever he saw me watching the sunset or the sunrise or the trees or the birds, he would ask me, "Why are you sitting here? You have come for a morning walk—do your exercise!"

I told him, "This is not an exercise for me. You are doing exercise; with me it is a love affair."

And when it rained he would never come out. Whenever it rained I would go and knock at his door and tell him, "Come on!"

He would say, "But it is raining!"

I said, "That's the most beautiful time to go for a walk, because the streets are absolutely empty. And to go for a walk without any umbrella while it is raining is so beautiful, is so poetic!"

He thought I was mad—but a man who has never gone in the rains, under the trees, cannot understand poetry. I told the head of the department, "This man is not poetic; he destroys everything. He is so scholarly and poetry is such an unscholarly phenomenon that there is no meeting ground between the two."

Universities destroy people's interest and love for poetry. They destroy your whole idea of how a life should be; they make it more and more a commodity. They teach you how to earn more, but they don't teach you how to live deeply, how to live totally—and these are where you can get glimpses. These are where small doors and windows open into the ultimate. You are told the value of money but not the value of a rose flower. You are told the value of being a prime minister or a president but not the value of being a poet, a painter, a singer, a dancer. Those things are thought to be for crazy people.

AFTER RECEIVING MY B.A. I LEFT JABALPUR BECAUSE ONE OF THE PRO-fessors in Sagar University, S. S. Roy, was persistently asking me, writing me, phoning me to say, "After your B.A. you join this university for your postgraduation."

From Jabalpur University to Sagar University there is not much distance—one hundred miles. But Sagar University was in many ways unique. It was a small university compared to Benares University or Aligarh University, which had ten thousand students, twelve thousand students. They are just like Oxford or Cambridge—big universities, big names. Sagar University had only one thousand students and almost three hundred professors, so for every three students, one professor. It was a rare place; perhaps nowhere in the world can you find another university where there is one professor for three students.

The man who had founded the university was acquainted with all the best professors around the world. Sagar was his birthplace; Doctor Harisingh Gaur was his name. He was a world-famous authority on law, and he earned so much money—and never gave a single paisa to any beggar, to any institution, to any charity. He was known as the most miserly person in the whole of India. And then he founded the university and donated his whole life's earnings. It was millions of dollars.

He said to me, "That's why I was a miser; otherwise there was no way—I was a poor man, I was born a poor man. If I were doing charity and giving to this hospital and to this beggar and to that orphan, this university would not have existed." He had carried his whole life only one idea, that his birthplace should have one of the best universities in the world. And certainly he created one of the best universities. While he was alive he managed to bring professors from all over the world. He gave them double salaries, triple salaries, whatsoever they wanted—and no work, because there were only one thousand students. And he opened all the departments that only a university like Oxford can afford. There were dozens of departments—without students, but with full staff: the head of the department, the assistant professor, the professor, the lecturer. He would say, "Don't be worried. First create the university—and make it the best. Students will come, will have to come."

Then the professors and the deans were all in search of the best students. And somehow this Professor S. S. Roy, who was the head of the department of philosophy, got his eye on me.

I used to go every year to Sagar University for the interuniversity debating competition. For four years I was winning the trophy, and for four years he was listening to me as a judge—he was one of the judges. The fourth year he invited me to his home and he said, "Listen, I wait for you for the whole year. I know that after one year, when the next interuniversity debating competition is held, you are bound to be there.

"The way you present your arguments is strange. It is sometimes so weird that I wonder . . . how did you manage to look from this angle? I have been thinking about a few problems myself, but I never looked from that aspect. It strikes me that perhaps you go on dropping any aspect that can occur to the ordinary mind, and you choose only the aspect that is unlikely to occur to anybody.

"For four years you have been winning the trophy for the simple reason that the argument is unique and there is nobody who is ready to answer it. They have not even thought about it, so they are simply in shock. Your opponents—you reduce them so badly, one feels pity for them, but what can we do? And I have been giving you ninety-nine percent marks out of a hundred. I wanted to give you more than a hundred, but even ninety-nine . . . It has become known to people that I am favorable to a certain student. They say this is too much, because nobody goes beyond fifty.

"I have called you to my home for dinner to invite you to leave Jabalpur University and come here. Now this is your fourth year, you are finished when you graduate. For postgraduation you come here. I cannot miss having you as my student; if you don't come here, then I am going to join Jabalpur University."

And he was a well-known authority; if he wanted to come, Jabalpur University would have been immensely happy to accept him as head of the department. I said, "No, don't go to that much trouble. I can come here, and I love the place." It is perhaps the best-situated university in the world, in the hills near a tremendously vast lake. It is so silent—such huge trees, ancient trees—that just to be there is enough education.

And Doctor Harisingh Gaur must have been a tremendous lover of books. He donated his entire library, and he managed to get as many books as possible from every corner of the world. A single man's effort . . . it is rare; he created Oxford just single-handedly, alone. Oxford was created over one thousand years; thousands of people have worked. This man's work is really a piece of art. Single-handedly, with his own money, he put himself at stake.

So I loved the place. I said, "You need not be worried, I will be coming—but you have seen me only in the debate competitions. You don't know much about me; I may prove a trouble for you, a nuisance. I would like you to know everything about me before you decide."

Professor S. S. Roy said, "I don't want to know anything about you. The little bit that I have come to know, just by seeing you, your eyes, your way of saying things, your way of approaching reality, is enough. And don't try to make me frightened about trouble and nuisance—you can do whatsoever you want."

THE FIRST DAY I JOINED HIS CLASS, PROFESSOR S. S. ROY WAS EXPLAINing the concept of the Absolute. He was an authority on Bradley and Shankara. Both believe in the Absolute—that is their name for God.

I asked him one thing, which made me very intimate to him and he opened his whole heart to me in every possible way. I just asked, "Is your 'absolute' perfect? Has it come to a full stop or is it still growing? If it is still growing, then it is not absolute, it is imperfect—only then can it grow. If something more is possible, some more branches, some more flowers—then it is alive. If it is complete, entirely complete—that's the meaning of the word *absolute;* now there is no possibility for growth—then it is dead." So I asked him, "Be clear, because 'absolute' represents God to Bradley and Shankara; that is their philosophical name for God. Is your God alive or dead? You have to answer this question."

He was really an honest man. He said, "Please give me time to think." He had a doctorate on Bradley from Oxford, another doctorate on Shankara from Benares, and he was thought to be the greatest authority on these two philosophers because he had tried to prove that Bradley, from the West, and Shankara, from the East, have come to the same conclusion. He said, "Please give me time to think."

I said, "Your whole life you have been writing about Bradley and Shankara and the Absolute—I have read your books, I have read your unpublished thesis. And you have been teaching here your whole life—has nobody ever asked you such a simple question?"

He said, "Nobody ever asked me; not only that, even I have never thought about it—that certainly, if something is perfect then it has to be dead. Anything alive has to be imperfect. This idea has never occurred to me. So please give me time."

I said, "You can take as much time as you want. I will come every day and ask the same question." And it continued for five, six days. Every day I would enter the class and he would come shaking, and I would stand up and say, "My question."

And he said, "Please forgive me, I cannot decide. With both sides there is difficulty. I cannot say God is imperfect; I cannot say God is dead. But you have conquered my heart."

He moved my things from the hostel to his house. He said, "No more, you cannot live in the hostel. You have to come and live with me and my family. I have much to learn from you—because such a simple question has not occurred to me. All my degrees you have canceled."

I lived with him for almost six months before he moved to another university. He wanted me to move with him, but my vice-chancellor was reluctant. He said, "Professor Roy, you can go. Professors will come and go but we may not find such a student again. So I am not going to give him his certificates and I am not going to allow him to leave the university. And I will write to your university telling them that my student should not be taken in there either!"

But he continued to love me. It was a rare phenomenon: He used to come almost every month to see me from his university, almost two hundred miles away. But he would come at least once every month just to see me, just to sit with me. And he said, "Now I am getting a better salary and everything is more comfortable there, but I miss you. The class seems to be dead. Nobody asks questions like you, questions that cannot be answered."

And I had told him, "This is an agreement between me and you, that I call a question a question only when it cannot be answered. If it can be answered, what kind of question is it?"

I USED TO WALK IN AN INDIAN SANDAL MADE OF WOOD. IT HAS been used by sannyasins for centuries, almost ten thousand years or perhaps longer. A wooden sandal . . . because it avoids any kind of leather, which is bound to be coming from an animal who maybe has been killed, and killed only for this purpose—and the best leather comes from very young children of animals. So sannyasins have been avoiding that and using a wooden sandal. But it makes so much noise when the person walks, you can hear from almost half a mile away that he is coming. And on a cement road, or walking on the veranda in the university . . . the whole university knows. The whole university used to know that I was coming or going; there was no need to see me, just my sandals were enough.

WHEN ON THE FIRST DAY I ENTERED THE UNIVERSITY'S PHILOSOPHY class, I met Dr. Saxena for the first time. Only for a few professors did I have really great love and respect. These two were my most loved professors—Dr. S. K. Saxena and Dr. S. S. Roy—and for the simple reason that they never treated me like a student.

When I entered Dr. Saxena's class the first day, with my wooden sandals, he looked a little puzzled. He looked at my sandals and asked me, "Why are you using wooden sandals? They make so much noise."

I said, "Just to keep my consciousness alert."

He said, "Consciousness? Are you trying to keep your consciousness alert in other ways too?"

I said, "Twenty-four hours a day I am trying to do that, in every possible way: walking, sitting, eating, even sleeping. And you may believe it or you may not, that just lately I have succeeded to be aware and alert even in sleep."

He said, "The class is dismissed—you just come with me to the office." The whole class thought I had created trouble for myself the first day. He took me into his office and took from the shelf his thesis for a doctorate that he had written thirty years before. It was on consciousness. He said, "Take it. It has been published in English, and so many people in India have asked permission to translate it into Hindi—great scholars, knowing both English and Hindi perfectly well. But I have not allowed anybody, because the question is not whether you know the language well or not; I was looking for a man who knows what consciousness is—and I can see in your eyes, on your face, by the way you answered . . . you have to translate this book."

I said, "This is difficult because I don't know much English, and I don't know much Hindi either. Hindi is my mother tongue, but I know only as much as everybody knows his mother tongue. And I believe in the definition of the mother tongue. Why is every language called the mother tongue? Because the mother speaks and the father listens—and that's how the children learn. That's how I have learned.

"My father is a silent man; my mother speaks and he listens—and I learned the language. It is just a mother tongue, I don't know much. Hindi has never been my subject of study. English I know just a little bit, and that is enough for your so-called examinations, but for translating a book that is a Ph.D. thesis . . . And you are giving it to a student?"

He said, "Don't be worried—I know you will be able to do it."

I said, "If you trust me, I will do my best. But one thing I must tell you, that if I find something wrong in it then I am going to make an editorial note underneath, and how it should be corrected. If I find something missing, I am going to put a footnote that something is missing, and this is the part that is missing."

He said, "I agree to that. I know there are many things missing in it. But you surprise me: you have not even seen the book, you have not even opened it. How do you know that things will be missing in it?"

I said, "By looking at you. Just the way you can see by looking at me that I am the right person to translate it, I can see perfectly, Dr. Saxena, you are not the right person to write it!"

And he loved that so much that he told it to everybody! The whole university knew about this dialogue that had happened between him and me. In the next two-month summer vacation I translated the book, and I made those editorial notes. When I showed him, there were tears of joy in his eyes. He said, "I knew perfectly well that something is missing here, but I could not figure it out because I have never practiced it. I was just trying to collect all the information about consciousness from the Eastern scriptures. I had collected a lot, and then from that I started sorting it out. It took me almost seven years to finish my thesis." He had done really a great scholarly job—but only scholarly. I said, "It is scholarly, but it is not the work of a meditator. And I have made all these notes—that this can be written only by a scholar, not by a meditator."

He looked at all those pages and he said to me, "If you had been one of my examiners for the thesis I would not have got the doctorate! You have found exactly the places that I was doubtful about, but those fools who examined it were not even suspicious. It has been praised very much."

He was a professor in America for many years, and his book is really a monumental work of scholarship; but nobody criticized him, nobody pointed out those things. So I asked him, "Now what are you going to do with the translation?"

He said, "I cannot publish it. I have finally found a translator—but you are more an examiner than a translator! I will keep it but I cannot publish it. With your notes and with your editorial commentary it will destroy my whole reputation—but I agree with you. In fact," he said, "if it were in my power I would have given you a doctorate just for your editorial notes and footnotes, because you have found exactly the places that only a meditator can find; a nonmeditator has no way to find them."

So my whole life from the very beginning has been concerned with two things: never to allow any unintelligent thing to be imposed upon me, to fight against all kinds of stupidities, whatsoever the consequences, and to be rational, logical, to the very end. This was one side, which I was using with all those people with whom I was in contact. And the other was absolutely private, my own: to become more and more alert, so that I didn't end up just being an intellectual.

I AM REMINDED OF ONE OF MY VICE-CHANCELLORS. HE WAS A world-famous historian. He had been a professor of history in Oxford for almost twenty years, and after his retirement from Oxford he came back to India. He had a world-famous name, and he was elected to be the vice-chancellor of the university I was studying in. He was a nice man, a beautiful personality, with immense knowledgeability, scholarship, recognition—so many books to his credit.

By chance, the day he took charge as vice-chancellor was Gautam Buddha's birthday. And Gautam Buddha's birthday is more important than anybody else's birthday, because Gautam Buddha's birthday is also his day of enlightenment, and also his day of leaving the body. The same day he was born, the same day he became enlightened, the same day he died.

The whole university gathered to hear this man speak on Gautam Buddha. And he was a great historian, he had written about Gautam Buddha; and he spoke with great emotion. Tears in his eyes, he said, "I have always felt that if I had been born in Gautam Buddha's time, I would have never left his feet."

According to my habit I stood up, and I said, "You please take your words back."

He said, "But why?"

I said, "Because they are false. You have been alive in Raman Maharshi's time. He was the same kind of man, his was the same enlightenment—and I know that you have not even visited him. So whom are you trying to befool? You would not have visited Gautam Buddha either. Wipe your tears, they are crocodile tears. You are simply a scholar and you don't know anything about enlightenment or people like Gautam Buddha."

There was a great silence in the auditorium. My professors were afraid that I might be expelled; they were always afraid that at any time I could be expelled. They loved me and they wanted me to be there. But to create such a situation, such an awkward situation . . . and nobody knew what to do, how to break the ice. In those few seconds it felt as if hours had passed. The vice-chancellor was standing there . . . but he was certainly a man of some superior quality. He wiped his tears and asked that he should be forgiven—perhaps he was wrong. And he invited me to his house so that we could discuss it in more detail.

But he said, in front of the whole university, "You are right. I would not have gone to Gautam Buddha, I know it. I was not aware when I said it; I was just being emotional, I was carried away. Yes, I never went to Raman Maharshi when he was alive, and I had been very close to his place many times. I used to give lectures in Madras University, from where it is only a few hours' journey to his place in Arunachal. I have been told by many friends, 'You should go and see this man'—and I always went on postponing till the man died."

The whole university could not believe it. My professors could not believe it. But his humbleness touched everybody. Respect for him grew tremendously, and we became friends. He was very old—he was almost sixty-eight—and I was only twenty-four, but we became friends. And he never for a moment allowed me to feel that he was a great scholar, that he was the vice-chancellor, that he was my grandfather's age.

On the contrary, he said to me, "I don't know what happened that day; I am not so humble a man. Being a professor in Oxford for twenty years, being a visiting professor to many of the universities of the world, I have become very egoistic. But you destroyed everything in a single stroke. And I will remain grateful to you for my whole life: If you had not stood up, I might have kept on believing that I would have done this. But now I would like it . . . if you can find someone, then I would like to sit by his feet and listen to him."

I said, "Then sit down and listen."

He said, "What!?"

I said, "Just look at me. Don't be bothered by my age, sit down and listen to me." And you will not believe it—that old man sat down and listened to me, to whatever I wanted to say to him. But rare are people who have so much courage and so much openness.

After that day he used to come to the hostel to visit me. Everybody was puzzled—what had happened? And I had created such an embarrassing situation for him! He used to take me to his house and we would sit together and he would ask me, "Say anything—I want to listen. My whole life I have been talking; I have forgotten listening. And I have been saying things that I don't know." And he listened the way a disciple listens to a master.

My professors were very much puzzled. They said, "Have you done some magic on that old man? Or has he gone senile? Or what is the matter? To see him, we have to make an appointment and we have to wait on a long list. When our time comes, only then can we meet him. And he comes to see you—not only that, he listens to you. What has happened?"

I said, "The same can happen to you too, but you are not that intelligent, not that sensitive, not that understanding. That old man is really rare."

1957–1966:
THE PROFESSOR

I enjoyed my student life immensely; whether people were against me, for me, indifferent, loved me, all those experiences were beautiful. All that helped me when I myself became a teacher, because I could see the students' viewpoint simultaneously when I was presenting mine.

And my classes became debating clubs. Everybody was allowed to doubt, to argue. Once in a while somebody started worrying about what would happen to the course, because on each single point there was so much argument. I said, "Don't be worried. All that is needed is a sharpening of your intelligence. The course is a small thing—you can read for it in one night. If you have a sharp mind, even without reading for it you can answer. But if you don't have a sharp mind, even the book can be provided to you and you will not be able to find where the answer is. In a five-hundred-page book the answer must be somewhere in one paragraph."

So my classes were totally different. Everything had to be discussed, everything had to be looked into, in the deepest possible way, from every corner, from every aspect—and accepted only if your intelligence felt satisfied. Otherwise, there was no need to accept it; we could continue the discussion the next day.

And I was amazed to know that when you discuss something and discover the logical pattern, the whole fabric, you need not remember it. It is your own discovery; it remains with you. You cannot forget it.

My students certainly loved me because nobody else would give them so much freedom, nobody else would give them so much respect. Nobody else would give them so much love, nobody else would help them to sharpen their intelligence.

Every teacher was concerned about his salary. I myself never went to collect the salary. I would just give my authority to a student and say, "Whenever the first day of the month comes, you collect the salary and you can bring it to me. And if you need any part of it you can keep it."

All the years I was in the university somebody or other was bringing me my salary. The man who was distributing the salaries once came to see me just to say, "You never appear. I have been hoping that sometime you would come and I would see you. But seeing that perhaps you will never come to the office, I have come to your house just to see what kind of man you are—because there are professors who start lining up early in the morning, on the first of each month, for their salary. You are always missing. Any student might appear with your signature and authority, and I don't know whether the salary reaches you or not."

I said, "You need not be worried, it has always reached me." When you trust someone, it is very difficult for him to deceive.

All the years I was a teacher, not a single student to whom I had given the authority had taken any part of it, although I had told them, "It is up to you. If you feel like having it all, you can have it. If you want to keep a part of it, you can keep it. And it is not lent to you so that you have to return it, because I don't want to be bothered by remembering who owes how much money to me. It is simply yours; it doesn't matter." But not a single student ever took any part of the salary.

All the teachers were interested only in the salary, in the competition of getting higher posts. I have seen nobody who was really interested in the students and their future and particularly in their spiritual growth.

Seeing that, I opened a small school of meditation. One of my friends offered his beautiful bungalow and garden, and he made a marble temple for me, for meditations, so at least fifty people could sit and meditate in the temple. Many students, many professors—even the vice-chancellors—came to understand what meditation is.

IN INDIA, MOHAMMEDANS HAVE A CERTAIN DRESS, HINDUS HAVE A certain dress, Punjabis have a certain dress, Bengalis have a certain dress, South Indians have a certain dress. For example, in South India you can wear a wrap-around lungi; just a dhoti that you wrap around. And not only that, they pull it up and tuck it over so it is just up to the knees. Even in the universities, professors go to teach in that dress.

I loved the lungi because it is very simple, the simplest: no need of a seamstress, no need of any tailoring, nothing; just any piece of cloth can be turned into a lungi very easily. But I was not in South India, I was in central India where the lungi is used only by vagabonds, loafers, unsocial elements. It is a symbol that the person is uncaring about the society, that he does not bother what you think about him.

When I started going to the university in a lungi, everything stopped for a moment: students came out of their classes, professors came out of their classes. As I passed along the corridor everybody was standing there watching, and I waved to everybody—a good reception!

The vice-chancellor came out: "What is the matter? The classes have stopped in the middle, professors are out, and there is a silence . . ." He saw me and I waved to him, and he had not even the guts to reply to my wave.

I said, "At least you should wave to me. All these people have come to see my lungi." I think they loved it because every day professors came with beautiful clothes, the costliest clothes. The vice-chancellor was very particular about his clothes and very famous for them. If you had gone into his house you would have been surprised: nothing but clothes all around the whole house, he and his servant and the clothes.

I said, "Even when you come in, nobody comes out of their classrooms. But a poor lungi—the poorest wear them—has brought them out! And I am going to come every day in this lungi."

He said, "A joke is okay, one day is okay, but don't carry it too far."

I said, "When I do something I do it to the very end."

He said, "What do you mean? You mean you really are going to come every day in a lungi?"

I said, "Right now that's what I intend to do. If I am interfered with I can come even without a lungi. You can take my word for it. If I am interfered with in any way, if you try to say that this is not proper for a professor and this and that, I don't bother . . . If you can keep quiet, I will remain in the lungi; if you start doing anything against me, then the lungi goes. I will come . . . and then you will see the real scene!"

And it was such a hilarious scene because all the students started clapping when they heard this and he felt so embarrassed, he simply went back into his room. He never said a single word about the lungi. I inquired many times, "What about my lungi? Is any action being taken against it or not?"

He said, "You just leave me alone—do whatsoever you want to do. And I don't want to say anything because anything said to you is dangerous, one never knows how you will take it. I was not saying, 'Drop the lungi,' I was saying, 'Come back to your old clothes.' "

I said, "Those are gone, and what is gone is gone—I never look back. Now I am going to be in a lungi."

So first I was going in a lungi, with a long robe. Then one day I dropped the robe and just started using a shawl. Again there was a great drama, but he kept his cool. Everybody came out but he didn't come—perhaps because he was afraid that I had dropped the lungi! He didn't come out of his room. I knocked on his door. He said, "Have you done it?"

I said, "Not yet. You can come out."

He opened the door and just looked out to see whether I was clothed or whether I had dropped everything. He said, "So you have changed now— the robe also?"

I said, "I have changed that too. Have you something to say?"

He said, "I don't want to say a single word. About you, I don't even talk to others. Journalists are phoning and asking, 'How is it being allowed in the university? Because that will become a precedent and students may start coming in lungis, and other professors.'

"I tell them, 'Whatsoever happens, even if everybody starts coming in lungis, it is okay with me. I am not going to disturb him, because he threatens me that if I disturb him in any way he can come nude. And he says that nudity is an acceptable spiritual way of life in India. Mahavira was nude, the twenty-four tirthankaras of the Jainas were nude, thousands of monks are still nude, and if a tirthankara can be nude then why not a professor? Nudity in India cannot be in any way disrespected.' "

So he said, "I am telling people, 'If he wants to really create chaos . . . and he has followers also in the university; there are many students ready to do anything he tells them to. So it is better to leave him alone.' "

I have found throughout my life that if you are just a little ready to sacrifice respectability, you can have your way very easily. The society has played a game with you. It has put respectability on too high a pedestal in your mind, and opposite it, all those things that it wants you not to do. So if you do them, you lose respectability. Once you are ready to say, "I don't care about respectability," then the society is absolutely impotent to do anything against your will.

WHEN I BECAME A TEACHER IN THE UNIVERSITY THE FIRST THING I did—because as I entered the class I saw the girls sitting in one corner, four or five rows just empty in front of me, and the boys sitting in the other corner— I said, "Who am I going to teach, these tables and chairs? And what kind of nonsense is this? Who told you to sit like this? Just get mixed together and come in front of me."

They hesitated. They had never heard a teacher tell them to get mixed. I said, "You get mixed immediately; otherwise I am going to report to the vice-chancellor that something absolutely unnatural, unpsychological, is happening."

Slowly, hesitantly . . . I said, "Don't hesitate! Just move and get mixed. In my class you cannot sit separately. And I don't mind if you try to touch the girl or the girl tries to pull your shirt; whatever is natural is accepted by me. So I don't want you to sit there frozen, shrunken. That is not going to happen in my class. Enjoy being together. I know you have been throwing slips, stones, letters. There is no need. Just sit by her side, give the letter to the girl, or whatever you want to do—because in fact you are all sexually mature; you should do something. And you are just studying philosophy, you are absolutely insane! Is this the time to study philosophy? This is the time to go out and make love. Philosophy is for the old age when you cannot do anything else—you can study philosophy then."

They all were so afraid. Slowly, slowly they got relaxed, but other classes started feeling jealous of them. Other professors started reporting to the vice-chancellor, "This man is dangerous. He is allowing boys and girls to do things that we have all been prohibiting. Rather than stopping them getting into contact, he is helping them! He says, 'If you don't know how to write a love letter, come to me. I will teach you. Philosophy is secondary—it is not much. We will finish the two years' course in six months. The remaining one year and six months, enjoy, dance, sing. Don't be worried.' "

The vice-chancellor finally had to call me, and he said, "I have heard all these things. What do you say?"

I said, "You must have been a student in the university."

He said, "Yes. I have been. Otherwise, how can I be the vice-chancellor?"

I said, "Then just go back a little and remember those days when girls were sitting far away and you were sitting far away. What was going on in your mind?"

He said, "You seem to be a strange fellow. I have asked you to come because I want to inquire about something."

I said, "That we'll take later on. First answer my question. And be sincere; otherwise I will give you an open challenge tomorrow before the whole university, all the professors, all the students. We can discuss the matter and let them vote."

He said, "Don't get excited. Perhaps you are right. I do remember. I am now an old man, and I hope that you will not say this to anybody—I was thinking of the girls. I was not listening to the professor; nobody was listening to the professor. The girls were throwing notes, we were throwing notes, letters were being exchanged."

"Then," I said, "can I go?"

He said, "Of course. You simply go and do whatsoever you want. I don't want a public encounter with you, I know you will win it. You are right. But I am a poor fellow; I have to look after my post. If I start doing such a thing, the government will throw me out of this vice-chancellorship."

I said, "I am not interested in your vice-chancellorship. You remain vice-chancellor, but remember: never call me again. Many complaints will come, but I make it clear to you right now that every time I will be right."

He said, "I have understood."

Then students—boys and girls who were not students of my subject—started asking me, "Can we also come?"

I said, "Philosophy has never been so juicy. Come! Anybody is welcome. I never take attendance. Every month, when the attendance register has to go back, I just fill it randomly—absent, present, absent, present. I just have to remember that everybody gets more than seventy-five percent present so they go to the examination. I don't bother. So you can come."

My classes were overpopulated. People were sitting in the windows. And they were really expected to be in some other class.

Then came complaints again, and the vice-chancellor said, "Don't bring any complaint about that man. It is your problem if people are not coming to your class. What can I do? What can he do if they prefer him? And they are not students of philosophy, but they don't want to come to your history, your economics, your politics. What can I do? And that man has challenged me: 'Never again call me in, otherwise you will have to face a public encounter.' "

But so many complaints came from every department that finally he had to come. He knew that it was better not to call me; he had to come to my class. He could not believe it.

In philosophy there are very few students, because philosophy is not a paying subject. But the class was overcrowded; there was not even space for him to enter. I saw him standing in the door behind the students. I told the students, "Let the vice-chancellor come in. Let him also enjoy the whole scene that is happening here."

He came in. He could not believe his eyes, that girls and boys were all sitting together and so joyously listening to me. Not a single disturbance, because I have prevented all disturbances from the very root. Now the boy is sitting by his girlfriend; there is no need to throw a stone, throw a letter. There is no need.

He said, "I cannot believe that it is such a crowded class and there is pin-drop silence."

I said, "There is bound to be because there is no repression. I have told the students that when they want to leave they need not ask my permission, they should simply go; when they want to come in they should simply come. They need not ask my permission. It is none of my business whether they are here or not. I enjoy teaching. I will go on teaching—if you want to sit here, sit; otherwise get lost. But nobody goes away."

The vice-chancellor said, "This should happen to every class. But I am not a strong man like you; I cannot say to the government that this is the way it should be."

I WAS CALLED TO A SEMINAR, MANY UNIVERSITY VICE-CHANCELLORS and chancellors had gathered there. They were very worried about the lack of discipline in the schools, colleges, and universities, and they were worried about the new generation's disrespectful attitude toward the teachers.

I listened to their views and I told them, "I see that somewhere the very basis is missing. A teacher is one who is respected naturally, so a teacher cannot demand respect. If the teacher demands respect, he simply shows that he is not a teacher; he has chosen the wrong profession, that is not his vocation. The very definition of a teacher is one who is naturally respected—not that you have to respect him. If you have to respect him, what type of respect is this going to be? Just look: '*have* to respect'—the whole beauty is lost, the respect is not alive. If it *has* to be done, then it is not there. When it is there, nobody is self-conscious about it. It simply flows. Whenever a teacher is there, it simply flows."

So I asked the seminar: "Rather than asking students to respect the teachers, you please look again—you must be choosing wrong teachers, who are not teachers at all."

Teachers are as much born as poets, it is a great art. Everybody cannot be a teacher, but because of universal education millions of teachers are required.

Just think of a society that thinks everybody has to be taught poetry and poetry has to be taught by poets. Then millions of poets will be required. Of course, then there will be poets' training colleges. Those poets will be bogus, and then they will ask. "Applaud us!—because we are poets. Why are you not respecting us?" This has happened with teachers.

In the past there were very few teachers. People used to travel thousands of miles to find a teacher, to be with him. There was tremendous respect, but the respect depended on the quality of the teacher. It was not demanded from the disciple or from the student or the pupil. It simply happened.

ON THE ROAD

❧

Just think of me—wandering in India for years, and in return getting stones, shoes, and knives thrown at me. And you don't know Indian railways, waiting rooms; you don't know the way Indians live. It is unhygienic, ugly, but they are accustomed to it. I suffered for those years as much, perhaps more, than Jesus suffered on the cross. To be on the cross is a question only of a few hours. To be assassinated is even quicker. But to be a wandering master in India is no joke.

THE SITUATION OF THE WORLD HAS CHANGED DRAMATICALLY. JUST three hundred years ago, the world was very big. Even if Gautam Buddha had wanted to approach all human beings, it would not have been possible; just the means of communication were not available. People were living in many worlds, almost isolated from each other. That has a simplicity.

As a Jew, Jesus had to face his fellow Jews, not the world. It would not have been possible, sitting on his donkey, to go around the world. Even if he had managed to cover the small kingdom of Judea, that would have been too much. The education of people was very limited. They were not even aware of each other's existence.

Gautam Buddha, Lao Tzu in China, Socrates in Athens—they were all contemporaries but they had no idea of each other.

Before the scientific revolution in communication and transportation, there were many worlds, sufficient unto themselves. They never thought of others, they had no idea even that others existed. As people became acquainted more and more with each other, the world became smaller. Now a Buddha will not be able to manage, nor Jesus nor Moses nor Confucius. They will all have very localized minds and very localized attitudes.

We are fortunate that the world is now so small that you cannot be local. In spite of yourself, you cannot be local; you have to be universal. You have to think of Confucius, you have to think of Krishna, you have to think of Socrates, you have to think of Bertrand Russell. Unless you think of the world as one single unit, and all the contributions of different geniuses, you will not be able to talk to the modern man. The gap will be so big—twenty-five centuries, twenty centuries . . . almost impossible to bridge it.

The only way to bridge it is that the person who has come to know should not stop at his own knowing, should not be contented to give expression only to what he has come to know. He has to make a tremendous effort to know all the languages.

The work is vast but it is exciting—the exploration into human genius from different dimensions. If you have within yourself the light of understanding, you can create, without any difficulty, a synthesis. And the synthesis is not only going to be of all the religious mystics—that will be partial. The synthesis has to include all the artists and their insights—all the musicians, all the poets, all the dancers, their insights. All the creative people who have contributed to life, who have made humanity richer, have to be taken into account. Nobody has thought ever of the artistic people, that their contribution is also religious.

And most important of all is scientific growth. To bring scientific growth into a synthetic vision with the heart and with religion was not possible in the past. In the first place there was no science—and it has changed a thousand and one things. Life can never be the same again.

In my vision it is a triangle—science, religion, art. And they are such different dimensions—they speak different languages, they contradict each other; they are not in agreement superficially, unless you have a deep insight in which they all can melt and become one.

My effort has been to do almost the impossible.

In my university days as a student, my professors were at a loss. I was a student of philosophy, and I was attending science classes—physics, chemistry, and biology. Those professors were feeling very strange: "You are here in the university to study philosophy. Why are you wasting your time with chemistry?"

I said, "I have nothing to do with chemistry; I just want to have a clear insight into what chemistry has done, what physics has done. I don't want to go into details, I just want the essential contribution."

I was rarely in my classes, I was mostly in the library. My professors were continually saying, "What are you doing the whole day in the library? Because so many complaints have come from the librarian that you are the first to enter the library and you have to be almost physically taken out at the end of the day. The whole day you are there—and not only in the philosophical section, you are roaming around the library in all the sections that have nothing to do with you."

I said to them, "It is difficult for me to explain to you, but my effort in the future is going to be to bring everything that has some truth in it into a synthetic whole. To create a way of life that is inclusive of all, that is not based on arguments and contradictions, that is based on a deep insight into the essential core of all the contributions that have been made to human knowledge, to human wisdom."

They thought I would go mad—the task I have chosen can lead anyone to madness, it is too vast. But they were not aware that madness is impossible for me, that I have left the mind far behind; I am just a watcher.

And the mind is such a delicate and complicated computer. Man has made great computers but none is yet comparable to the human mind. Just a single human mind has the capacity to contain all the libraries of the world. And just a single library—the British Museum Library—has books, which if you go on arranging them like a wall, one by one, they will go three times round the earth. And that is only one big library. Moscow has the same kind of library, perhaps bigger. Harvard has the same kind of library. But a single human mind is capable of containing all that is written in all these books, of memorizing it. In a single brain there are billions of cells, and each single cell is capable of containing millions of pieces of information. Certainly one will go mad if one is not already standing outside of the mind. If you have not reached the status of meditation, madness is sure. They were not wrong, but they were not aware of my efforts toward meditation.

So I was reading strange books, strange scriptures from all over the world; yet I was only a watcher, because as far as I was concerned I had come home. I had nothing to learn from all that reading; that reading was for a different purpose, and the purpose was to make my message universal, to make it free from local limitations. And I am happy that I have succeeded in it completely.

Because people love me, they have called me a "master of masters." It is out of their love. As far as I am concerned, I simply think of myself as just an ordinary human being who was stubborn enough to remain independent, resisted all conditioning, never belonged to any religion, never belonged to any political party, never belonged to any organization, never belonged to any nation, any race. I have tried in every possible way just to be myself, without any adjective. And that has given me so much integrity, individuality, authenticity, and the tremendous blissfulness of being fulfilled.

But it was the need of the time. After me, anybody trying to be a master will have to remember that he has to pass through all the things I have passed through; otherwise, he cannot be called a master. He will remain just localized— a Hindu teacher, a Christian missionary, a Mohammedan priest—but not a master for human beings as such. After me it is going to be really difficult to be a master!

THE AWAKENED MAN UNDERSTANDS HUMANITY SO DEEPLY. BY UNDER-standing himself he has understood the miserable state of all human beings. He feels sorry for people; he is compassionate. He does not return evil for evil, for the simple reason that he does not feel offended in the first place. Second, he feels sorry for you; he does not feel antagonistic toward you.

Once it happened in Baroda. I was talking to a big crowd. Somebody sitting just in the front row became so disturbed by what I was saying, he went out of control; he lost his senses. He threw one of his shoes at me. At that moment I remembered that I used to play volleyball when I was a student, so I caught hold of his shoe in the air and asked him for the other one. He was at a loss! I said, "You throw the other one too—what am I going to do with just one? If you want to present something to me . . ." He waited. I said, "Why are you waiting? Throw the other one too, because this way neither will I be able to use the shoe nor will you be able to use it. And I am not going to return it, because evil should not be returned for evil! So you please give the other one too."

He was so shocked because he could not believe it. First, what he had done he could not believe—he was a very good man, a scholar, a well-known Sanskrit scholar, a pundit. He was not expected to behave like that, but it had happened—people are so unconscious. If I had acted the way he was unconsciously expecting, then everything would have been okay. But I asked for the other shoe and that shocked him very much. He was dazed. I told somebody who was sitting by his side, "You pull off his other shoe. I am not letting him off, I want both shoes. In fact, I was thinking of purchasing some shoes, and this man seems to be so generous!" And the shoe was really new.

The man came in the night, fell at my feet and asked to be forgiven. I said, "You forget all about it, there is no question . . . I was not angry, so why should I forgive you? To forgive, one first has to be angry. I was not angry, I enjoyed the scene. In fact, it was something so beautiful that many people who had fallen asleep were suddenly awakened! I was thinking on the way that it is a good idea, that I should plant a few of my people so that once in a while they can throw a shoe and all the sleepers will wake up. At least for a few moments they will remain alert, because something is happening! I am thankful to you."

For years he went on writing to me, "Please forgive me! Unless you forgive me I will go on writing."

But I told him, "First I have to be angry. Forgiving you simply means that I accept that I was angry. How can I forgive you? You forgive me, because I am unable to be angry with you, unable to forgive you—you forgive me!" I don't know whether he has forgiven me or not, but he has forgotten me. Now he writes no more.

I WOULD HAVE LOVED NOT TO BE ASSOCIATED IN ANY WAY WITH the word *religion*. The whole history of religion simply stinks. It is ugly, and it shows the degradation of man, his inhumanity, and all that is evil. And this is not about any one single religion, it is the same story repeated by all the religions of the world: man exploiting man in the name of God. I still feel uneasy being associated with the word *religion*. But there are a few problems: in life sometimes one has to choose things that one hates.

In my youth I was known in the university as an atheist, irreligious, against all moral systems. That was my stand, and that is still my stand. I have not changed even an inch; my position is exactly the same. But being known as an atheist, irreligious, amoral, became a problem. It was difficult to communicate with people, almost impossible to bridge any kind of relationship with people. In my communing with people, those words—*atheist, irreligious, amoral*—functioned like impenetrable walls. I would have remained so—for me there was no problem—but I saw that it was impossible to spread my experience, to share.

The moment people heard that I was an atheist, irreligious, amoral, they were completely closed. That I don't believe in any God, that I don't believe in any heaven and hell, was enough for them to withdraw from me. Even very educated people—because I was a professor in the university and I was sur-rounded by hundreds of professors, research scholars, intelligent, educated people—simply avoided me because they had no courage to defend what they believed; they had no argument for themselves.

And I was continually arguing on street corners, in the university, in the pan wallah's shop—anywhere that I could get hold of somebody. I would hammer religion and try to clean people completely of all this nonsense. But the total result was that I became like an island; nobody even wanted to talk with me, because even to say hello to me was dangerous: where would it lead? Finally I had to change my strategy.

I became aware that, strangely, the people who were interested in the search for truth had got involved in religions. Because they thought me irreligious, I could not commune with them; and they were the people who would be really interested to know. They were the people who would be ready to travel with me to unknown spaces. But they were already involved in some religion, in some sect, in some philosophy; just their thinking of me as irreligious, atheistic, became a barrier. And those were the people I had to seek out.

There were people who were not involved in religions but they were not seekers at all. They were interested just in the trivia of life: earning more money, being a great leader—a politician, a prime minister, a president. Their interests were very mundane. They were no use to me, and they were also not interested in what I had to offer to them. The man who wants to become the prime minister of the country is not interested in finding the truth. If truth and the prime ministership are both presented to him, he will choose the prime ministership. He will say about truth, "There is no hurry. We can do that—the whole of eternity is available—but the opportunity of the prime ministership may or may not come again. It rarely comes, and only to very rare people, once in a while. Truth is everybody's nature, so any day we can find that. First let us do that which is momentary, temporal, fleeting. This beautiful dream may not happen again. Reality is not going anywhere but this dream is fleeting."

Their interest was in dreaming, imagination. They were not my people, and communication with them was also impossible because our interests were diametrically opposite. I tried hard, but these people were not interested in religion, not interested in truth, not interested in anything that is significant.

The people who *were* interested were Christians or Hindus, Moham-medans, Jainas, Buddhists. They were already following some ideology, some religion. Then it was obvious to to me that I would have to play the game of being religious; there was no other way. Only then could I find people who were authentic seekers.

I hate the word *religion*, I have always hated it, but I had to talk about reli-gion. But what I was talking about under the cover of religion was not the same as people understood by religion. Now, this was simply a strategy. I was using their words—*God, religion, liberation, moksha*—and I was giving them my meanings. In this way I could start finding people, and people started coming to me.

It took a few years for me to change my image in people's eyes. But peo-ple listen only to words, they don't understand meanings. People understand only what you say, they don't understand what is conveyed unsaid. So I used their own weapons against them! I commented on religious books and gave a meaning that was totally mine.

I would have said the same thing without commenting—it would have been far easier because then I would have been directly speaking to them. There was no need to drag in Krishna, Mahavira, and Jesus and then make them say what they had never said. But such is the stupidity of humanity that the same thing that I had been saying before, and they were not ready even to hear it . . . now thousands started gathering around me because I was speaking on Krishna.

Now, what have I to do with Krishna? What has he done for me? What relationship have I got with Jesus? If I had met him while he was alive I would have said to him, "You are a fanatic and you are not in your senses. I cannot say that the people who want to crucify you are absolutely wrong, because they have no other way to deal with you."

So this was the only way. When I started speaking on Jesus, Christian col-leges and Christian theological institutes started inviting me to speak. And I was really continually giggling inside, because those fools thought that this was what Jesus had said. Yes, I used Jesus' words—one has just to understand a little game with words and one can make any word mean anything—and they thought that this was the real message of Jesus . . . "Our own Christian missionaries and priests have not done so much for Jesus as you have done."

And I had to keep quiet, knowing that I have nothing to do with Jesus, and that what I was saying Jesus might not have been able to even understand. What I said in the name of Jesus I had been saying before also, but no Christian community, no Christian college, no Christian theological institute would have invited me. What to say of invitation? If I had wanted to enter they would have closed the doors. That was the situation: I was prohibited from entering my own city's central temple, and they had the support of the police so that I should not be allowed in. So whenever there was a Hindu monk speaking inside, a policeman was on guard outside to prevent me coming in.

I said, "But I want to listen to that man."

The police officer said, "We know, and everybody knows that when you are there, everybody has to listen to *you*. And we have been called here just to prevent you, not anybody else; everybody else is allowed. If you stop coming we would not be bothered because we are unnecessarily standing here for two or three hours every day. While the discourse session continues I will be standing here just for you, one person."

But now the same temple started inviting me. Again the police were there—to prevent overcrowding! One officer who was still there said to me, "You are something! We were standing here to keep you out, now we are standing here because too much crowding is dangerous—the temple is old."

It had balconies and at least five thousand people could sit inside. But when I used to speak there, nearabout fifteen thousand people would turn up. So people would go onto the balconies, which were normally never used. One day it became so serious that it was possible the balconies might fall down—so many people on the balconies, and it was such an old temple. Then naturally they had to arrange it so the next day only a certain number of people were to be allowed in.

That created trouble. That officer said, "Now new trouble! You speak for two hours there, but people start coming two hours early because if they come late they won't get in." He said to me, "But you are something! I thought you were against God."

I said in his ear, "I still am—don't tell anybody because nobody will believe it. And I will always remain against God. Before I depart from the world I will expose everything. But you are not to tell, because nobody is going to believe you and I will flatly deny that I have ever said anything to you."

But I had to find my own ways. I would speak on God and then tell people that *godliness* was a far better word. That was a way of disposing of God. But because I was speaking on God, the people who were involved—who were true seekers being exploited by the religious priesthood—started becoming interested in me. I found from all the religions, the cream.

There was no other way, because I would not have been able to enter their folds and they would not have been able to come to me. Just a few words would have been enough to prevent them. And I could not have blamed them, I would have blamed myself. I had to find some way so that I could approach them. And I found the way; it was very simple. I simply thought, "Use their words, use their language, use their scriptures. And if you are using somebody else's gun, that does not mean you cannot put your own cartridges in it. Let the gun be anybody's, the cartridges are mine! Because the real work is going to happen through the cartridges, not the gun. So what's the harm?"

And it was easy, very easy, because I could use Hindu words and play the same game; I could use Mohammedan words and play the same game; I could use Christian words and play the same game.

Not only were these people coming to me, but Jaina monks, nuns, Hindu monks, Buddhist monks, Christian missionaries, priests—all kinds of people started coming to me. And you will not believe it . . . you have not seen me laughing because I have laughed so much inside that there was no need. I have been telling jokes to you, but I have not been laughing because I have been playing a joke my whole life! What can be more funny? And I managed to befool all those priests and great scholars so easily. They started coming to me and asking me questions. I just had to be alert in the beginning to use their vocabulary, and just between the lines, between the words, to go on putting the real stuff in which I was interested.

I learned the art from a fisherman.

I used to sit by the bank of the river for hours because that was the most beautiful place in my village. The morning was beautiful, the evening was beautiful; and even in the hot summer there were spots where there were thick trees, just leaning over the river. You could just sit in the river, in the water, and it was so cool you could forget it was summer.

I was just sitting looking at the morning sun, and fishermen were there. Everywhere fishermen put out bait. And they will cut small insects into pieces, which are delicious to the fishes, and hook them to their fishing line. The fishes will come and catch the insect, and with the insect there is a hook; the hook will catch the fish. The fish will come to get the insect, but once she swallows the insect the fish is caught by the hook and she can be pulled out immediately.

Looking at this fisherman I thought, "I have to find some way that I can catch my people. Right now they are in different camps, nobody is mine." I was alone: Nobody was courageous enough even to associate with me or to walk with me because people would think that person was also gone, was lost.

I found the bait: Use their words. In the beginning, people were really shocked. Those who knew me for years, who knew that I had always been against God, were really puzzled, absolutely puzzled. And this was happening again and again.

Once I was speaking in a Mohammedan institute in Jabalpur. One of my old Mohammedan teachers had become the principal of this institute, and he was not aware that this speaker was going to be the same person he had known as a student. Somebody had told him that they heard me speaking on Sufis, and that it was something incredible: "We had not thought about Sufis that way, and our institute will be honored if this man comes."

If a Mohammedan comes and speaks on the Bible, the Christian will feel very flattered, his ego tremendously strengthened. Or if a Mohammedan, a Hindu, a Buddhist is speaking on Jesus, praising him and his words . . . And particularly in India, where Mohammedans and Hindus are continuously killing each other, if somebody who is not a Mohammedan can speak on Sufism . . . my old teacher was very happy and he invited me to talk. I was in search of all these invitations because I wanted to find my people, and they were all hiding in different places.

When my teacher saw me he said, "I have only *heard* of miracles, but this is a miracle! You are speaking on Sufism, on Islam, on the fundamental philosophy of Islam?"

I said, "To you I will not lie—you are my old teacher. I will be speaking only on my philosophy. Yes, I have learned the art of throwing the word *Islam* to people once in a while. That much I will do."

He said, "My God! But now there is no way out—people are waiting in the auditorium. And you are the same mischievous person, you have not changed. Are you kidding or something? Because one of our trusted teachers who is an authority on Sufism has praised you. Because of his praise I have invited you."

I said, "He has spoken rightly, and you will also praise what I say. But remember always, I will say only what I want to say. It does not matter, it is so simple a thing: if a Buddhist calls me I have only to change a few words. And starting from Sufism I talk about Zen, not about Sufis. I say the same thing; it is just that Sufism is changed a little here and there. And I have to be alert—I should not forget about whom I am speaking, that's all."

And I spoke. Of course he had been sitting there very unhappy, but when he heard me he was so joyous. He came and hugged me and he said, "You must have been joking."

I said, "I am always joking—don't take it seriously."

"You *are* a Sufi," he said.

I said, "That's what people say!"

I was speaking in Amritsar in the Golden Temple of the Sikhs. Everywhere, all around the country, people had asked me thousands of times, "Why do you grow a beard?" I had become accustomed to the question and I enjoyed answering in different ways to different people. But in the Golden Temple when I was speaking on Nanak and his message, a very old sardar came to me, touched my feet and said, "Sardarji, why have you cut your hair?" That was a new question, asked for the first time. He said, "Your beard is perfectly okay, but why have you cut your hair? And you being such a religious man."

Only five things are needed to be a Sikh—very simple things, you can manage them, anybody can. They are called the "five *k*'s" because each word starts with *k*. *Kesh* means hair, *katar* means a knife; *kachchha* means underwear—that I have not been able to figure out. It is the only question I cannot answer. What philosophy is being taught? Strange, but there must be some reason. I inquired of the Sikh priests and their high priest, "Everything is okay—grow your hair and have a sword, or a knife—but this *kachchha* . . . ? What theological, theosophical, philosophical meaning does *kachchha* have?"

They said, "Nobody has ever asked about it; we just have to follow these five *k*'s."

This old sardar thought that I was a sardar too, because nobody who was not a sardar had ever spoken in the Golden Temple. It was unprecedented. He was certainly puzzled about why I, such a religious man, had cut my hair. And I was only thirty at that time.

So I told him, "There is some reason in it. I don't feel yet a perfect sardar, and I don't want to claim anything that I am not. So I have kept four things, but I have been cutting my hair. I will grow my hair when I am a perfect sardar."

He said, "That's right. It is tremendously significant that a man should think about this, that he should not pretend to be a perfect sardar. You are a better sardar than we are! We think we are perfect because we have all five things."

From among these people I found my people. It was not difficult, it was very easy. I was speaking their language, using their religious idioms, quoting their scriptures, and giving my message. The intelligent people immediately understood and they started gathering around me.

All over India I started creating groups of my own people. Now there was no need for me to speak on Sikhism, Hinduism, Jainism; there was no need, but for ten years I had been continually speaking on them. Slowly, when I had my own people, I dropped speaking on others. I stopped traveling also, because there was no need. Now I had my people: if they wanted to come to me they could come.

So it was an absolute necessity; there was no other way to hook my people. Everybody is already divided, it is not an open world: somebody is a Christian, somebody is a Hindu, somebody is a Mohammedan. It is very difficult to find a person who is nobody. I had to find my people from these closed flocks, but to enter their flock I had to talk their language. Slowly, slowly, I dropped their language. Proportionately, as my message became more and more clear, their language I slowly dropped.

In those days I had to speak in the name of religion, in the name of God. It was compulsory, there was no alternative. It was not that I had not tried it— I had tried it, but found it simply closes people's doors.

Even my father was puzzled, more so than anybody else, because he knew me from my very childhood—that I am against religion, against the priests. When I started speaking in religious conferences, he asked me, "What is happening? Have you changed?"

I said, "Not a bit. I have just changed my strategy; otherwise it is difficult to speak in the World Hindu Conference. They won't allow an atheist on their stage; an amoralist, a godless person they won't allow. But they invited me— and in the name of religion I said everything *against* religion."

The *shankaracharya,* the head of the Hindu religion, was presiding over the conference. The king of Nepal—Nepal is the only Hindu kingdom in the world—inaugurated the conference. The *shankaracharya* was in great difficulty because what I was saying was absolutely sabotaging the whole conference, but the way I was presenting it, people were getting impressed. He became so angry that he stood up and tried to snatch away the microphone—this old man. While he was trying to snatch it away, I said, "Just one minute, and I will be finished." So just for one minute he stopped—and in one minute I managed!

I asked the people—there must have been at least one hundred thousand people—I asked them, "What do you want? He is the president, he can stop me if he wants, and certainly I will stop. But you are the people who have come here to listen. If you want to listen to me, then you all raise your hands— and to make it clear raise both your hands."

Two hundred thousand hands . . . I looked at the old fellow and said, "Now you sit down. You are no longer president: two hundred thousand hands have canceled you completely. Whom do you represent? You were president— these people had made you president, now these people have canceled you. Now I will speak as long as I want to speak."

It would have been impossible otherwise. And I found hundreds of people from that gathering; Bihar became a source of many of my sannyasins.

In the same way I was moving around the country going into religious conferences and catching hold of people. And once I had my own group in that city then I never bothered about their conferences; then my group was holding its own conferences, its own meetings. But it takes time.

IT HAPPENED ONCE THAT I WAS SPEAKING IN A CONFERENCE WITH Chandan Muni, a Jaina monk who was very much respected among the Jainas. He spoke first, and he talked about the self, the realization of self, and the blissfulness of self. I was sitting by his side, watching the man. All those words were empty; there was no support from his experience. I could see in his eyes, there was no depth.

I spoke after him, and the first thing I said was, "Whatever Chandan Muni has said is simply a repetition of scriptures, parrotlike. He has done a good job. His memory is good, but his experience is nil."

There was great trouble because it was the conference of the Jainas. A few people started standing up and going. I said, "Wait! You will have to listen for at least five minutes to me and then you can go. I am new to you; you don't know me. At least five minutes just to have a little introduction as to what kind of a man you have left behind, and then you are free; everybody can go."

Speaking for five minutes was enough, and after five minutes I asked, "Now, anybody who wants to go should immediately leave."

Not a single man left. I spoke for almost two hours. I was not supposed to speak for that long, I was asked to speak for only ten minutes. But seeing that now people were listening and nobody had left, the president was afraid. Even Chandan Muni was listening very intensely and alertly. The president was afraid to disturb me because he knew that I am not a man who can be stopped. And I was not going to stop, I was going to throw out that president. He understood it, so he was sitting silently.

But having heard me for two hours, Chandan Muni sent me a message that afternoon saying, "I want to meet you alone, in private. I cannot come to the place where you are staying because a Jaina monk cannot go anywhere except the Jaina temple. So please forgive me, you will have to come here."

I said, "There is no problem. I will come."

I went there, and at least two hundred people had gathered. But he wanted absolute privacy, so he took me in, closed the doors of the room, sat down with me on the floor and said, "You were right. I don't have courage enough to say it in public, but I wanted to say to you that you were right. I don't have any experience of self, I don't have any experience of self-realization. I don't know whether such a thing exists or not—and you were absolutely right that I was just like a parrot repeating the scriptures.

"But help me. I am imprisoned, I cannot go anywhere. I am the head of a community; I cannot even ask questions to you in front of others. They think I am already self-realized, so why should I be asking questions? I should know the answer myself." And there were tears in his eyes.

I said, "I will do my best to help you, because I have seen many religious leaders but not with such a sincere heart. And I know perfectly well that you cannot remain in this bondage for long. You have met a dangerous man, and you have invited me yourself!"

And it happened within two years. He was in contact with me—letters, learning meditation, doing meditation—and after two years he dropped out of the Jaina community. He was so well respected, and the Jaina community is very rich . . . and he dropped out.

He came to meet me. I could not believe it. When he came to my house and said, "I am Chandan Muni," I said, "You have changed so much!"

He said, "To be free of a prison, to be free of borrowed knowledge has been such a great relief that I have again become young"—and he was seventy years old. He said, "Now I am ready to do whatever you want. I have risked everything; I was rich, I renounced that to become a Jaina monk. Now I have renounced Jainism, the monkhood, just to be nobody so that I can have total freedom to experiment."

IF I SEE PEOPLE SILENTLY SITTING, ATTENTIVE, DRINKING IN EVERY single word, focused, meditative, I can say far higher things; far more complicated things can be explained to them.

But if no friends are sitting in front of me, I always have to begin from ABC. Then the plane can never take off; then the plane has to function like a bus. You can use a plane like a bus—but it can take off only when it gains speed; a certain situation is needed for it to gain speed.

I used to talk to millions of people in India; then I had to stop. I was talking to thousands—in a single meeting, fifty thousand people. I traveled around that country for fifteen years, from one corner to another corner. I simply became tired of the whole thing, because each day I would have to start from ABC. It was always ABC, ABC, ABC, and it became absolutely clear that I would never be able to reach XYZ. I had to stop traveling.

EXPRESSING THE
INEXPRESSIBLE: THE SILENCES
BETWEEN WORDS

For thirty-five years I have been continually speaking for no purpose. With this much speaking I could have become a president, a prime minister; there was no problem in it. With so much speaking I could have done anything. What have I gained?

But I was not out for gain in the first place—I enjoyed. This was my painting, this was my song, this was my poetry. Just those moments when I am speaking and I feel the communion happening, those moments when I see your eyes flare up, when I see that you have understood the point . . . they give me such tremendous joy that I cannot think anything can be added to it.

YOU DON'T KNOW ABOUT THOUSANDS OF ENLIGHTENED PEOPLE who have lived and died, because they had no special talents so that they became visible to the ordinary man. They may have had something unique; for example they may have had the immense quality of being silent, but that would not be noticed much.

I knew an enlightened man who was in Bombay when I was there, and his only talent was to make beautiful statues out of sand. I have never seen such beautiful statues. The whole day he would make them on the beach, and thousands of people would see them and would be amazed. They had seen Gautam Buddha's statues, Krishna's, Mahavira's, but there was no comparison. And he was not working in marble, just with the sea sand. People would be throwing rupee notes; he was not at all bothered. I have seen others taking the notes away; he was not concerned about that either. He was so absorbed in making those statues. But those statues didn't last. Just an ocean wave would come and the Buddha was gone.

Before his enlightenment he was earning a living that way, moving from one city to another city and making sand statues. And they were so beautiful that it was impossible not to give something to him. He earned much, enough for one man.

Now he had become enlightened—but he had only one talent, to make sand statues. Of course he will make sand statues that point toward enlightenment, but that is the only offering he can give. Existence will use that. His statues are more meditative. Just sitting by the side of his sand statues you can feel that he has given a proportion to the statue, a certain shape, a certain face that creates something within you.

I asked him, "Why do you go on making Gautam Buddha and Mahavira? You can earn more—because this country is not Buddhist, and Jainas are very few. You can make Rama, you can make Krishna."

But he said, "They will not serve the purpose; they do not point to the moon. They will be beautiful statues—I have made all those statues before—but now I can make only that which is a teaching, even though it will be invisible to millions of people, almost to all."

By the time I went to live in Bombay permanently he had died, but before that whenever I used to go there, I made it a point to go and visit him. He worked on Juhu Beach at that time. It is silent there the whole day, people came only in the evening and by that time his statue was ready. The whole day, no disturbance.

I told him, "You can make statues, why don't you work in marble? They will remain forever."

He said, "Nothing is permanent"—that is a quotation of Buddha—"and these statues represent Gautam Buddha better than any marble statue. A marble statue has a certain permanence and these statues are momentary: just a strong wind and they are gone, an ocean wave and they are gone. A child comes running and stumbles on the statue, and it is gone."

I said, "Don't you feel bad when you have been working the whole day, and the statue was just going to be complete, and then something happens and the whole day's work is gone?"

He said, "No. All of existence is momentary; there is no question of frustration. I enjoyed making it, and if an ocean wave enjoys unmaking it, then the two of us enjoyed! I enjoyed making it, the wave enjoyed unmaking it. So in existence there has been a double quantity of joy—why should I be frustrated? The wave has as much power over the sand as I have; perhaps it has more."

When I was talking to him he said, "You are a little strange because nobody talks to me. People simply throw rupees. They enjoy the statue, but nobody enjoys me. But when you come I feel so blissful that there is somebody who enjoys me, who is not concerned only with the statue but with its inner meaning, with why I am making it. I cannot do anything else. My whole life I have been making statues; that is the only art I know. And now I am surrendered to existence; now existence can use me."

These people will remain unrecognized. A dancer may be a buddha, a singer may be a buddha, but these people will not be recognized for the simple reason that their way of doing things cannot become a teaching. It cannot help people really to come out of their sleep. But they are doing their best; whatever they can do, they are doing.

The very few people who become masters are those who have earned in their many lives a certain articulateness, a certain insight into words, language, the sound of words, the symmetry and the poetry of language. It is a totally different thing. It is not a question of linguistics or grammar, it is more a question of finding in ordinary language some extraordinary music, of creating the quality of great poetry in ordinary prose. They know how to play with words so that you can be helped to go beyond words.

It is not that they have chosen to be masters, and it is not that existence has chosen them to be masters. It is just a coincidence: before enlightenment they had been great teachers and they became masters because of enlightenment. Now they can change their teaching into mastery—and certainly that is the most difficult part.

Those who remain silent and disappear peacefully with nobody knowing them have an easy way, but a man like me cannot have an easy way. It was not easy when I was a teacher—how can it be easy when I am a master? It is bound to be difficult.

THE QUESTION ARISES ALMOST FOR EVERYONE, THAT THE WAY I TALK IS a little strange. No speaker in the world talks like me—technically it is wrong; it takes almost double the time! But those speakers have a different purpose—my purpose is absolutely different from theirs. They speak because they are prepared for it; they are simply repeating something that they have rehearsed. Second, they are speaking to impose a certain ideology, a certain idea on you. Third, to them speaking is an art—they go on refining it.

As far as I am concerned, I am not what they call a speaker or an orator. It is not an art to me, or a technique; technically I go on becoming worse every day! But our purposes are totally different. I don't want to impress you in order to manipulate you. I don't speak for any goal to be achieved through convincing you. I don't speak to convert you into a Christian, into a Hindu or a Mohammedan, into a theist or an atheist—these are not my concerns.

My speaking is really one of my devices for meditation. Speaking has never been used this way: I speak not to give you a message but to stop your mind functioning.

I speak nothing prepared—I don't know myself what is going to be the next word; hence I never commit any mistake. One commits a mistake if one is prepared. I never forget anything, because one forgets if one has been remembering it. So I speak with a freedom that perhaps nobody has ever spoken with.

I am not concerned whether I am consistent, because that is not the purpose. A man who wants to convince you and manipulate you through his speaking has to be consistent, has to be logical, has to be rational, to overpower your reason. He wants to dominate through words.

One of the very famous books of Dale Carnegie is about speaking and influencing people as an art—it has been sold second only to the Holy Bible—but I will fail his examinations. He used to run a course in America to train missionaries, to train professors and orators. I will fail on all counts. First, I have no motivation to convert you; I have no desire anywhere to impress you. And I don't remember what I have said yesterday, so I cannot bother about being consistent—that is too much worry. I can easily contradict myself because I am not trying to have a communication with your intellectual, rational mind.

My purpose is so unique—I am using words just to create silent gaps. The words are not important so I can say anything contradictory, anything absurd, anything unrelated, because my purpose is just to create gaps. The words are secondary; the silences between those words are primary. This is simply a device to give you a glimpse of meditation. And once you know that it is possible for you, you have traveled far in the direction of your own being.

Most of the people in the world don't think that it is possible for mind to be silent. Because they don't think it is possible, they don't try. How to give people a taste of meditation was my basic reason to speak, so I can go on speaking eternally—it does not matter what I am saying. All that matters is that I give you a few chances to be silent, which you find difficult on your own in the beginning.

I cannot force you to be silent, but I can create a device in which spontaneously you are bound to be silent. I am speaking and in the middle of a sentence, when you were expecting another word to follow, nothing follows but a silent gap. And your mind was looking to listen, and waiting for something to follow, and does not want to miss it—naturally it becomes silent. What can the poor mind do? If it was well known at what points I will be silent, if it was declared to you that on such and such points I will be silent, then you could manage to think—you would not be silent. Then you know: "This is the point where he is going to be silent, now I can have a little chitchat with myself." But because it comes absolutely suddenly . . . I myself don't know why at certain points I stop.

Anything like this, in any orator in the world, will be condemned. Because an orator stopping again and again means he is not well prepared, he has not done the homework. It means that his memory is not reliable, that sometimes he cannot find what word to use. But because it is not oratory, I am not concerned about the people who will be condemning me—I am concerned with you.

And it is not only here, but far away . . . anywhere in the world where people will be listening to the video or to the audio, they will come to the same silence. My success is not to convince you, my success is to give you a real taste so that you can become confident that meditation is not a fiction, that the state of no-mind is not just a philosophical idea, that it is a reality; that you are capable of it, and that it does not need any special qualifications.

You may be a sinner, you may be a saint—it does not matter. If the sinner can become silent, he will attain to the same consciousness as the saint.

Existence is not so miserly as religions have been teaching you. Existence is not like the KGB or FBI—watching everybody to see what you are doing, whether you are going to the movie with your own wife or with somebody else's wife. Existence is not interested at all. The problem of whether the wife is yours or not is just a man-created problem. In existence, there is nothing like marriage. Whether you are stealing money, taking it out from somebody's safe or from your own, existence does not and cannot decide the difference. You are taking out the money from the safe—that is a fact—but to whom the safe belongs, that is absolutely of no concern to existence.

Once George Bernard Shaw was asked, "Can a man live his life so lazily, just keeping his hands in his pockets and enjoying?" George Bernard Shaw said, "Yes, just the pockets should be somebody else's!"

Keeping your hands in your own pockets, you cannot survive! And the fact is that almost everybody has his hand in somebody else's pocket. And that fellow may have *his* hand in somebody else's pocket, so he cannot stop you because by stopping you, he will be stopped. So he has to accept it, and if he has his hands in a richer pocket, he does not care about you: "Go on doing whatsoever you are doing, just don't create a disturbance."

Existence has no morality as such—it is amoral. For existence there is nothing wrong and nothing right. Only one thing is right—your being alert and conscious. Then you are blissful.

It is very strange that no religion has defined "right" as being blissful, or defined "virtue" as being blissful. They were in a difficulty to define it exactly as I am defining it because their concern was that in the world, the people they think are sinners look happier than the people they think are saints! The saints look absolutely unhappy. And if they say that blissfulness is the criterion of whether you are right or wrong, this will destroy their whole superstructure. The saints will look like sinners and the sinners will look like saints.

But this is my criterion because I don't care about the scriptures, I don't care about the prophets, I don't care about the past—that was their business and their problem. I have my own eyes to see, why should I depend on anybody else's eyes? And I have my own consciousness to be aware, why should I be dependent on Gautam Buddha, or Bodhidharma, or Jesus Christ? They lived their lives according to their own understanding and insight; I live my life according to my understanding and my insight.

My effort here to speak to you is to give you a chance to see that you are as capable of becoming a no-mind as any Gautam Buddha—that it is not a special quality given to a few people, that it is not a talent. Everybody cannot be a painter and everybody cannot be a poet—those are talents. Everybody cannot be a genius—those are given qualities from birth. But everybody can be enlightened—that is the only thing about which communism is right. And strangely enough, that is the only thing communism denies.

Enlightenment is the only thing, the only experience, where everybody is equal—equally capable. And it does not depend on your acts, it does not depend on your prayers, it does not depend on whether you believe in God or not. It depends only on one thing and that is a little taste—and suddenly you become confident that you are capable of it. My speaking is just to give you confidence. So I can tell a story, I can tell a joke—absolutely unrelated!

Every intellectual will condemn me, saying, "What kind of speech is this?" But he has not understood my purpose; it is not a speech, it is not a lecture. It is simply a device to bring confidence to you and to your heart that you can be silent. The more you become confident, the more you will be able. Without my speaking you will start finding devices yourself. For example, you can go on listening to the birds—they suddenly stop, and they suddenly start. Listen . . . there is no reason why this crow should make noises and then stop. It is just giving you a chance. You can find these opportunities, once you know—even in the marketplace where there is so much noise, everything is going on, crazy.

So my speaking is not oratory; it is not a doctrine that I am preaching to you. It is simply an arbitrary device to give you a taste of what silence is, and to make you confident that it is not a talent—that it does not belong to any specially qualified people, that it does not belong to long austerities, that it does not belong to those who call themselves virtuous. It belongs to all, without any conditions; you just have to become aware of it. That's my whole purpose in speaking to you.

Once you are certain that you can be silent, then your whole focus will change. It is not a question of discipline, it is not a question of being prayerful, it is not a question of believing in God and all kinds of nonsense. It is a question of feeling your own possibility, and once you have known the possibility and become confident about it, your whole vision will have a different color.

My own experience is that if you can be silent, and if you can transcend mind and your consciousness can grow, it does not matter what you are doing; your actions are not counted at all, only your consciousness. Actions are very small things, but up to now all the religions have been counting your actions, not your consciousness. They have been training you how to act rightly and what has to be avoided. But nobody was saying that unless your consciousness rises you will not be authentically religious.

And it was a surprise to me that as you become silent, as you become conscious, more alert, your actions start changing—but not vice versa. You can change your actions, but that will not make you more conscious. You become more conscious, and your actions will change—that's absolutely simple and scientific. You were doing something stupid; as you become more alert and more conscious, you cannot do it.

It is not a question of reward or punishment. It is simply your consciousness, your silence, your peace, which makes you look so far away and so deep into everything that you do. You cannot do harm to anybody; you cannot be violent, you cannot be angry, you cannot be greedy, you cannot be ambitious. Your consciousness has given you so much blissfulness . . . what can greed give you except anxieties? What can ambition give you? Just a continuous struggle to reach high on some ladder.

As your consciousness becomes more settled, all your life patterns change. What religions have called sin will disappear from your life, and what they have called virtue will automatically flow from your being, from your actions. But they have been doing just vice versa: first change the acts. It is as if you are in a dark house and you are stumbling over furniture and things, and you are told that unless you stop stumbling, light is not possible. What I am saying is, bring light in and stumbling will disappear, because when there is light why should you stumble over things? Every time you stumble, every time you hit your head on the wall, it hurts. It is a punishment in itself—a wrong act is a punishment in itself; there is nobody recording your acts. And every beautiful action is a reward unto itself. But first bring light in your life.

Meditation is an effort to bring light and to bring joy and to bring silence and to bring blissfulness, and out of this beautiful world of meditation it is impossible for you to do anything wrong.

So I have changed it completely. Religions were insisting on action; my insistence is on consciousness, and consciousness can grow only in silence. Silence is the right soil for consciousness. When you are noisy, you cannot be very alert and conscious. When you are conscious and alert, you cannot be noisy—they cannot coexist.

So my speaking, my talking should not be categorized with any other kind of oratory. It is a device for meditation, to bring the confidence in you that has been taken away by religions. Instead of confidence they have given you guilt, which pulls you down and keeps you sad. Once you become confident that great things are available to you, you will not feel inferior, you will not feel guilty—you will feel blessed. You will feel that existence has prepared you to be one of the peaks of consciousness.

It will take a little time to gain confidence—that's why I have been speaking, morning and evening, for almost thirty years continuously. Perhaps two or three times in these thirty years, I have stopped because I was not feeling well; otherwise I have continued to speak. But because I cannot go on speaking the whole day to keep you in meditative moments, I want you to become responsible. Accepting that you are capable of being silent will help you when you are meditating alone. Knowing your capacity . . . and one comes to know one's capacity only when one experiences it. There is no other way.

Pay more attention to it, to why you become silent. Don't make me wholly responsible for your silence, because that will create a difficulty for you. Alone, what are you going to do? Then it becomes a kind of addiction, and I don't want you to be addicted to me. I don't want to be a drug to you.

The so-called masters and teachers of the religions of the whole world—I have come across almost all kinds and all categories of teachers—want their disciples to be addicted to them, to be dependent on them. That is their power trip. I don't have any power trip. I love you, whether you are with me or not with me. I want you to be independent and confident that you can attain these precious moments on your own.

If you can attain them with me, there is no reason why you cannot attain them without me, because I am not the cause. You have to understand what is happening: listening to me, you put your mind aside. Listening to the ocean, or listening to the thundering of the clouds, or listening to the rain falling heavily, just put your ego aside, because there is no need . . . The ocean is not going to attack you, the rain is not going to attack you, the trees are not going to attack you—there is no need of any defense. To be vulnerable to life as such, to existence as such, you will be getting these moments continuously—soon it will become your very life.

PART TWO

Reflections in an Empty Mirror: The Many Faces of a Man Who Never Was

Q: *Who are you?*

A: Whomsoever you think, because it depends on you. If you look at me with total emptiness, I will be different. If you look at me with ideas, those ideas will color me; if you come to me with a prejudice, then I will be different. I am just a mirror. Your own face will be reflected. There is a saying that if a monkey looks into the mirror he will not find an apostle looking at him through the mirror. Only a monkey will be looking through the mirror.

So it depends on the way you look at me. I have disappeared completely so I cannot impose on you who I am. I have nothing to impose. There is just a nothingness, a mirror. Now you have complete freedom.

If you really want to know who I am, you have to be as absolutely empty as I am. Then two mirrors will be facing each other, and only emptiness will be mirrored. Infinite emptiness will be mirrored: two mirrors facing each other. But if you have some idea, then you will see your own idea in me.

SEX GURU

Q: *It has been written, and people have talked about you as a "free sex guru," believing in promiscuous sex with violent encounter sessions and mind control. True or false?*

A: Do you think sex should be charged for? Should it not be free? Should it be paid for?

To me, sex is a simple, beautiful, natural phenomenon. If two persons want to share energy with each other, it is nobody's business to interfere. And to say "free sex" implies that you want sex also to be a commodity, that is has to be purchased—either from a prostitute for one night, or from a wife for the whole life, but it has to be purchased and paid for.

Yes, I believe in free sex. I believe that sex is everybody's birthright to share, to enjoy. It is fun. There is nothing serious about it. The people who have been talking about me as teaching "free sex" are really pathetic. They are sexually repressed people.

•from an interview with Ken Kashiwahara,
Good Morning America

I HAVE WRITTEN ONE BOOK—NOT WRITTEN, MY DISCOURSES HAVE been collected in it—it is called *From Sex to Superconsciousness*. Since then, hundreds of my books have been published but nobody seems to read any other—not in India. They all read *From Sex to Superconsciousness*. They all criticize it also, they are all against it. Articles are still being written, books are written against it, and mahatmas go on objecting to it. And no other book is mentioned, no other book is looked at. Do you understand? As if I have written only one book.

People are suffering from a wound. Sex has become a wound; it needs to be healed.

SEXUAL ORGASM, ACCORDING TO ME, GIVES YOU THE FIRST GLIMPSE of meditation—because the mind stops, time stops. For those few moments there is no time and there is no mind, you are just utterly silent and blissful. I say it—it is my scientific approach to the subject, because there was no other way for man to find out that if there is no mind and no time, you enter into a blissful state. Except for sex there was no other possibility for the mind to understand that there is some way of going beyond mind, beyond time. It was certainly sex that gave the first glimpse of meditativeness. And I am being condemned all over the world because I am telling people the truth.

Nobody has come up with any other idea to explain how you have found meditation. You cannot find it by just walking on the side of the road—it is lying there and you go over and pick up meditation. Where have you found meditation?

I have been discussed around the world, condemned, just because I am talking about going from sex to superconsciousness. But nobody has given any explanation why they are condemning me—because of my book, which has been translated into thirty-four languages, has gone into dozens of editions, and is read by all the monks! Whether they are Hindu, Jaina, Christian, or Buddhist, monks are the best customers for that book. There was a Jaina conference here in Pune just a few months ago and my secretary informed me, "It is strange. Jaina monks come and they ask for one book only, *From Sex to Superconsciousness*. Then they hide it in their clothes and just go out of the door silently so nobody finds them out."

The book, *From Sex to Superconsciousness*, is not about sex, it is about superconsciousness. But the only possible way for man to find that there is some door, some way to go beyond his thoughts into eternal silence, is the sexual orgasm. Even though it lasts only a moment, that moment is eternity—everything stops. You forget all the worries, all the tensions.

I HAVE BEEN TELLING YOU IT IS POSSIBLE TO GO "FROM SEX TO SUPER-consciousness," and you have been very happy—you hear only "from sex," you don't hear "to superconsciousness."

And this is the case with those who are against me *and* with those who are in favor of me—the same! Man is almost the same; friends and enemies are not very different. I am being misunderstood by the opponents, and that is under-standable. But I am also being misunderstood by the supporters; that is not understandable at all. The opponents can be forgiven, but the supporters can-not be forgiven.

Because I have said that sex is stupid, many angry questions have come to me. One of my sannyasins has written to me, "You have some nerve to say that sex is stupid!" She must have felt hurt. And I can understand: when you are liv-ing in a certain way you don't want it to be described as stupid. Nobody wants to be called stupid. It is not over the question of sex that you are disturbed—it is your life; if it is stupid and you are living it, then *you* are being stupid. That hurts. But I have to say it even if it hurts, because that is the only way to make you aware that there is something more in life, something higher, something greater, something far more blissful, far more orgasmic.

Sex is only a beginning—not the end. And nothing is wrong if you take it as a beginning. If you start clinging to it, then things start going wrong.

After making love, at least for one hour sit in *zazen* and you will see what I am saying. You will understand what I mean when I say sex is stupid. After making love, make it a point to sit in *zazen* for one hour just watching what has happened. Were you the master of it or just a slave? If you were the master of it, then it is not stupid. If you were a slave, it is stupid—because by repeating it you are making your slavery stronger and stronger, you are feeding your slavery.

It is only through meditation that you will be able to understand what I have been telling you. It is not a question to be decided by argument, it can be decided only by your own meditation, your own understanding, your own awareness.

I HAVE NEVER TAUGHT "FREE SEX." WHAT I HAVE BEEN TEACHING IS the sacredness of sex. I have been teaching that sex should not be degraded from the realm of love to the realm of law. The moment you have to love a woman because she is your wife, and not because you simply love her, it is prostitution, legalized prostitution. I have been against prostitution, whether it has been legalized or illegalized. I believe in love. If two persons love each other they can live together as long as they love. The moment love is gone, they should gracefully separate.

I have never taught anything concerning free sex. This is the idiotic Indian yellow journalism that has confined my whole philosophy to two words. I have published four hundred books—only one book is concerned with sex. Three hundred ninety-nine books nobody bothers about; only one book that is concerned with sex—and that too is not *for* sex. That too is about how to transform sex energy into spiritual energy. It is really antisex!

What they have been doing all along is misinforming people and then condemning that misinformation. They have never represented me fairly; otherwise, I don't think India is so unintelligent. A country that has produced the philosophy of Tantra, a country that has made temples like Khajuraho, Konarak, cannot be so stupid that it will not understand what I am saying. Khajuraho is my proof. All the literature of Tantra is my proof. And this is the only country where something like Tantra has existed. Nowhere else in the world has any effort been made to transform sexual energy into spiritual energy—and that's what I was doing. But the journalists are not interested in reality; they are interested in sensationalism.

CULT LEADER

Q: *What has grown around you has been presented by newspapers as a cult, as a sect. Is it? And if not, can you explain what it is?*

A: It is simply a movement; neither a cult nor a sect nor a religion but a movement for meditation, an effort to create a science of the inner. It is a science of consciousness. Just as the science is there for the objective world, this movement is preparing a science for the subjective world.

The scientist will study everything, and we are going to study the scientist.

Otherwise he will be left out! He will be able to know everything except himself. And that will be a real shame, that Albert Einstein knows so much about physics that only twelve other persons in the whole world can understand it, but he knows nothing about himself. This is a very ugly state of affairs.

So my work is a movement not to create a religion but to create religiousness. I take religiousness as a quality—not as a membership in an organization, but an inner experience of one's being.

•from an interview with
Private National Network, Italy

YOU ARE CERTAINLY BRAINWASHED. I USE A DRY CLEANING MACHINE. I am not old-fashioned. And naturally you are addicted. Who will not be?

Addiction is not always bad. If you are addicted to beauty, to poetry, to drama, to sculpture, to painting, nobody tells you to drop the addiction. Addiction has to be dropped only when it makes you unconscious. Alcoholics are told to drop the addiction, but here my teaching is of consciousness—be addicted to it more and more.

And what is wrong in being brainwashed? Wash it every day, keep it clean. Do you like cockroaches? When I brainwash people, I find cockroaches. Cockroaches are very special animals. It has been found scientifically that wherever you find man you find cockroaches, and wherever you find cockroaches you find man. They are always together, they are the oldest companions.

What have you got in your brain? So just washing it is perfectly right. But people have given it a very wrong connotation; those are the wrong people.

Christians are afraid of somebody brainwashing Christians, because then they will not be Christians. Hindus are afraid because then those people will not be Hindus. Mohammedans are afraid, communists are afraid. Everybody is afraid of brainwashing.

I am in absolute favor of it.

There used to be an old saying: "Cleanliness is next to God." Now there is no God, so there is only cleanliness left. Cleanliness is God.

And I am not afraid of brainwashing because I am not putting cockroaches in your mind. I am giving you an opportunity to experience a clean mind, and once you know a clean mind you will never allow anybody to throw rubbish and crap into your mind. They are the criminals.

Brainwashing is not a crime—who has made it dirty? Dirtying other people's minds is a crime, but all over the world all the religions, all the political leaders, are using your mind as if it is a toilet. These ugly fellows have condemned brainwashing; otherwise, brainwashing is a perfectly good job.

I am a brainwasher.

And those who come to me should come with the clear conception that they are going to a man who is bound to brainwash, to clean their minds of all kinds of cockroaches. Hindu, Mohammedan, Christian—they are all against me for the simple reason that they go on putting in their cockroaches, and I go on washing people's minds.

It is just an up-to-date religious laundry.

MY EFFORT IS TO TAKE AWAY ALL TRADITIONS, ORTHODOXIES, SUPER-stitions, and beliefs from your mind, so that you can attain a state of no-mind, the ultimate state of silence, where not even a thought moves—not even a ripple in the lake of your consciousness.

And the whole thing has to be done by you. I am not saying, "Just follow me, I am the savior. I will save you." All that is crap. Nobody can save you, except yourself. And spiritual independence is the only independence worth calling independence. All other independences—political, economic—are just so-so, superficial. The real and authentic independence is that you are not dependent on anybody for your inner growth.

Those who have come to me have become more and more independent, more and more themselves. That's why they love me. I am not making them a crowd, I am making them absolutely individuals. I am not even giving them ideologies to be practiced, disciplines to be practiced—I am simply sharing my own experience. Out of that experience they have to find their own discipline.

This is a company, not of a master and disciples, this is a company of a master and potential masters.

CON MAN

I have to work on two levels: one is the level where you live, where you are, and one is the level where I am and I want you also to be.

From the top of a hill I have to come into the valley where you are; otherwise you won't listen, you won't believe the sunlit top. I have to take your hand in my hand and persuade you—and on the way, tell stories that are not true! But they keep you engaged, and you don't create any trouble in walking; you go on, engaged with the story. And when you have reached the hilltop, you will know why I was telling long stories, and you will feel grateful that I told those stories; otherwise you would not have been able to travel that long, that far uphill.

It is something to be remembered: All the masters of the world have been telling stories, parables—why? The truth can be simply said, there is no need to give you so many stories. But the night is long, and you have to be kept awake; without stories you are going to fall asleep.

Till the morning comes there is an absolute necessity to keep you engaged, and the stories the masters have been telling are the most intriguing things possible.

The truth cannot be said, but you can be led to the point from where you can see it.

I AM REMINDED OF A STORY:

A king used to go every night into the city for a round to see how things were going—of course, in disguise. He was very much puzzled about one man, a young, very beautiful man, who was always standing under a tree by the side of the street, the same tree every night.

Finally, the curiosity took over, and the king stopped his horse and asked the man, "Why don't you go to sleep?"

And the man said, "People go to sleep because they have nothing to guard, and I have such treasures that I cannot go to sleep, I have to guard them."

The king said, "Strange, I don't see any treasures here."

The man said, "Those treasures are inside me, you cannot see them."

It became a routine thing for the king to stop every day, because the man was beautiful, and whatever he said made the king think over it for hours. The king became so much attached to and interested in the man that he started feeling that he was really a saint, because awareness and love and peace and silence and meditation and enlightenment, these are his treasures that he is guarding; he cannot sleep, he cannot afford sleep. Only beggars can afford . . .

The story had started just by curiosity, but slowly, slowly the king started respecting and honoring the man, almost as a spiritual guide. One day he said to him, "I know you will not come with me to the palace, but I think of you, day in, day out. You come to my mind so many times, I would love it if you can become a guest in my palace."

The king was thinking that he will not agree—he had the old idea that saints renounce the world—but the young man said, "If you are missing me so much, why did you not say it before? So bring another horse, and I will come with you."

The king became suspicious, "What kind of saint is he, so easily ready?" But now it was too late, he had invited him. He gave him his best room in the palace, which was preserved only for rare guests, other emperors. And he was thinking the man would refuse, that he would say, "I am a saint, I cannot live in this luxury." But he did not say anything like this. He said, "Very good."

The king could not sleep the whole night, and he thought, "It seems this fellow has deceived me; he is not a saint or anything." Two, three times he went to look from the window—the saint was asleep. And he had never been asleep, he was always standing under the tree. Now he was not guarding. The king thought, "I have been conned. This is a real con man."

The second day he ate with the king—all delicious foods, no austerity—and he enjoyed the food. The king offered him new clothes, worthy of an emperor, and he loved those clothes. And the king thought, "Now, how to get rid of this fellow?" Just in seven days he was tired, thinking, "This is a complete charlatan, he has cheated me."

On the seventh day he said to this strange fellow, "I want to ask a question."

And the stranger said, "I know your question. You wanted to ask it seven days before, but just out of courtesy, manners, you kept it repressed—I was watching. But I will not answer you here. You can ask the question, and then we will go for a long morning ride on the horses, and I will choose the right place to answer it."

The king said, "Okay. My question is, now what is the difference between me and you? You are living like an emperor, but you used to be a saint. Now you are no longer a saint."

The man said, "Get the horses ready!" They went out, and the king many times reminded him, "How far are we going? You can answer."

Finally they reached the river that was the boundary line of his empire. The king said, "Now we have come to my boundary. The other side is somebody else's kingdom. This is a good place to answer."

He said, "Yes, I am going. You can take both the horses, or if you like, you can come with me."

The king said, "Where are you going?"

He said, "My treasure is with me. Wherever I go, my treasure will be with me. Are you coming with me or not?"

The king said, "How can I come with you? My kingdom, my palace, my whole life's work is behind me."

The stranger laughed and he said, "Now, do you see the difference? I can stand naked under a tree, or I can live in a palace like an emperor because my treasure is within me. Whether the tree is there or the palace is there makes no difference. So you can go back; I am going into the other kingdom. Now your kingdom is not worth remaining in."

The king felt repentance. He touched the feet of the stranger and said, "Forgive me. I was thinking wrong thoughts about you. You are really a great saint. Just don't go and leave me like this; otherwise this wound will hurt me my whole life."

The stranger said, "There is no difficulty for me; I can come back with you. But I want you to be alert. The moment we reach the palace, the question will again arise in your mind. So it is better—let me go.

"I can give you some time to think. I can come back. To me it makes no difference. But to you it is better that I should leave the kingdom; it is better. In this way at least you will think of me as a saint. Back in the palace you will again start doubting: 'This is a con man.' But if you insist, I am ready. I can leave again after seven days when the question becomes too heavy on you."

"SELF-APPOINTED" BHAGWAN

The critics who have been writing against me have always made it a point that I am a "self-appointed" *bhagwan*. And I have always wondered, do they know of anybody—Rama, Krishna, Buddha, Mohammed—who was appointed by somebody else? If Rama is appointed by somebody else as *bhagwan,* then certainly the appointing authority is higher—and if you can be appointed, you can be disappointed too!

This is absolutely stupid. Basically, they have not understood the idea: *bhagwan* is a state of experience—nothing to do with an appointment, an election, a title, or a degree. It is the experience of *bhagwatta,* of godliness, that the whole existence is full of godliness, that there is nothing other than godliness.

There is no God, but in every flower and in every tree, in every stone, there is something that can only be called godliness. But you can see it only when you have seen it within yourself; otherwise you don't know the language.

I AM VERY STRANGE IN A WAY BECAUSE YOU CANNOT CATEGORIZE me. There are three categories—theist, atheist, agnostic. There is no fourth category—and I belong to the fourth, the unnamed category. I have looked, searched. I have not found God, true, but I have found something far more significant: godliness.

I am not an atheist, I am not a theist, I am not an agnostic. My position is absolutely clear.

So if there is no God, why was I called by my people *bhagwan*?

This question is a little complex. You will have to go into the linguistics of the word *bhagwan*. It is a very strange word. In Hindu scriptures, *bhagwan* is almost synonymous with God. I say almost, because in English there is only one word, *God*. In Sanskrit, in Hinduism, there are three words: *bhagwan* is one, *iswar* is the second, *paramatma* is the third. Hindus use these three words for three different reasons.

Paramatma means "the supreme soul"; *param* means "the supreme," *atma* means "the soul"; *paramatma* means "the supreme soul." So those who really understand use the word *paramatma* for God.

The second word is *iswar*. It is a beautiful word. *Iswar* means "the richest"; literally one who has everything, who is everything. It's certainly true. The moment you experience godliness, you have everything, everything that is of worth. You may not have anything at all, that doesn't matter, but you have everything that is of any significance to life.

And the third is *bhagwan*. *Bhagwan* is very difficult to understand or to be explained in any other language. In Hindu scriptures . . . remember that, because *bhagwan* is used by two kinds of people in India: Hindus, one; Jainas and Buddhists, two. Jainas and Buddhists don't believe in a God, still they use the word *bhagwan*. For Buddha, Buddhists use *bhagwan*—Bhagwan Gautam Buddha. And Jainas also don't believe in a God, but for Mahavira they use Bhagwan Vardhman Mahavira. So their meaning is totally different.

Hindus are very down to earth. You will be surprised, even shocked, but the original root in Hinduism of *bhagwan* is *bhag*—*bhag* means "vagina." You could not have imagined! And *bhagwan* means "one who used the vagina of the universe to create"—the creator. Hindus worship the female vagina and the male phallic symbol, *shivalinga*. If you have seen a *shivalinga,* the marble emerging is just a symbol of the male sexual organ, and it is standing in the vagina. Underneath it, if you have looked, there is a marble vagina, out of which it is emerging. Hindus have worshiped it symbolically, and it seems meaningful in their reference, that any creation is bound to be the meeting of the male and the female, yin and yang. So for the "creator" they use the word *bhagwan*. But the origin of the word is very strange.

Buddhists and Jainas don't believe in God, don't believe that anybody created the world, but they also use the word *bhagwan*. They have a different origination for their word. In the Jaina and Buddhist reference, *bhag* means "fortune," and *bhagwan* means "the fortunate one, the blessed one;" one who has attained to his destiny, who has matured.

So when I started talking thirty-four years ago, people started using it . . . because in India, if you respect a man you don't use his name; that is thought to be disrespectful. So when I started speaking and when people started feeling something for me, on their own they began to call me "acharya." *Acharya* means "the master"—but not just the master, it is something more. Actually it means the person who says only that which he lives, one whose actions and thoughts are absolutely in harmony. So for almost twenty years people called me "acharya." This was before I started initiating people.

For years people had been telling me that they would like to be initiated into sannyas by me, and I said to them, "Wait. Let the moment come when I feel it is right." The day came. I was holding a meditation camp deep in the Himalayas, in Kulu-Manali—it is one of the most beautiful places in the world. It is called the Valley of the Gods, it is so beautiful, so otherworldly. Once you enter Kulu-Manali you start feeling you are entering into another world. On the last day of the camp it came to me, "Now the moment has come." And I declared, "Whosoever wants to be initiated, I am ready." Twenty-one persons immediately stood up. They entered into sannyas. Now for them it became a question what to call me. Everybody else used to call me acharya; now it was not enough for them. For them I had become far more important, far more significant, far more intimate. They had come very close to my being, and they decided that they would call me *bhagwan*.

They asked me. I said, "That's perfectly good, because that's a very meaningful word for me: the blessed one."

It does not mean God to me, it does not mean the creator, it simply means the blessed one—one who is at home, has arrived; one who has found, one who has encountered himself. Then there is nothing else but blessings, and blessings go on raining over him. Day in, day out, the blessing goes on showering. So remember, *bhagwan* has nothing to do with God. It has certainly something to do with godliness, because that is what arriving is: coming home. That is what makes you the blessed one.

BHAGWAN IS A NONCOMPARATIVE TERM. YOU CANNOT BE GODLIER than God; godder than God you cannot be. It is a noncomparative term. And it does not show any achievement; it simply shows your nature. Not that one has to become God; one is God, one has simply to recognize it.

1965

1975

1985

If you really want to know who I am, you have to be as absolutely empty as I am. Then two mirrors will be facing each other, and only emptiness will be mirrored. Infinite emptiness will be mirrored: two mirrors facing each other. But if you have some idea, then you will see your own idea in me.

1951, All-India debating championship portrait

In college I used to wear a long robe, with a wrap-around lungi as it is used in India, and with no buttons on the robe so the chest is open. The principal told me, "Coming to the college without buttons is not according to the etiquette." I said, "Then change the etiquette, because my chest needs fresh air. And I decide according to my needs, not according to anybody's idea of etiquette."

1955

Many people have asked me why I kept silent about the fact that I became enlightened in 1953. For almost twenty years I never said anything about it to anybody, unless somebody suspected it himself, unless somebody said to me on his own, "We feel that something has happened to you." In those years not more than ten people asked me, and even then I avoided them as much as I could unless I felt that their desire was genuine. I told them only when they had promised to keep it a secret.

Greece, 1986

Kulu Manali, 1985

Rajneeshpuram, 1983

꙰

My mother came to me; she was a little worried. She said, "It is beautiful to see you dancing, but now you have started dancing with girls!" She was concerned that if people in India see this, in the pictures, on the video, they will be very much shocked. I said, "So far, so good."

But I am free—more free than Gautam Buddha, more free than Mahavira. Gautam Buddha did not have the guts to dance with a girl.

Rajneeshpuram, 1985

☙

I am a terrific driver. And I don't believe in any
rules—I may drive right, I may drive left, I may drive
in the middle—so my poor people had to create a
road just for me so I could drive anywhere,
any way, at any speed.

Rajneeshpuram, 1983

I want the world to know that we have ninety-three
Rolls Royces because that is the only way to make
any bridge. And then I can talk about truth and
enlightenment, too, on the side.
Without Rolls Royces there is no
communication at all.
I know my business perfectly well.

Posing with a motorbike in Greece, 1986

On the plane to America, 1981

Millions of people miss meditation because meditation has taken on a wrong connotation. It looks very serious, looks gloomy, has something of the church in it, looks as if it is only for people who are dead, or almost dead. A really meditative person is playful: Life is fun for him, life is a play. He enjoys it tremendously. He is not serious.
He is relaxed.

Soon after arrival at the Big Muddy Ranch, Oregon, 1981

Festival visitors line up at the "shoe check" before entering the meditation hall at Rajneeshpuram, 1982

Inside the meditation hall at festival time, 1983

Osho in a sequined celebration robe, 1984

In America they were worried we were going to take over Oregon, Wasco County. I am not interested in taking small things—if I was interested in taking over I would have taken over the whole world! I am not interested in taking over.

But political idiots are a very special kind of idiots.

❧

I can't speak without my hands.
If you tie my hands I cannot
speak a single word, because it is
not only that a part of me is
speaking, it is my whole being
that is involved in it. My eyes,
my hands, my whole body is
involved. My whole body is saying something, is supporting what
I am saying in words.

Press interview, Rajneeshpuram, 1984

With his hands and feet in chains, Charlotte, North Carolina, 1985

Greece, 1986

After enlightenment, nothing happens. All happening stops, disappears. One simply is. Not that the sun does not rise, not that the night is not full of stars, not that the flowers don't bloom anymore—all this goes on. But nothing happens in you. All remains calm and quiet. After enlightenment there is no biography.

Kulu Manali, 1985

Osho checks out his new "bedroom," designed as the place
where his ashes will be kept after his death.

Only that which cannot be taken away by death is real.
Everything else is unreal; it is made of the same stuff
dreams are made of.

*January 19, 1990. Osho's body is brought into the meditation hall,
and then carried to the ghats for burning.*

It does not show any talent. There is somebody who is a great poet, somebody who is a great seer, a great visionary—somebody a great painter, somebody a great musician, somebody a great dancer—these are all talents. All cannot be great dancers; you cannot all be Nijinskys. And all cannot be great painters; you cannot all be van Goghs. And you all cannot be great poets; you cannot all be Tagores and Pablo Nerudas.

But *bhagwan* you all are. It does not show an achievement; it simply shows your universality, your very nature. Already you are God.

When people suggested to call me *bhagwan,* I loved the term. I said, "That will do. At least for a few years it will do; then we can drop it."

I chose it for a specific purpose and it has been serving well, because people who used to come to me to gather knowledge, stopped coming. The day I called myself *bhagwan,* they stopped. It was too much for them, it was too much for their egos. Somebody calling himself *bhagwan*? It hurts the ego. They stopped. They were coming to me to gather knowledge. Now I've changed my function absolutely. I started working on a different level, in a different dimension. Now I give you being, not knowledge. I was an acharya and they were students; they were learning. Now I am no longer a teacher and you are not here as students.

If you are here as students, sooner or later you will have to leave, because you will find yourself in a wrong place; you will not fit here. Only if you are a disciple, then you can fit with me. Because now I am giving something more. If you are here for knowledge, then sooner or later you will see—you have to go somewhere else.

I am here to impart being. I am here to make you awake. I am not going to give you knowledge, I am going to give you knowing—and that is a totally different dimension. Calling myself *bhagwan* was simply symbolic—that now my work had entered a different dimension. And it has been tremendously useful. All wrong people automatically disappeared, and a totally different quality of people started arriving.

It worked well, it sorted out well. Only those who were ready to put aside their knowledge remained, all others escaped. They created space around me. Otherwise they were crowding too much, and it was very difficult for the real seekers to come closer to me. The crowds disappeared. The word *bhagwan* functioned like an atomic explosion. I am happy that I chose it.

Now people who come to me are no longer argumentative. Now people who come to me are great adventurers of the soul, and they are ready to risk—to risk any and everything.

Calling myself *bhagwan* is a device. Sooner or later, when you have grown up and you have understood the point, and when your presence here has created a different quality of vibrations, I will stop calling myself *bhagwan*. Then there will be no need. Then the whole atmosphere will be throbbing with godliness. Then people who will come, it will shower on them. It will penetrate into their hearts. There will be no need to call me anything—you will know. But in the beginning it was needed, and it has been of tremendous help.

The last thing about it:

I am not a philosopher. Always remember me as a poet. My approach toward life is that of poetry, is that of romance. It is romantic, it is imaginative. I would like you all to be gods and goddesses. I would like you to reveal your true being. Calling myself God is a challenge. It is a subtle challenge. There are only two ways to settle with it. One is, you say, "This man is not God, so go away—what are you doing here? If this man is not God, then why waste your time?" You go away. Or you accept that this man is God, and then you start being with me and your own godliness starts flowering.

One day you will also be a god, a goddess. Accepting me as God is in fact deep down accepting the possibility that you can also be a god, that's all. The very acceptance that this man can be a god stirs something that has been fast asleep within you. Then you cannot remain as you are; something has to be done. Something has to be transformed, something has to be known . . .

If you decide to go with me, you will become more and more watchful. And the more watchful you will become, the more you will be able to understand me, the more you will be able to understand what has happened, what has transpired within my soul. You will become more and more a participant in this happening, in this dance, in this singing.

And by and by you will see—the master is coming. And it is not coming from the outside, it is coming from your innermost core, it is arising from your depths. I looked in, and I found him there. My message is simple—that I have found the god within me. My whole effort is to persuade you to look within. The only question is of becoming a watcher on the hills. Become a witness—alert, observing—and you will be fulfilled.

BY THE WAY, I HAVE BEEN CALLING MYSELF BHAGWAN JUST AS A challenge—to the Christians, to the Mohammedans, to the Hindus. They have condemned me, but none has been courageous enough to explain the condemnation. From faraway sources there have been articles and letters sent to me saying, "Why do you call yourself *bhagwan*?" And I have laughed, because why does Ram call himself *bhagwan*? Is he appointed by a committee? And a *bhagwan* appointed by a committee will not be much of a *bhagwan,* because the committee does not consist of *bhagwans*. What right have they?

Is Krishna elected by the people as *bhagwan*? Is it an election matter? Who has appointed these people? No Hindu has the answer. And a man like Krishna has stolen sixteen thousand women from different people—they were mothers, they were married, unmarried, with no discrimination—and yet no Hindu has the courage to object that a man with such a character has no right to be called *bhagwan*. They can even call their god Kalki, a horse, *bhagwan*. Strange people! And they ask me why I call myself *bhagwan*. I don't have any respect for the word. In fact I have every condemnation of it. It is not a beautiful word— although I have tried in my own way to transform the word, but the stupid Hindus won't allow it. I have tried to give it a new name, a new meaning, a new significance. I have said that it means the blessed one, a man with a blessed being, although it was my invention.

The word *bhagwan* is a very ugly word. But the Hindus are not even aware of it. They think that it is something very special. Its root meaning—*bhag* means a woman's genital organs. And *wan* means a man's genital organs. The meaning of the word *bhagwan* is symbolically that he brings about, in the feminine energy of existence, through his male chauvinistic energy, the creation.

I hate the word! I have been waiting for some Hindu idiot to come forward, but they think that it is something very dignified and I have no right to call myself *bhagwan*. Today I say absolutely, "Yes, but I have every right to denounce the word." Nobody can prevent me. I don't want to be called *bhagwan* again. Enough is enough! The joke is over!

THE RICH MAN'S GURU

I always spend before I get. Just the idea that some money is coming, and I tell my people: Spend! Because who knows about tomorrow? Spend today. We don't have any money, but we are perfectly sufficient. Nothing is missing, everything is perfectly okay. And money goes on coming. I have lived thirty-five years without any money. It has always been coming. Somebody somewhere feels to send, and it comes. And now I have started believing that existence takes care, even of an expensive man like me.

YOU ASK, "ARE YOU NOT A RICH MAN'S GURU?" I AM—BECAUSE ONLY a rich man can come to me. But when I say a rich man I mean one who is very poor inside. When I say a rich man I mean one who is rich in intelligence, I mean one who has everything that the world can give to him and has found that it is futile.

Yes, only a rich person can become religious. I am not saying that a poor person cannot become religious, but it is very rare, exceptional. A poor person goes on hoping. A poor person has not known what riches are, he is not yet frustrated. How can he go beyond riches if he is not frustrated with them? A poor man also sometimes comes to me, but then he comes for something that I cannot supply. He asks for success. His son is not getting employed; he asks, "Bless him, Osho." His wife is ill, or he is losing money in his business. These are symptoms of a poor man, one who is asking about things of this world.

When a rich person comes to me, he has money, he has employment, he has a house, he has health—he has everything that one can have. And suddenly he has come to a realization that nothing is fulfilling. Then the search for God starts.

Yes, sometimes a poor man can also be religious, but for that very great intelligence is needed. A rich man, if he is not religious, is stupid. A poor man, if he is religious, is tremendously intelligent. If a poor man is not religious, he has to be forgiven. If a rich man is not religious, his sin is unpardonable.

I am a rich man's guru. Absolutely it is so.

If it were not for your money, you would not have been here. You are here because you are frustrated with your money. You are here because you are frustrated with your success. You are here because you are frustrated with your life. A beggar cannot come because he is not yet frustrated.

Religion is a luxury—the ultimate luxury I call it, because it is the highest value. When a man is hungry, he does not bother about music—he cannot. And if you start playing the sitar before him, he will kill you! He will say, "You are insulting me! I am hungry and you are playing a sitar—is this the time to play the sitar? Feed me first! And I am so hungry I cannot understand music. I am dying!" When a man is dying of hunger, what use is a van Gogh painting or a Buddha sermon or beautiful Upanishads or music? Meaningless. He needs bread.

When a man is happy with his body, has enough to eat, has a good house to live in, he starts becoming interested in music, poetry, literature, painting, art. Now a new hunger arises. The bodily needs are fulfilled, now psychological needs arise. There is a hierarchy in needs: the first is the body; it is the base, it is the ground floor of your being. Without the ground floor, the first story cannot exist.

When your bodily needs are fulfilled, psychological needs arise. When your psychological needs are also fulfilled, then your spiritual needs arise. When a person has listened to all the music that is available in the world, and has seen all the beauty, and has found that it is all dream—has listened to all the great poets and has found that poetry is just a way to forget yourself, to intoxicate yourself, but it does not lead you anywhere—has seen all the paintings and the great art, amusing, entertaining . . . then what? The hands remain empty, more empty than they ever were before. Then music and poetry are not enough. Then the desire to meditate, the desire to pray, a hunger for God, a hunger for truth arises. A great passion takes possession of you, and you are in search of truth because you now know: Unless you know what the secretmost truth of this existence is, nothing can satisfy. All else you have tried and it has failed.

Religion is the ultimate luxury. Either you have to be very rich to come to this luxury, or you have to be tremendously intelligent. But in both the cases you are rich—rich with money or rich with intelligence. I have never seen a person who is really poor—poor in intelligence, poor in riches—ever become religious.

A Kabir becomes religious. He was not a millionaire, but he was tremendously intelligent. Buddha became religious because he was tremendously rich. Krishna and Ram and Mahavir became religious because they were tremendously rich. Dadu, Raidas, Farid—they became religious because they were tremendously intelligent. But a certain sort of richness is needed.

Yes, you are right: I am the rich man's guru.

THE JOKER

Q: *Who is the better showman—in metaphysical terms, if you like—you or President Ronald Reagan?*

A: Nobody can beat me! I am the best showman in the whole history of man.

Q: *If that is true, what kind of show do you enjoy? Is this theater, or circus?*

A: This is my circus, my carnival. And I enjoy it immensely!

•from an interview with Jeff McMullen,
60 Minutes, Australia

Q: *IN ONE PRESS CONFERENCE, YOU DESCRIBED YOUR COMMUNE AS A CIRCUS and yourself as a great showman, the greatest in the world. Were you mocking yourself and your commune? Why did you say it?*

A: You are bringing the past here. Forget all about that nonsense. I am a showman? And my people a circus? I contradict it completely.

Q: *How would you describe it now?*

A: There is no circus here. This is the only place where a circus is not happening.

Q: *And you are a serious teacher?*

A: I am a very nonserious teacher! And I have already forgotten what news conference you are talking about! I just respond to you. Why drag the dead unnecessarily out of their graves? Let them sleep silently. You are alive, I am alive, we can have an existential encounter.

And I see the potentiality in you, that's why I am saying that. I would not have said it to another person. I have been interviewed every evening for weeks, but I would not have said that to another journalist. I don't see you just as a journalist, I see you more as a seeker. I see you more as a human being. And I see your heart throbbing with me, in tune with me, that's why I am saying it. Otherwise, I can go on answering about the past, anything that comes to my mind, there is no problem about it.

I love jokes. And to joke on other people's account is not very good, not nice. So, once in a while, I joke upon myself, upon my people. It was simply a joke, and those idiotic newspaper journalists thought it is something serious. Do you think a showman will sit here in the desert? Is this the place for a showman? Then I would have chosen Hollywood! But on the contrary, I have pulled all my Hollywood people here.

In this desert, one hundred and twenty-six square miles, I am sitting the whole day in my room. I come out only twice: in the morning to talk with the sannyasins, in the evening to talk with an interviewer. What kind of a showman do you think I am? This is not the way of being a showman.

And I don't have any time for showmanship. I will tell you my routine and you will see: Where would I get the time? Six o'clock in the morning, I wake up. Furthermore, my caretaker, Vivek, has to wake me up; otherwise I will not wake up. Who cares to wake up again? I have been waking for half a century again and again, it is enough!

But she wakes me up, gives me a cup of tea. Just to be respectful to her, I drink the tea. My tea is not much, it is just water and tea leaves. No sugar, no milk—if that kind of tea is served in heaven, all the saints will start moving toward hell. Then—I have always loved water, from my very childhood—for one and a half hours in the morning I am in my bathroom enjoying the bathtub, the shower; and the same in the evening, one and a half hours again.

After my bath, immediately I have to get into the car and move to the auditorium where my people are waiting. Back to my place, it is lunchtime. I take my lunch at eleven and go to sleep again, which I have done most of my life. I had to miss my classes when I was a student—and my teachers allowed it because if they did not allow, then I used to sleep in the class. I said, "There is no way . . . I have to sleep these two hours."

At two o'clock I wake up, and for one hour I go for a ride. I love driving, and I have certainly one of the most beautiful roads because it is made by my sannyasins only for me. There is no traffic, so I need not bother whether I am driving on the right or on the left. The whole road belongs to me. One hour there and back home.

One and a half hours I simply sit silently in my chair doing nothing and let the grass grow by itself. Then my bath.

After the bath I take my supper, and after the supper I am here for the press interview. I will be back in my room near about nine, nine-thirty. Then comes my personal secretary with letters from all over the world; news cuttings about me from all over the world, anything that the personal secretary feels I need to know—because I don't read. I have stopped reading anything, books, newspapers, magazines, anything. The clippings that my personal secretary brings, *she* has to read; I simply listen. Near about eleven, I go to bed again. Now, where will I find the time to be a showman? Yes, you can look at my dress and think it looks like the dress of a showman. It is not, it is the love of my people. I am dressing for them. They make beautiful dresses, they enjoy making them for me; I cannot refuse them. And to whom am I going to show? I never go out of this place.

You see my watch? I have hundreds. My people are really intelligent people—no master in the whole of history can claim such an intelligent group. Now, this watch is made by my sannyasins. It has already defeated Piaget—and it is made of real stones, not diamonds.

Q: *Real stones?*

A: Real stones, not diamonds. So don't carry the idea that it is a fake watch. Real stones are as real as real diamonds, there is no question of its being fake. I just heard on television one stupid journalist saying that I have been using fake watches. I cannot understand: such authentic stones, and you call it a fake watch? Its time is absolutely perfect; in a year it will lose only one second, and that is the best any watch can do. It is as beautiful as any diamond. The same watch from Piaget is a half million dollars, just because of an idiotic idea that diamonds have some value. This watch costs nothing, but I would not sell it even for ten million dollars because it is invaluable. It is made with such great love that it is not a salable thing. Love cannot be sold.

But to whom am I going to show the watch? My people know my

dresses, my people know my watches, my people know me. I don't mix with anybody else, I don't go anywhere else. As far as I am concerned, the third world war has happened and only this place is saved. There is nowhere else to go.

I was simply joking. And my people are working hard, twelve hours, fourteen hours a day, transforming a desert into an oasis—do you think these people constitute a circus? You will not find anywhere in the world such hardworking people—and they are not being paid, because we don't believe money should be used inside the commune in any way. There is no need. We fulfill our needs, our food, our clothes, everything, so nobody needs any money. Whatsoever he needs, he can get. These people are working so hard, and for what? To entertain somebody? These people are creative people. They love me and now they want to materialize my vision into reality.

•from an interview with Willem Sheer,
Pers Unie, The Hague, Netherlands

I HAVE TO TELL JOKES BECAUSE, I AM AFRAID, YOU ARE ALL RELIGIOUS people. You tend to be serious. I have to tickle you so that sometimes you forget your religiousness, you forget all your philosophies, theories, systems, and you fall down to earth. I have to bring you back to the earth again and again; otherwise you will tend to become more and more serious. And seriousness is a cancerous growth.

Now, even medical science says that laughter is one of the most deep-going medicines nature has provided for man. If you can laugh when you are ill, you will get your health back sooner. If you cannot laugh, even if you are healthy, sooner or later you will lose your health and you will become ill.

Laughter brings some energy from your inner source to your surface. Energy starts flowing, it follows laughter like a shadow. Have you watched it? When you really laugh, for those few moments you are in a deep meditative state. Thinking stops. It is impossible to laugh and think together. They are diametrically opposite: either you can laugh or you can think. If you really laugh, thinking stops. If you are still thinking, laughter will be just so-so, lagging behind. It will be a crippled laughter.

When you really laugh, suddenly mind disappears. The whole Zen methodology is how to get into no-mind—laughter is one of the beautiful doors to get to it.

As far as I know, dancing and laughter are the best, most natural, easily approachable doors. If you really dance, thinking stops. You go on and on, you whirl and whirl, and you become a whirlpool—all boundaries, all divisions are lost. You don't even know where your body ends and where the existence begins. You melt into existence and the existence melts into you; there is an overlapping of boundaries. And if you are really dancing—not managing it but allowing it to manage you, allowing it to possess you—if you are possessed by dance, thinking stops.

The same happens with laughter. If you are possessed by laughter, thinking stops. And if you know a few moments of no-mind, those glimpses will promise you many more rewards that are going to come. You just have to become more and more of the quality of no-mind. More and more, thinking has to be dropped.

Laughter can be a beautiful introduction to a nonthinking state.

AND I HAVE TO TELL JOKES, BECAUSE THE THINGS THAT I AM SAYING are so subtle, so deep and profound, that if I simply go on telling you those things you will fall asleep and you will not be able to listen or to understand. You will remain almost deaf.

The more profound the truth I have to tell you, the worse joke I choose for it. The highest truth I am trying to relate, then the lowest I have to go in search of a joke. That's why even dirty jokes . . . I don't bother. Even a dirty joke can be helpful—more so because it can shock you to the very roots, to the very guts. And that's the whole point! It helps you to come again and again to your alertness. When I see you are alert, I again go relating that which I would like to relate to you. When I see again that you are slipping into your sleep, I have to bring in a joke again.

If you really listen with alertness, there will be no need—I can say the truth directly. But it is difficult. You start yawning . . . and it is better to laugh than to yawn.

THE ROLLS-ROYCE GURU

A: I would like the whole world to live so luxuriously that people start becoming bored with luxury. You should ask me how I am bored with Rolls-Royces.

Q: *How are you bored with Rolls-Royces?*

A: Ninety Rolls-Royces, anybody will be bored! And my people are going to try to have three hundred sixty-five. They are bent upon boring me. What can you do? And the whole earth is capable for the first time to be so luxurious that you don't feel any material need. When all material needs are fulfilled, then what are you going to do? There is nothing else than meditation. That is the only door that is left still open. All other doors you have knocked upon, and seen there is nothing. Only one door is still open, inviting.

And whoever has entered that door has never come back frustrated, disappointed—not a single case in the whole history of humanity that anybody who has reached the center of his being was disappointed, felt meaningless, was miserable, committed suicide. Not a single exception! That's why I say meditation is a scientific thing. That's how science works: If you can find something without any exception, then it becomes a rule. Meditation is a scientific method because in the whole of history nobody has said that it does not lead you to the ultimate blissfulness.

•from an interview with Ted Viramonte,
Madras Pioneer, Madras, Oregon

1978: PUNE, INDIA

Just a few days ago I told my secretary Laxmi to purchase the most costly car possible in the country. One thing good about Laxmi, she never asks why. She purchased it. It worked—it was a device. Laxmi was knocking on the doors of the banks to get money for the new commune. We need much money; near-about a million dollars will be needed. Who is going to lend that much money to me? The day she purchased the car, seeing that we have the money, banks started coming to her office, offering, "Take as much money as you want." Now she is puzzled: from whom to take? Everybody wants to give on better terms, and they are after her.

I have been working in India for twenty years continuously. Thousands of people have been transformed, millions have listened to me and many more have been reading what I am saying, but the *Times of India*—the most conventional newspaper of India, still the most British—has not published a single article about me or my work. But the day Laxmi purchased the car there was a big article—on the car, not on me!

Now they are all interested. The news of the car has been published all over the country, in all the newspapers, in all the languages. Now what kind of people are these? Their interest is not in me, not in meditation, not in the thousands of people who are meditating here. They are completely unaware of what is happening here, but they became interested in the car.

They come here. Many people come to the office, not to see me or to see the commune—they inquire, "Can we see the car?" Laxmi says to them, "You can come to the morning discourse, and you can see the car too." And poor fellows—they have to come and listen for ninety minutes just to see the car. What a torture! And these are rich people, educated people. Can you think of a more materialistic country?

And they are very worried, and editorials have been written on the car. They ask, "Why? Why can't you live a simple life?" My life is absolutely simple—so simple, really, that I am always satisfied with the best kinds of things. It is absolutely simple, what more simplicity is possible? In a single sentence it can be said: the best kinds of things. There is no complexity about it. I like quality. I'm not interested in how much it costs but in the quality. I like quality in people, not quantity. I like quality in everything, not quantity. We could have purchased thirty Indian cars instead of this one, but that would have been quantity—and even thirty wouldn't have been of any use.

But their puzzle, why they can't understand it, is that they pretend to be religious but deep down their whole obsession is materialistic. They carry a hypocrisy, and to fulfill their hypocrisy the whole Indian religious world has to compromise. If somebody wants to become a saint he has to live in utter poverty. It is almost a kind of masochism; he has to torture himself. The more he tortures himself, the more people think he is religious: "See how religiously he is living!"

To live religiously means to live joyously, to live religiously means to live meditatively. To live religiously means to live this world as a gift of God! But their minds are obsessed and they can't understand. Once the purpose of the car is served, it will be gone.

I can even come in a bullock cart. It would be even more colorful, and I would enjoy the ride more.

They come here and they look, and their whole concern is, "Why such a beautiful ashram?" They want something dirty, shabby—a sloppy place, and then it is an ashram. They cannot believe that the ashram can be clean, beautiful, with trees and flowers, and comfortable. They cannot believe it. And not that they don't want comfort for themselves; they are hankering for it. They are, in fact, jealous. The Indian mind has become materialistic, grossly materialistic.

A spiritual mind makes no distinctions between matter and spirit; it is undivided. The whole existence is one—that is the spiritual mind. The materialist, even if he loves a woman, reduces her to a thing. Then who is a spiritualist? A spiritualist is a person who, even if he touches a thing, transforms it into a person.

You will be surprised by my definition. A spiritual person is one who, even if he drives a car, the car becomes a person. He feels for the car, he listens for its humming sound. He has all affection and care for it. Even a thing starts becoming a person, alive; he has communion with the thing too. And a materialistic person is one who, even if he loves a man or a woman, a person, immediately reduces him or her into a thing. The woman becomes a wife—the wife is a thing. The man becomes a husband—the husband is a thing, an institution. And all institutions are ugly, dead.

1981–1985: OREGON

The Americans think they are the richest people in the world. But I created a simple joke with ninety-three Rolls-Royces, and all their pride was gone. Even the president became jealous, the governors became jealous, the clergymen became jealous. One clergyman in Wasco County, every Sunday may have forgotten Jesus Christ completely but he could not forget ninety-three Rolls-Royces. He would bring up some way to condemn them. And you will be surprised that when I was bailed out of jail, he wrote a letter to me. He asked, "Now you will be going back to your own land—what about donating at least one Rolls-Royce to my church? It will be a great act of charity." Now you can see the mind . . . I was teaching meditation to thousands of people; America was not interested in it. Thousands of people were coming to the commune; America was not interested in it. Each festival, there were twenty thousand people coming from all over the world; America was not interested in it. The whole of the news media was continuously talking about ninety-three Rolls-Royces.

I used to think, perhaps in a poor country this could be expected . . . but I destroyed the pride of America! I don't need ninety-three Rolls-Royces. It was a practical joke.

PEOPLE ARE SAD, JEALOUS, AND THINKING THAT ROLLS-ROYCES DON'T fit with spirituality. I don't see that there is any contradiction. Sitting in a Rolls-Royce I have been as meditative . . . In fact, sitting in a bullock cart it is very difficult to be meditative; a Rolls-Royce is the best for spiritual growth.

THE MASTER

One beautiful morning, Gautam Buddha had gone for a walk with his caretaker, his disciple Ananda. It was in the fall; the trees were getting almost naked and all the leaves were on the path. The wind was fluttering the trees, and the leaves were making beautiful sounds. Walking on those leaves, Buddha was immensely happy . . . the music of the dry leaves.

He took a few leaves in his hand. Ananda asked him, "Bhagwan, I have always been thinking to ask one thing, but privacy is so difficult. You are always surrounded by people. Today you are alone in this forest, and I cannot resist the temptation. I want to ask you: Have you said everything to us, or have you kept some secrets?"

Buddha said, "Do you see the leaves in my hand? And do you see the leaves all over the forest?"

Ananda said, "Yes, I do see, but I don't understand . . ."

Buddha said, "You will understand. I have said only this much, and I have kept secret all these leaves that are in the whole forest."

My situation is different. I have said the whole forest; only one thing I have kept secret, just one leaf.

Buddha declared before his death that he would be coming again after twenty-five centuries, and that his name would be Maitreya. *Maitreya* means "the friend." Buddhas don't come back; no enlightened person ever comes back, so it is just a way of saying . . .

What he was saying is of tremendous importance. It has nothing to do with his coming back; he cannot come back. What he meant was that the ancient relationship between the master and the disciple would become irrelevant in twenty-five centuries. It was his clarity of perception—he was not predicting anything—just his clarity to see that as things are changing, as they have changed in the past and as they go on changing, it would take at least twenty-five centuries for the master and disciple relationship to become out of date. Then the enlightened master will be only the friend.

I had always wanted not to be a master to anybody. But people want a master, they want to be disciples; hence, I played the role.

MASTERS DO NOT TELL THE TRUTH. EVEN IF THEY WANT TO THEY cannot; it is impossible. Then what is their function? What do they go on doing? They cannot tell the truth, but they can call forth the truth that is fast asleep in you. They can provoke it, they can challenge it. They can shake you up, they can wake you up. They cannot give you God, truth, nirvana, because in the first place you already have it all with you. You are born with it. It is innate, it is intrinsic. It is your very nature. So anybody who pretends to give you the truth is simply exploiting your stupidity, your gullibility. He is cunning—cunning and utterly ignorant too. He knows nothing; not even a glimpse of truth has happened to him. He is a pseudo master.

Truth cannot be given; it is already in you. It can be called forth, it can be provoked. A context can be created, a certain space can be created in which it arises in you and is no longer asleep, becomes awakened.

The function of the master is far more complex than you think. It would have been far easier, simpler, if truth could be conveyed. It cannot be conveyed; hence indirect ways and means have to be devised.

The New Testament has the beautiful story of Lazarus. Christians have missed the whole point of it. Christ is so unfortunate—he has fallen into the wrong company. Not even a single Christian theologian has been able to discover the meaning of the story of Lazarus, his death and resurrection.

Lazarus dies. He is the brother of Mary Magdalene and Martha, and a great devotee of Jesus. Jesus is far away; by the time he gets the information and the invitation—"Come immediately"—two days have already passed. And by the time he reaches Lazarus's place, four days have passed. But Mary and Martha are waiting for him—their trust is such. The whole village is laughing at them. They are being stupid in others' eyes because they are keeping the corpse in a cave; they are watching day in, day out, guarding the corpse. The corpse has already started stinking; it is deteriorating.

The village people are saying, "You are fools! Jesus cannot do anything. When somebody is dead, somebody is dead!"

Jesus comes. He goes to the cave—he does not enter into the cave—he stands outside and calls Lazarus forth. The people have gathered. They must be laughing: "This man seems to be crazy!"

Somebody says to him, "What are you doing? He is dead! He has been dead for four days. In fact, to enter into the cave is difficult—his body is stinking. It is impossible! Whom are you calling?"

But, unperturbed, Jesus shouts again and again, "Lazarus, come out!"

And the crowd is in for a great surprise: Lazarus walks out of the cave—shaken, shocked, as if out of a great slumber, as if he had fallen into a coma. He himself cannot believe what has happened, why he was in the cave.

This, in fact, is just a way of saying what the function of a master is. Whether Lazarus was really dead or not is not the point. Whether Jesus was capable of raising the dead or not is not the point. To get involved in those stupid questions is absurd. Only scholars can be so foolish. No man of understanding will think that this is something historical. It is far more! It is not a fact, it is a truth. It is not something that happens in time, it is something more—something that happens in eternity.

You are all dead. You are all in the same situation as Lazarus. You are all living in your dark caves. You are all stinking and deteriorating . . . because death is not something that comes one day suddenly. You are dying every day; since the day of your birth you have been dying. It is a long process; it takes seventy, eighty, ninety years to complete it. *Each moment* something of you dies, but you are absolutely unaware of the whole situation. You go on as if you are alive; you go on living as if you know what life is.

The function of the master is to call you forth: "Lazarus, come out of the cave! Come out of your grave! Come out of your death!"

The master cannot give you the truth but he can call forth the truth. He can stir something in you. He can trigger a process in you that will ignite a fire, a flame. Truth you are—just so much dust has gathered around you. The function of the master is negative: he has to give you a bath, a shower, so the dust disappears.

That's exactly the meaning of Christian baptism. That's what John the Baptist was doing in the River Jordan. But people go on misunderstanding. Today also baptism happens in the churches; it is meaningless. John the Baptist was preparing people for an inner bath. When they were ready he would take them symbolically into the River Jordan. That bath in the River Jordan was symbolic—symbolic that the master can give you a bath. He can take the dust, the dust of centuries, away from you. And suddenly all is clear, all is clarity. That clarity is enlightenment.

The great Zen master Daie says, "All the teachings of the sages, of the saints, of the masters, have expounded no more than this: they are commentaries on your sudden cry, *Ah, This!*"

When suddenly you are clear, and a great joy and rejoicing arises in you and your whole being, every fiber of your body, mind, and soul dances and you say, "Ah, this! Alleluia!"—a great shout of joy arises in your being—that is enlightenment. Suddenly stars come down from the rafters. You become part of the eternal dance of existence.

Auden says:

Dance till the stars come down from the rafters!
Dance, dance, dance till you drop!

Yes, it happens—it is not something that you have to do. It is something that even if you want not to do you will find it impossible; you will find it impossible to resist. You will have to dance.

The beauty of *this,* the beauty of *now,* the joy that existence *is* and the closeness of it . . . Yes, stars come down from the rafters. They are so close you can just touch them; you can hold them in your hands.

Daie is right. He says: All the teachings the sages expounded are no more than commentaries on your sudden cry, *Ah, This!*

The whole heart saying "Aha!" and the silence that follows it, and the peace, and the joy, and the meeting, and the merger, and the orgasmic experience, the ecstasy . . .

Masters don't teach the truth; there is no way to teach it. It is a transmission beyond scriptures, beyond words. It is a transmission. It is energy provoking energy in you. It is a kind of synchronicity.

The master has disappeared as an ego; he is pure joy. And the disciple sits by the side of the master slowly, slowly partaking of his joy, of his being. Eating and drinking out of that eternal, inexhaustible source—*Aes Dhammo Sanantano*. One day—and one cannot predict when that day will come; it is unpredictable—one day suddenly it has happened. A process has started in you, which reveals the truth of your being to you. You come face to face with yourself. God is not somewhere else, he is now, here.

You have to approach the master with great love, with great trust, with an open heart. You are not aware who you are. He is aware who he is, and he is aware who you are. The caterpillar might be said to be unaware that it may become a butterfly. You are caterpillars—bodhisattvas. All caterpillars are bodhisattvas and all bodhisattvas are caterpillars. A bodhisattva means one who can become a butterfly, who can become a buddha, who is a buddha in the seed, in essence. But how can the caterpillar be aware that he can become a butterfly? The only way is to commune with butterflies, to see butterflies moving in the wind, in the sun. Seeing them soaring high, seeing them moving from one flower to another flower, seeing their beauty, their color, maybe a deep desire, a longing arises in the caterpillar: "Can I also be the same?" In that very moment the caterpillar has started awakening, a process has been triggered.

The master-disciple relationship is the relationship between a caterpillar and a butterfly, a friendship between a caterpillar and a butterfly. The butterfly cannot prove that the caterpillar can become a butterfly; there is no logical way. But the butterfly can provoke a longing in the caterpillar—that is possible.

The master helps you to reach your own experience. He does not give you the Vedas, the Koran, the Bible; he throws you to yourself. He makes you aware of your inner sources. He makes you aware of your own juice, of your own godliness. He liberates you from the scriptures. He liberates you from the interpretations of others. He liberates you from all belief. He liberates you from all speculation, from all guesswork. He liberates you from philosophy and from religion and from theology. He liberates you, in short, from the world of words—because the word is the problem.

You become so much obsessed with the word *love* that you forget that love is an experience, not a word. You become so obsessed with the word *God* that you forget that God is an experience, not a word. The word *God* is not God, and the word *fire* is not fire, and the word *love* is not love either.

The master liberates you from words, he liberates you from all kinds of imaginative philosophies. He brings you to a state of wordless silence.

The failure of religion and philosophy is that they all become substitutes for real experience. Beware of it!

THE MASTER IS A PHYSICIAN—NOT OF YOUR ORDINARY DISEASES BUT of your existential conflicts.

That's why I have been fighting on two fronts. I have to fight the old traditions, old religions, old orthodoxies, because they will not allow you ever to be healthy and whole. They will cripple you. The more crippled you are, the greater saint you become. So on one hand, I have to fight with any kind of thinking or theology that divides you.

Second, I have to work on the growth of your inner being.

Both are part of the same process: how to make you a whole person, how to destroy all the rubbish that is preventing you from becoming whole—that is the negative part. And the positive part is how to make you aflame with meditation, with silence, with love, with joy, with peace. That is the positive part of my teaching.

With my positive part there is no problem; I could have gone around the world teaching people meditation, peace, love, silence—and nobody would have opposed me.

But I would not have been of any help to anybody, because who is going to destroy all that rubbish? And the rubbish has to be destroyed first, it is blocking the way.

THE WISE MAN WANTS YOU ONLY TO HAVE INSIGHT INTO THINGS, so that you have your own light. But you don't want insight, you want clear-cut instructions. You don't want to see yourself, you want to be guided. You don't want to accept your responsibility toward yourself, you want to throw the whole responsibility on the shoulders of the master, on the shoulders of the wise man. Then you feel at ease. Now he is responsible; if something goes wrong, he is responsible. And everything is going to be wrong, because unless you take your responsibility, nothing is ever going to be right.

Nobody can put you right except you yourself.

A real religious person is born the moment you accept your responsibility for yourself, the moment you say, "Whatsoever I am is my choice—not of the past but of the present. It is my choice of this moment, and if I want to change it I am absolutely free to change it. Nobody can hinder me—no social force, no state, no history, no economics, no unconscious, can hinder me. If I am determined to change it, I can change it."

FROM YOUR VERY CHILDHOOD YOU HAVE BEEN TAUGHT NOT TO BE responsible. You have been taught to depend. You have been taught to be responsible to your father, to your mother, to your family, to your motherland, to all kinds of nonsense. But you have not been told that you have to be responsible for yourself, that there is nobody who is going to take your responsibility. . . .

I teach you not to be responsible to anybody—the father, the mother, the country, the religion, the party line, don't be responsible to anybody. You are not!

Just be responsible to yourself. Do whatsoever you feel like doing. If it is wrong, the punishment will immediately follow. If it is right, the reward will follow immediately, instantly; there is no other way. In this way you will start finding what is wrong, what is right, on your own. You will grow a new sensitivity—Indians call it the third eye. You will start seeing with a new vision, a new eye. Instantly you will know what is wrong, because in the past so many times you have done it and always suffered in consequence. You will know what is right, because whenever you did existence showered great blessings on you. Cause and effect are together, they are not separated by years and lives. . . .

This is what I mean by being responsible to yourself. There is no God on whom you can dump your responsibility, but you are always searching to dump on somebody, even on a poor man like me, who is continuously telling you that I am not responsible for anything, for anybody. Still, somehow, deep down you go on carrying the illusion that I must be joking. I am not joking. "He is our master," you must be thinking. "How can he say that he is not responsible?" But you don't understand. Dumping your responsibility on me, you will remain retarded, childish. You will never grow.

The only way to grow is to accept all the good, the bad, the joyful, the sorrowful. Everything that happens to you, you are responsible for. That gives you great freedom.

If I am responsible for something, then the key to your actions is in my hands. Then you are a slave to me. Then you are a puppet and the strings are in my hand. I say dance, you dance; I say stop, you stop. Of course, the puppet cannot be responsible for anything. The puppeteer, who is behind the screen, is always responsible. God is the great puppeteer.

The moment I say there is no puppeteer, no God, no saint, it is all rubbish, I am trying to give you total freedom. I am making you absolutely responsible for everything that happens to you or does not happen. Rejoice in this freedom. Rejoice in this great understanding that you are responsible for everything in your life. This will make you what I call an *individual*. And to become an individual is to know all that is worth knowing, is to experience all that is worth experiencing. To be an individual is to be liberated, is to be enlightened.

THE SANNYAS MOVEMENT IS NOT MINE. IT IS NOT YOURS. IT WAS here when I was not here, it will be here when I will not be here. The sannyas movement simply means the movement of the seekers of truth. They have always been here. Of course, they have been always tortured by the ignorant masses: killed, murdered, crucified—or worshiped. Remember: It is the same whether you crucify or you worship; both are ways to get rid of those people. Worship is more cultured. We say, "You are an incarnation of God, we will worship you. But we will not do what you say—how can we? We are ordinary human beings, you were extraordinary. Either you were a prophet sent by God, or a messenger, or the only begotten Son of God, or you were an incarnation of God—you could do miracles."

We have created all kinds of miracles for only one reason: to create a distance between the people who have been seeking the truth and the people who have ultimately found the truth. We were not ready to go with them.

There has always been a line of seekers of truth. . . . I call it sannyas. It is eternal. It has nothing to do with me.

Millions of people have contributed to it. I have also contributed my own share. It will go on becoming more and more rich. When I am gone there will be more and more people coming and making it richer. The old sannyas was serious; I have contributed to it a sense of humor. The old sannyas was sad; I have contributed to it singing, dancing, laughing . . . I have made it more human.

The old sannyas was somehow life-negative. I have made it life-affirmative. But it is the same sannyas. It is the same search. I have made it more rich, I have made it more grounded in the world because my whole teaching is "be in the world, but don't be of the world."

There is no need to renounce the world. Only cowards renounce it. Live in the world, experience it. It is a school. You cannot grow in the Himalayas, you can grow only in the world.

Each step is an examination. Each step you are passing through is a test. Life is an opportunity.

I will be gone. That does not mean that the sannyas movement will be gone. It does not belong to anybody.

Just as science does not belong to Albert Einstein—why should the search for truth belong to somebody? To Gautam Buddha? To J. Krishnamurti? Or to me? Or to you?

Just as science goes on growing and every scientific genius goes on contributing to it and the Ganges goes on becoming bigger and wider, oceanic—in the same way the inner world needs a science. The objective world has a science. The inner world needs a science and I call sannyas the science of the inner world. It has been growing but because it goes against humanity's attachments, ignorance, superstitions—so-called religions, churches, priests, popes, *shankaracharyas* . . . these are the enemies of the inner search because the inner search needs no organization.

The sannyas movement is not an organization, that is why I call it a movement. It is individual. People join—I had started alone and then people started coming and joining me and slowly, slowly the caravan became bigger and bigger. But it is not an organization, I am nobody's leader. Nobody has to follow me. I am grateful that you have allowed me to share my bliss, my love, my ecstasy. I am grateful to you. Nobody is my follower, nobody is lower. There is no hierarchy. It is not a religion, it is pure religiousness, the very essence. Not a flower, but only a fragrance; you cannot catch hold of it. You can have the experience of it, you can be surrounded by the perfume but you cannot catch hold of it.

Religions are like the dead flowers you can find in Bibles, in Gitas. . . .

When they were put in the Bible they were living, they were fragrant, but now it is only a corpse. All holy books are corpses, dead flowers and nothing else.

Truth, the living truth, has to be discovered by each individual *by himself.* Nobody can give it to you.

Yes, somebody who has achieved it can trigger a thirst in you, a tremendous desire for it. I cannot give you the truth but I can give you the desire for it.

I cannot give you the truth but I can show you the moon . . . please don't get attached to the finger that is indicating the moon. This finger will disappear. The moon will remain and the search will continue.

As long as there is a single human being on the earth the flowers of sannyas will go on blossoming.

PART THREE

The Legacy

I may be gone, but I am creating a certain ripple that will remain. You may be gone, but you loved somebody and that love created a ripple that will remain and remain and remain. It can never disappear; it will have its own repercussions . . . it will go on vibrating. You throw a small pebble in the lake, and ripples arise. The pebble settles very soon at the bottom, but the ripples continue. They go on moving toward the shore—and there is no shore to this existence.

I am talking to you. . . . In this moment something is transpiring between me and you. I will be gone, you will be gone, but that which is transpiring will abide. So these words will go on echoing, reechoing. The speaker will not be there, the listener will not be there, but what is transpiring between the two in this moment has become part of eternity. And there is no shore, so these ripples will go on and on and on.

RELIGIONLESS RELIGION

I have been constantly inconsistent so that you will never be able to make a dogma out of me. You will simply go nuts if you try. I am leaving something really terrible for scholars; they will not be able to make any sense out of it. They will go nuts—and they deserve it, they should go nuts! But nobody can create an orthodoxy out of me, it is impossible. From my words you can get burned, but you will not be able to find any kind of theology, dogmatism.

You can find a way to live but not a dogma to preach. You can find a rebellious quality to be imbibed, but you will not find a revolutionary theme to be organized. My words are not only on fire, I am putting gunpowder also here and there, which will go on exploding for centuries. I am putting more than needed—I never take any chances. Almost each sentence is going to create trouble for anybody who wants to organize a religion around me.

Yes, you can have a loose community, a commune. Remember the word *loose*: everybody independent, everybody free to live his own way, to interpret me in his own way, to find whatsoever he wants to find. He can find the way he wants to live—and everybody unto himself.

There is no need for somebody to decide what my religion is. I am leaving it open-ended. You can work out a definition for yourself—but it is only for yourself, and that too you will have to continuously change. As you understand me more and more, you will have to change it. You cannot go on holding it like a dead thing in your hand. You will have to change it, and it will go on changing you simultaneously.

CHRISTIANITY, HINDUISM, BUDDHISM, JAINISM, MOHAMMEDANISM—these are only ideologies, dogmas, creeds; they are only cults. The true religion has no name, it cannot have any name. Buddha lived it, Jesus lived it—but remember, Jesus was not a Christian and Buddha was not a Buddhist, he had never heard of the word. The truly religious people have been simply religious, they have not been dogmatic. There are three hundred religions in the world—this is such an absurdity! If truth is one, how can there be three hundred religions? There is only one science and three hundred religions?

If the science that is concerned with the objective truth is one, then religion is also one because it is concerned with the subjective truth, the other side of the truth. But that religion cannot have any name, it cannot have any ideology.

I teach only that religion. Hence if somebody asks you what my teaching is, in short, you will not be able to say—because I don't teach principles, ideologies, dogmas, doctrines. I teach you a religionless religion, I teach you the taste of it. I give you the method to become receptive to the divine. I don't say anything about the divine, I simply tell you, "This is the window—open it and you will see the starry night."

Now, that starry night is indefinable. Once you see it through the open window you will know it. Seeing is knowing—and seeing should be *being* too. There should be no other belief.

So my whole effort is existential, not intellectual at all. And the true religion is existential. It has always happened to only a few people and then it disappears from the earth because the intellectuals immediately grab it and they start making beautiful ideologies out of it—neat and clean, logical. In that very effort they destroy its beauty. They create philosophies, and religion disappears. The pundit, the scholar, the theologian, is the enemy of religion.

So remember it: you are not getting initiated into a certain religion; you are getting initiated into just religiousness. It is vast, immense, unbounded—it is like the whole sky.

Even the sky is not the limit, so open your wings without any fear. This whole existence belongs to us; this is our temple, this is our scripture. Less than that is man-made, manufactured by man. Where it is manufactured does not matter much—beware of manufactured religions so that you can know the true, which is not man-made. And it is available in the trees, in the mountains, in the rivers, in the stars—in you, in people that surround you—it is available everywhere.

SCIENCE IS THE SEARCH FOR TRUTH IN THE OBJECTIVE WORLD AND RELIGION is the search for truth in the subjective world. In fact, they are two wings of one bird, of one inquiry—two sides. Ultimately there is no need to have two names. My own suggestion is that *science* is a perfectly beautiful name, because it means "knowing." So science has two sides, just like every coin has two sides. Knowing in the dimension of matter you can call objective science, and knowing in the dimension of your interiority—of your inner being, of your consciousness—you can call subjective science. There is no need for the word *religion*.

Science is perfectly good—and it is the same search, just the directions are different. And it will be good that we make one supreme science, which is a synthesis, a synchronicity of the outer science and the inner science. There will be no need of so many religions then, and there will be no need then even for somebody to be an atheist. When theists are gone, then there is no need for atheists—they are only reactions. There are believers in God so there are disbelievers in God. When the believers are gone, what is the need of disbelievers?

There is no need to believe in anything—that is the fundamental of science. That is the scientific approach to reality: do not believe, inquire. The moment you believe, inquiry stops. Keep your mind open—neither believe nor disbelieve. Just remain alert and search and doubt everything until you come to a point that is indubitable—that's what truth is. You cannot doubt it. It is not a question of believing in it, it is a totally different phenomenon. It is so much a certainty, overwhelming you so much, that there is no way to doubt it.

This is knowing. And this knowing transforms a man into a buddha, into an enlightened one. This is the goal of all human growth.

THE CREDIT OF BRINGING A QUANTUM LEAP TO RELIGION GOES BACK twenty-five centuries before Gautam Buddha to Adinatha, who for the first time preached a religion without God. It was a tremendous revolution because nowhere in the whole world had it ever been conceived that religion could exist without God.

God has been an essential part—the center—of all the religions: Christianity, Judaism, Mohammedanism. But to make God the center of religion makes man just the periphery. To conceive of God as the creator of the world makes man only a puppet.

That's why in Hebrew, which is the language of Judaism, man is called Adam. *Adam* means "mud." In Arabic, man is called *admi*; it is from the same root as *adam*, and again it means "mud." In English, which has become the language of Christianity by and large, the word *human* comes from *humus*, and *humus* means "mud." Naturally, if God is the creator he has to create from something. He has to make man like a statue, so first he makes man with mud and then breathes life into him. But if this is so, man loses all dignity.

And if God is the creator of man and everything else, the whole idea is whimsical. What has God been doing for eternity, before he created man and the universe? According to Christianity he created man only 4004 years before Jesus Christ. So what was he doing all along through eternity? It seems whimsical. There must not be any cause, because to have a cause for which God had to create existence means there are powers higher than God, there are causes that can make him create. Or there is a possibility that suddenly desire arose in him—that too is not very philosophically sound, because for eternity he was desireless—and to be desireless is so blissful. It is impossible to imagine that out of an experience of eternal blissfulness, a desire arose in God to create the world. Desire is desire, whether you want to make a house or become the prime minister or create the world. God cannot be conceived as having desires, so the only thing that remains is that he is whimsical, eccentric. Then there is no need for a cause and no need for desire—just a whim.

But if this whole existence is just created out of a whim it loses all meaning, all significance. And tomorrow another whim may arise in God to destroy, to dissolve the whole universe. So we are simply puppets in the hands of a dictatorial God who has all the powers but who has not a sane mind, who is whimsical.

Adinatha must have been a very deep meditator, contemplative, and he must have come to the conclusion that with a God, there is no meaning in the world. If we want meaning in the world then God has to be disposed of. He must have been a man of tremendous courage. People are still worshiping in the churches, in the synagogues, in the temples—yet that man Adinatha, five thousand years before us, came to a very clear-cut scientific conclusion that there is nothing higher than man, and that any evolution that is going to happen is within man and in his consciousness.

Adinatha is the first of twenty-four masters in Jainism, and this was the first quantum leap—God was disposed of. The credit does not go to Buddha, because Buddha comes twenty-five centuries later than Adinatha. But another credit goes to Buddha—Adinatha disposed of God but could not manage to put meditation in its place. On the contrary, he created asceticism, austerities, torturing the body—fasting, remaining naked, eating only once a day, not drinking in the night, not eating in the night, eating only certain foods. He had come to a beautiful philosophical conclusion but it seems the conclusion was only philosophical, it was not meditational.

When you depose God you cannot have any ritual, you cannot have worship, you cannot have prayer; something has to be substituted. He substituted austerities, because man became the center of his religion and man has to purify himself. Purity in his conception was that man has to detach himself from the world, has to detach himself from his own body. This distorted the whole thing. He had come to a very significant conclusion, but it remained only a philosophical concept.

Adinatha disposed of God but left a vacuum, and Buddha filled it with meditation. Adinatha made a godless religion, Buddha made a meditative religion.

Meditation is Buddha's contribution. The point is not to torture the body; the point is to become more silent, to become more relaxed, to become more peaceful. It is an inward journey to reach to one's own center of consciousness, and the center of one's own consciousness is the center of the whole existence.

Twenty-five centuries have again passed. Just as Adinatha's revolutionary concept of godless religion got lost in a desert of austerities and self-torture, Buddha's idea of meditation—something inner, that nobody else can see; only you know where you are, only you know whether you are progressing or not—got lost in another desert, and that was organized religion.

Religion says that single individuals cannot be trusted, whether they are meditating or not. They need communities, masters, monasteries where they can live together. Those who are on a higher level of consciousness can watch over others and help them. It became essential that religions should not be left in the hands of individuals; they should be organized and should be in the hands of those who have arrived at a high point of meditation.

In the beginning it was good; while Buddha was alive there were many people who reached self-realization, enlightenment. But as Buddha died and these people died, the very organization that was supposed to help people to meditate fell in the hands of a priesthood, and rather than helping you to meditate they started creating rituals around the image of Buddha. Buddha became another god. Adinatha disposed of God, Buddha never accepted that God exists—but this priesthood cannot exist without a god. So there may not be a god who is a creator but Buddha has reached godhood. For others the only thing is to worship Buddha, to have faith in Buddha, to follow the principles of Buddha, to live life according to his doctrine; Buddha got lost in the organization, the imitation. And they all forgot the basic thing, which was meditation.

My whole effort is to create a religionless religion. We have seen what happened to religions that have God as the center. We have seen what happened to Adinatha's revolutionary concept, godless religion. We have seen what happened to Buddha, organized religion without God.

Now my effort is, just as they dissolved God, to dissolve religion also. Leave only meditation so it cannot be forgotten in any way. There is nothing else to replace it. There is no God and there is no religion. By religion I mean an organized doctrine, creed, ritual, priesthood.

For the first time, I want religion to be absolutely individual. Because all organized religions, whether with God or without God, have misled humanity. And the sole cause has been organization because organization has its own ways, which go against meditativeness. Organization is really a political phenomenon, it is not religious. It is another way of power and will to power. Now every Christian priest hopes some day to become a bishop at least, to become a cardinal, to become a pope. This is a new hierarchy, a new bureaucracy—and because it is spiritual, nobody objects. You may be a bishop, you may be a pope, you may be anything. It is not objectionable because you are not going to obstruct anybody's life; it is just an abstract idea.

My effort is to destroy the priesthood completely. It remained with God, it remained with godless religion; now the only way is that we should dispose of God and religion both, so that there is no possibility of any priesthood. Then man is absolutely free, totally responsible for his own growth.

My feeling is that the more a man is responsible for his own growth, the more difficult it is for him to postpone it for long. Because it means if you are miserable, *you* are responsible. If you are tense, *you* are responsible. If you are not relaxed, *you* are responsible. If you are in suffering, *you* are the cause of it.

There is no God, there is no priesthood that you can go to and ask for some ritual. You are left alone with your misery—and nobody wants to be miserable.

The priests go on giving you opium, they go on giving you hope: "Don't be worried, it is just a test of your faith, of your trust. And if you can pass through this misery and suffering silently and patiently, in the other world beyond death you will be immensely rewarded." If there is no priesthood, you have to understand that whatever you are, you are responsible for it—nobody else. And the feeling that "I am responsible for my misery" opens the door. Then you start looking for methods and means to get out of this miserable state.

And that's what meditation is. It is simply the opposite state of misery, suffering, anguish, anxiety. It is the state of a peaceful, blissful flowering of being, so silent and so timeless that you cannot conceive that anything better is possible. And there is nothing that is better than the state of a meditative mind.

So you can say these are the three quantum leaps:

Adinatha drops God because he finds God is becoming too heavy on man; rather than helping man in his growth, God has become a burden. But he forgets to replace him with something. Man will need something in his miserable moments, in his suffering. He used to pray to God—you have taken God away, you have taken his prayer away and now when he is miserable, what will he do? In Jainism, meditation has no place.

It is Buddha's insight to see that God has been dropped, now the gap should be filled; otherwise the gap will destroy man. He puts in meditation—something really authentic, which can change the whole being. But he was not aware—perhaps he could not be aware because there are things you cannot be aware of unless they happen—that there should be no organization, that there should be no priesthood, that as God is gone, religion should also be gone. But he can be forgiven because he had not thought about it and there was no past to help him to see it. It came after him.

The real problem is the priest, and God is the invention of the priest. Unless you drop the priest, you can drop God but the priest will always find new rituals, he will create new gods.

My effort is to leave you alone with meditation, with no mediator between you and existence. When you are not in meditation you are separated from existence, and that is your suffering. It's the same as when you take a fish out of the ocean and throw it on the bank—the misery and the suffering and the torture he goes through, the hankering and the effort to reach back to the ocean because it is where he belongs, he is part of the ocean and he cannot remain apart. Any suffering is simply indicative that you are not in communion with existence, that the fish is not in the ocean.

Meditation is nothing but withdrawing all the barriers—thoughts, emotions, sentiments—that create a wall between you and existence. The moment they drop, you suddenly find yourself in tune with the whole; not only in tune, you really find you *are* the whole. When a dewdrop slips from a lotus leaf into the ocean it does not find that it is part of the ocean, it finds it *is* the ocean. And to find it is the ultimate goal, the ultimate realization. There is nothing beyond it.

So Adinatha dropped God but did not drop organization, and because there was no God, the organization created rituals. Buddha, seeing what had happened to Jainism, that it had become ritualism, dropped God, he dropped all rituals, and single-pointedly insisted on meditation. But he forgot that the priests who had created rituals in Jainism are going to do the same with meditation. And they did it, they made Buddha himself a God. They talk about meditation but basically Buddhists are worshipers of Buddha—they go to the temple and instead of Krishna or Christ, there is Buddha's statue. God was not there, ritual was difficult—around meditation, ritual was difficult. They created a statue and they started saying, in the same way all religions have been doing, "Have faith in Buddha, have trust in Buddha and you will be saved."

Both the revolutions were lost. I would like that what I am doing is not lost. So I am trying in every possible way to drop all those things that in the past have been barriers for the revolution to continue and grow. I don't want anybody to stand between the individual and existence. No prayer, no priest; you alone are enough to face the sunrise, you don't need somebody to interpret for you what a beautiful sunrise it is.

You are here, every individual is here, the whole existence is available. All that you need is just to be silent and listen to existence. There is no need of any religion, there is no need of any God, there is no need of any priesthood, there is no need of any organization.

I trust in the individual categorically. Nobody up to now has trusted in the individual in such a way. So all things can be removed. Now all that has been left to you is a state of meditation, which simply means a state of utter silence.

The word *meditation* makes it look heavier. It is better to call it just a simple, innocent silence and existence opens all its beauties to you.

And as it goes on growing, you go on growing, and there comes a moment when you have reached the very peak of your potentiality—you can call it buddhahood, enlightenment, *bhagwatta*, godliness, whatever—it has no name, so any name will do.

MEDITATION FOR THE
TWENTY-FIRST CENTURY

I was working for ten years continuously, teaching direct relaxation. It was simple for me, so I thought it would be simple for everyone. Then, by and by, I became aware that it is impossible. I was in a fallacy, it was not possible. I would say, "Relax," to those I was teaching. They would appear to understand the meaning of the word, but they could not relax. Then I had to devise new methods for meditation, which create tension first—more tension. They create such tension that you become just mad. And then I say, "Relax."

When you have come up to the climax, your whole body, your whole mind, becomes hungry for relaxation. With so much tension you want to stop, and I go on pushing you to continue, continue to the very end. Do whatsoever you can do to create tensions, and then, when you stop you just fall down from the peak into a deep abyss. The abyss is the end, the effortlessness is the end, but you can use tension as the means.

ONE OF MY COLLEAGUES WHEN I WAS A PROFESSOR IN THE UNIVERSITY wanted to learn meditation. I had a small school of meditators there. He participated, and the first day he experienced silence he simply jumped out of the small temple where we used to sit and ran away! I could not understand what had happened. I had to follow him. He would look back at me, and as he looked at me following him, he ran faster. I thought, "This is something! What happened to this man?"

I yelled, "You wait, Nityananda!"—his name was Nityananda Chatterji—

"just wait for a moment!" He just waved his hand, meaning "finished," and said, "I don't want to meditate. You are a dangerous man!"

Finally I got hold of him just before he entered his house. He could not run anywhere else now. I said, "You had better tell me what happened."

He said, "What you did I don't know, but I became so silent—and you know me, I am a chatterbox"—Chatterji was his name too. He was a Bengali. "In the morning I start talking, and I talk till I fall asleep, almost in the middle of a sentence—I continuously talk. It keeps me engaged, unworried, with no problems. I know there are problems, but talking to anybody . . . if nobody is there I talk to myself.

"And there, sitting with you, suddenly talking stopped. I was blank. And I said, 'My God, I am going mad! If this happens to me for twenty-four hours—finished! Nityananda Chatterji,' I said, 'your life is finished. If the mind does not come back again . . . before this silence goes further, escape from here. And why are these thirty, forty people sitting here with closed eyes? But that is their problem. Everybody has to take care of himself.' So I escaped."

I said, "Don't be worried. Silence is not something that destroys your mind, it simply helps the mind to rest. And to you it happened so easily because you are a chatterbox; the mind is tired. It does not usually happen so easily for those other people who are sitting. It is not so easy that when for the first time you sit to meditate, your mind becomes silent.

"You have bothered the mind so much your whole life, people are afraid of you. Your wife is afraid, your children are afraid. In the university, the professors are afraid. If you are sitting in the common room, the whole common room becomes empty; everybody escapes from there. It is because of too much use of the mind. It is a mechanism, it needs a little rest.

"Scientists say that even metal gets tired; it also needs rest. The mind is a very sophisticated phenomenon, the most sophisticated thing in the whole universe, and you have used it so much that finding a chance to become silent it immediately became silent. You should be happy."

He said, "But will it start again or not?"

I said, "It will, whenever you want."

He said, "I became afraid that if it does not start again . . . then Nityananda Chatterji, your life is finished. You will be in a madhouse—why, in the first place, did you ask this man about meditation!"

And I said, "I was also asking myself why you want to meditate."

He said, "I was simply talking about it, just the way I talk about everything— and you grabbed me. You said, 'That's perfectly okay. You come with me in the car.' I had never meant . . . I talk about everything, whether I know about it or not. It does not matter, I can talk for hours. Just because you were sitting in the common hall and there was nobody else, I thought, 'What subject will be right?' Seeing you, I thought meditation is the only subject you might be interested to talk about, so I talked. And you grabbed me; you brought me in the car . . . and I thought, 'What harm can it do? My house is just a few minutes away from his house, so it is good to have a ride in the car. And all the way I will talk.' And all the way I talked about meditation. And that's how I got into your trap, because then I could not turn back. You pushed me into that temple where forty people were sitting, so I had to sit. I wanted to escape from the very beginning! I never wanted to meditate, because I don't want to get into anything if I don't know where it will lead.

"And just as I was sitting there, everything became silent. I opened my eyes, I looked around, and everybody was with closed eyes, silent. I thought, 'This is the time that I should escape.' And you are such a man that you won't let me even run away. The whole street sees that I am escaping and you are following . . . and I was saying to myself, 'I am not going to stop.' Just . . . I became very much afraid. I am afraid of silence. Talking is perfectly okay."

I said, "You are fortunate because you have talked so much that your mind is ready to relax. Don't miss this opportunity—and don't be afraid! Can't you see me? I can talk. You will be able to talk whenever you want. Right now, talking is not within your power. It simply goes on by itself, you are simply a gramophone record. Silence will make you a master."

He said, "Well, if you promise . . . I trust you and I will come every day. But remember, I don't want to lose my mind. I have children, I have a wife, I have old parents. . . ."

I said, "Don't be worried. You will not lose your mind."

And you will be surprised: that man progressed in meditation better than anyone else. That gave me the idea of a special meditation, and I started using a new technique, gibberish. It was not absolutely new, but nobody had used it as a device for many people to meditate. . . .

I told Nityananda Chatterji, "You don't be worried. You have been doing gibberish so much that you are going to certainly attain a deep silence."

And he became very silent. The whole university was shocked. They could not believe it—what had I done to him? Now people would approach him, want him to talk, and he would say, "No, enough. When I used to talk, you all used to escape. I am finished. Just leave me alone."

He was promoted, but he refused and went on pension so his wife and children could live and he could continue his silence. I saw him after ten years. He had become a totally new man, so fresh and so young, as if a bud is just opening and becoming a rose—with that freshness. And he didn't talk; for hours he would come and sit, and there would be no talk.

Mind is only a mechanism—it can talk, it can be silent. The only problem is, it should not be the master; it should be the servant. As a servant it is great; as a master it is dangerous. You should be the master of it.

YOU CANNOT DO MEDITATION, YOU CAN ONLY BE IN MEDITATION. IT is not a question of doing something, it is a question of being. It is not an act but a state.

IT HAPPENS MANY TIMES: AN ATHEIST COMES TO ME AND HE ASKS, "Can I also meditate?" Because the idea has become prevalent that unless you believe in God you cannot meditate. Now, that is a very foolish notion. Meditation has nothing to do with God. In fact, the truth is that if you believe in God it will be difficult to meditate. Your very belief will become a disturbance.

The person who does not believe in anything can simply move beyond thoughts; the person who believes clings to thinking, because his belief is a thought. Belief is part of the mind—if you believe too much in God you cannot leave the mind because leaving the mind will mean, obviously, leaving your belief. The man who cannot believe is in a better situation.

And remember, the English word *meditate* gives a wrong connotation. When we use the word *meditation* it gives a feeling that you are meditating *upon* something. You have to have some object to meditate upon—and that is the problem. In the East we have another word, *dhyana*. Dhyana simply means there is no question of focusing, concentrating on something; rather, it is dropping all contents of the mind and just being. Meditation in the sense of dhyana needs no object; it is an objectless, contentless state of consciousness. You go on dropping—*neti, neti*, neither this nor that—you go on rejecting all thoughts, good and bad. When all thoughts are eliminated what is left? That is you, and that is godliness.

But what you call it does not matter. You can call it God if the word appeals to you; if it doesn't appeal to you, you can call it nirvana, you can call it Tao, or whatever. But don't be worried about it, that you can't believe in God. It is good! This is my approach: If somebody says, "I believe in God," I say, "It is good. Now let us start from there, that will do." If somebody says, "I don't believe in God," I say, "It is good. Now let us start from there."

You have to start from the point where you are. And all points are good, because all points are on the circumference and from every point on the circumference the center is available. So move toward the center, don't be worried about where you are.

One afternoon Mulla Nasruddin was getting a haircut in a barber's shop. He noticed a price list on the wall of the shop and on the list was, "Singe—5 Dollars." He asked the barber why it cost so much.

"Every hair on your head," said the barber, "is a little hollow tube, open at the ends, so the body's energy sort of bleeds out of it. After you get a haircut it is a good idea to get a singe because it closes up the hole at the end of each hair and seals in the energy. Otherwise the hair and your whole body just keep getting weaker and weaker every time you get it cut."

"Now, wait a minute," said the mulla, "what about the hair on my chin? I shave it every day and cut off the ends and it just keeps getting thicker and stronger. How do you explain that?"

"Easy!" said the barber. "You just ain't the kind of a fella this story was made up to tell to!"

These are all just stories. If it appeals, good; if it doesn't appeal, very good! There is no need to believe; you need not do anything about it. Don't waste your time with God. Just because of this word so many people go on wasting time. Somebody is trying to prove, somebody is trying to disprove, great treatises are being written. As many books are written about God as about anything else—millions of books, libraries full of books. Don't be wasting your time. If you can't believe, then that story is not for you. But we have other stories too, so why be worried? For godless people too there is a way.

And my way is for all. Whosoever comes is accepted. The Hindu, the Mohammedan, the Christian, the Jain, the Sikh, the Buddhist, the Parsee—

whosoever comes is accepted. I love all kinds of stories! Any kind of beginning is good, but begin. Don't remain stuck where you are; move toward the center. Meditate, and that will bring you home. And then you can call it whatsoever you like; that is none of my business what you call it. You can give it any name of your own fancy.

THERE ARE ONE HUNDRED AND TWELVE METHODS OF MEDITATION*; they were discovered ten thousand years ago. I have made a few new methods for the modern man, because those methods were created for a totally different kind of humanity, for very simple people. The contemporary man is not simple, he is very complex. Those methods were for people who were not repressed, who were natural. In these ten thousand years religions have made everybody repressed. Sexually, and in other ways, they have driven humanity against its own nature.

So I have created new methods that are cathartic, so that you can throw out all repressions, all garbage out of your being, and can become clean, a tabula rasa. Then those one hundred and twelve methods—any one method that appeals to you will be enough to transform your being.

FOR SIXTY MINUTES EVERY DAY, JUST FORGET ABOUT THE WORLD. LET the world disappear from you, and you disappear from the world. Take an about-turn, a 180-degree turn, and just look inside. In the beginning you will see only clouds. Don't be worried about them; those clouds are created by your repressions. You will come across anger, hatred, greed, and all kinds of black holes. You have repressed them, so they are there. And your so-called religions have taught you to repress them, so they are there like wounds. You have been hiding them.

That's why my emphasis is first on catharsis. Unless you go through great catharsis you will have to pass through many clouds. It will be tiring, and you may be so impatient that you may turn back into the world. And you will say, "There is nothing. There is no lotus and no fragrance, there is only stink, rubbish."

*Osho gives detailed instructions and guidance for these methods in *The Book of Secrets* (St. Martin's Press).

You know it. When you close your eyes and you start moving in, what do you come across? You don't come across those beautiful lands buddhas talk about. You come across hells, agonies, repressed there, waiting for you. Anger of many lives, accumulating—it is all a mess there, so one wants to remain outside. One wants to go to the movie, to the club, to meet people and gossip. One wants to remain occupied till one is tired and falls asleep. That's the way you are living, that's your style of life.

So when one starts looking in, naturally one is very much puzzled. Buddhas say that there is great benediction, great fragrance—you come across lotus flowers blooming and such fragrance that it is eternal. They talk about this paradise, they talk about this kingdom of God that is within you. And when you go in, you only come across hell. You see not Buddha lands but Adolf Hitler concentration camps. Naturally, you start thinking that this is all nonsense, it is better to remain outside. And why go on playing with your wounds? It hurts too, and pus starts oozing out of the wounds and it is dirty.

But catharsis helps. If you cathart, if you go through chaotic meditations—you throw all these clouds outside, all these darknesses outside—then mindfulness becomes easier. That is my reason why I emphasize first chaotic meditations and then silent meditations. First active meditations, then passive meditations. You can move into passivity only when all that is there like junk has been thrown out. Anger has been thrown out, greed has been thrown out . . . layer upon layer, these things are there. But once you have thrown them out, you can easily slip in. There is nothing to hinder you.

And suddenly—the bright light of the Buddha land. Suddenly you are in a totally different world.

1972: MEDITATION CAMP, MT. ABU, RAJASTHAN, INDIA

The morning meditation is in four stages. For the first ten minutes you are to do fast breathing. You are to enter into existence through breathing, you are to give vigor and energy to breathing. You are to put your very life into breathing—so much so that when the breath goes out, your very soul goes out with it, and when the breath comes in, the whole existence comes in with it. You have to breathe so intensely that you forget everything else, only the breathing remains—as if you yourself have become the breathing.

This intense breathing for ten minutes will awaken all the energies that are asleep within you. It will arouse and activate all those energies that you have never even touched. But miserliness won't do. Don't think along the lines, "I will breathe slowly. After all, if not much at least *some* energy will awaken." No, not at all—because the process of awakening begins only after a certain limit has been reached. It is the same as when you heat water; it heats up to one hundred degrees and then turns into steam. Don't think that at thirty degrees it will turn into steam "to some extent" or "some of it will turn into steam." No, mathematics won't work here. It turns into steam at one hundred degrees. Don't think that at fifty, at least half of it will turn into steam, no—none of it will turn into steam. It will begin to turn into steam only at one hundred degrees.

And what is that one hundred degrees? For water, it is the same anywhere. You heat water anywhere, in any corner of the world, and it turns into steam at one hundred degrees. Whether it is water from a pond, a river, or a tap, or rainwater from the sky—no matter from where—the water does not insist that "I am from a well" or from a river, it just turns into steam at one hundred degrees.

With man, there is a difficulty because he has a personality, an individuality. Each individual turns into steam at individual temperatures—or, in other words, the one hundred degrees of every person is different. Man also turns into steam only at one hundred degrees, but every man's one hundred degrees is different. So it is difficult to tell you at what point you will turn into steam. One thing is certain: You can judge your own hundred-degree point. The criterion is that if you did not withhold yourself at all, then you are at one hundred degrees—if you stake yourself totally in your effort, if you are absolutely certain that you are not withholding yourself at all. And the other person has nothing to do with it—it is your own thing. Hence, others may or may not know about it, that is not the point. Only you have to know that you are not withholding yourself and that you are putting yourself totally into it. If you are putting yourself totally into it, you are at one hundred degrees. Then there is nothing to worry about.

This too is possible—your neighbor may be making more effort than you and yet may not reach his one hundred degrees. He may still be withholding something of himself. And it is also possible that someone else may be making less effort than you are and may be at one hundred degrees—he has put himself completely on the line. Hence, you are not to be concerned about others;

you be clear within yourself whether you are putting yourself at stake completely or not.

Meditation is a gamble. In all other gambling we put some thing at stake, and in meditation we put ourselves at stake. It certainly is an act for a gambler and not for a businessman, because a businessman's concern is that there be the least risk, even if the gains are small. A gambler's concern is that the gains be great even if there is a risk of losing everything. This is the difference between a gambler and a businessman.

Meditation is not at all an undertaking for a businessman. Meditation is absolutely for a gambler. He puts himself totally at stake, no matter what.

There is one difference: In outside gambling, perhaps, a gain rarely happens. I say "perhaps" because the illusion continues that it *will* happen— although it doesn't happen. It never happens. In outside gambling, even if there is a win, it is only the beginning of some bigger defeat. Even if there is a win, it is only a temptation for some bigger loss. Hence, a gambler never wins; no matter how may times he wins, he still isn't a winner because finally he only loses.

The inner gambling is just the opposite: Even a defeat is only a beginning for some win that is to come. A meditator never loses ultimately—he loses many times, but finally he wins. Don't think that a Mahavira or a Buddha wins the very first day, that a Mohammed or a Christ wins the very first day. No, nobody wins the first day. They lose badly! But finally, they win.

So, intense breathing for ten minutes, with your whole totality involved in it.

Then, after ten minutes of intense breathing, when the energy is awakened, it is to be thrown out—from whatever route it wants to go out. Your body may jump, leap, dance, weep, shout, make sounds, may appear to have gone completely insane; you are not to stop it. You are to give it a completely free rein and support it. If your body wants to go completely mad, let it.

Why? Because there are endless numbers of madnesses accumulated within us. You are to let it go mad completely. Completely mad means you don't carry any fear— "What am I doing? Me shouting? I'm a professor in the college and what is this I'm doing?" Or "I'm a doctor and I'm doing this jumping and hopping! What am I doing? What if some patient of mine sees me!"

A doctor remains in fear of his patient, a teacher remains in fear of his student, and a shopkeeper remains in fear of his customer. No matter who you are afraid of, to go mad means you drop each of those fears—no matter with whom the fear is concerned. The husband is in fear of the wife and the wife of the husband. The father is in fear of the son and the son of the father—whatever fears you may have, to go mad means, "Now I drop all fears." Fearlessly, you will have to let whatsoever wants to happen, happen.

We accumulate madnesses day by day. It is as if there is rubbish in the house and you go on hiding and piling it in a corner. This will make the whole house dirty! One day the house will start stinking. One day the situation will be such that except rubbish, there will be nothing else in the house. As we are now, this is what we do with ourselves. Whatsoever rubbish is in the mind, we go on accumulating it. Whether it is anger, whether it is dishonesty, or whether it is hatred—we go on piling up anything.

Slowly, slowly this accumulation becomes so big that our lives pass only in somehow managing it, lest it come out, lest it fall out, is exposed—lest someone sees it. We then become so afraid of it that we stop looking within ourselves completely. Because the fear has gotten so big, and there is so much rubbish. We fear it will be exposed.

Only those can enter meditation who are ready to throw out all this rubbish. As it is thrown out, everything becomes light in you. The second stage is that of catharsis, of throwing everything out so that a cleanliness descends within. Until you gather courage, you won't be able to throw the rubbish out. But once you are able to do that, you will be a totally different man. The second stage is that of completely going mad.

The third stage is that of making the sound "Hoo." One has to make this sound "Hoo" while continuously jumping up and down for ten minutes. The sound of "Hoo" is like a hammer—you have to hammer with it. In your body, there is energy that resides right near your sex center and which yoga calls kundalini—or one can give it any other name one wants to; scientists now call it bioelectricity. It is hidden there, and if a deep and strong sound of "Hoo" is made, that dormant energy, that sleeping energy gets activated. The analogy that the ancient sages have used for it is that of a snake sitting coiled up—and when the snake is hit upon, it rises with an open hood and its coil disappears. If a snake is sufficiently aroused, it stands almost on its tail. Exactly like that, this energy is lying dormant within us. If it is hit, it starts rising up.

But this hitting should be done only when you have had the opportunity to throw out your madness from within. Otherwise, if it rises in the middle of all your madness, you can *actually* go mad. Hence, many times seekers go mad. The reason for it is that they start arousing their kundalini without any deep cleaning. The reason for that madness is that they do not have a scientific attitude. It is necessary to do this cleansing first.

So the first two stages are for cleansing you deeply. The first stage is for arousing all the energies in you, the second stage is for throwing out all that stuff that is in conflict with the aroused energies. Then the third stage is for arousing the kundalini lying dormant below.

So, for ten minutes you have to use the sound "Hoo" with the utmost intensity. And then in the fourth stage you are to lie down like a corpse, as if you are not there at all—absolutely quiet. You are to leave your body completely relaxed, just as if you are dead. With closed eyes, you are to be in a waiting, quietly within. Much will happen. In that inner awaiting, much will happen.*

MY UNDERSTANDING IS THAT SOONER OR LATER, THIS MEDITATION that I am giving you is going to be a therapy of great significance, and it will become a way of treating the mentally ill and restoring them to health. And if it be possible that every child in school goes through this meditation, he will be saved from insanity for the whole of his life. He will never go mad; he will be immune from this disease because then he will be his own master, master of his body and mind.

WHEN A PERSON MEDITATES, HE LOSES ALL RESTLESSNESS. HIS THINKING stops, his body movements stop; he becomes like a marble statue . . . totally still, unmoving. In that moment he is a pool of energy. He is tremendously powerful. If you see somebody meditating, sit by his side and you will be benefited. Sitting

---

*Over time, Osho changed the fourth stage of Dynamic Meditation to be a sudden "STOP!" in place, rather than lying down, and added a five-minute stage of dancing and celebration at the end. Dynamic Meditation is meant to be done in the morning, and Osho designed a complementary Kundalini Meditation to be done in the evening. These two techniques, and a number of other active meditations Osho has developed, are accompanied by music composed to support each of the processes. All these, plus many more meditation methods, are described in detail in Osho's book, *Meditation: The First and Last Freedom* (St. Martin's Press).

by the side of someone who is in a meditative mood, you will move into meditation also. His energy will pull you out of your mess. Meditation is nothing but absolute rest.

How you bring that absolute rest depends on many things. There are a thousand and one methods to create that rest. My own methods are such that first I would like you to become as restless as possible, so nothing is hanging inside you; restlessness has been thrown out   then move into rest. And there will be no disturbance, it will be easier.

In Buddha's time, such dynamic methods were not needed. People were more simple, more authentic. They lived a more real life. Now people are living a very repressed life, a very unreal life. When they don't want to smile, they smile. When they want to be angry, they show compassion. People are false, the whole life pattern is false. The whole culture is like a great falsity. People are just acting, not living. Much is left hanging, many incomplete experiences go on being collected, piled up, inside their minds.

So just sitting directly in silence won't help. The moment you will sit silently, you will see all sorts of things moving inside you. You will feel it almost impossible to be silent. First throw those things out so you come to a natural state of rest. But real meditation starts only when you are in rest.

All the dynamic meditations are preparatory to real meditation. They are just basic requirements to be fulfilled so that the meditation can happen. Don't treat them as meditations; they are just introductory, just a preface. The real meditation starts only when all activity has ceased—activity of the body and activity of the mind.

MEDITATION IS NOT "MEDITATING UPON" SOMETHING BUT JUST BEING oneself—no movement away from the center, no movement at all . . . just being yourself so totally that there is not even a flickering. The inner flame remains unmoving. The other has disappeared; only you are. Not a single thought is there. The whole world has disappeared. The mind is no longer there; only you are, in your absolute purity.

THE THIRD PSYCHOLOGY:
THE PSYCHOLOGY
OF THE BUDDHAS

I n the commune I had hundreds of different therapeutic schools working, but I was working to destroy every therapy. The therapists were working to destroy your problems, and I was trying to destroy therapies and the therapists!—because a therapy can be only a temporary relief, and the therapist can be only a very superficial help.

SIGMUND FREUD INTRODUCED PSYCHOANALYSIS INTO THE WORLD. IT is rooted in analyzing the mind. It is confined to the mind. It does not step out of the mind, not even an inch. On the contrary, it goes deeper into the mind, into the hidden layers of the mind, into the unconscious, to find out ways and means so that the mind of man can at least be normal.

The goal of Freudian psychoanalysis is not very great. The goal is to keep people normal. But normality is not enough. Just to be normal is not of any significance; it means the normal routine of life and your capacity to cope with it. It does not give you meaning, it does not give you significance. It does not give you insight into the reality of things. It does not take you beyond time, beyond death. It is at the most a helpful device for those who have gone so abnormal that they have become incapable of coping with daily life—they cannot live with people, they cannot work, they have become shattered. Psychotherapy provides them a certain togetherness—not integrity, mind you, but only a certain togetherness. It binds them into a bundle. They remain still fragmentary; nothing becomes crystallized in them, no soul is born. They don't become blissful, they are only less unhappy, less miserable.

Psychology helps them to accept the misery. It helps them to accept that this is all that life can give to you, so don't ask for more. In a way, it is dangerous to their inner growth—because the inner growth happens only when there is a divine discontent. When you are absolutely unsatisfied with things as they are, only then do you go in search; only then do you start rising higher, only then do you make efforts to pull yourself out of the mud.

Jung went a little farther into the unconscious; he went into the collective unconscious. This is getting more and more into muddy water, and this is not going to help. Assagioli moved to the other extreme. Seeing the failure of psychoanalysis he invented psychosynthesis. But it is rooted in the same idea. Instead of analysis he emphasizes synthesis.

The psychology of the buddhas is neither analysis nor synthesis; it is transcendence, it is going beyond the mind. It is not work *within* the mind, it is work that takes you *outside* the mind. That's exactly the meaning of the English word *ecstasy*—to stand out.

When you are capable of standing out of your own mind, when you are capable of creating a distance between your mind and your being, then you have taken the first step of the psychology of the buddhas. And a miracle happens: When you are standing out of the mind, all the problems of the mind disappear because mind itself disappears; it loses its grip over you.

Psychoanalysis is like pruning leaves of the tree, but new leaves will be coming up. It is not cutting off the roots. And psychosynthesis is sticking the fallen leaves back onto the tree again—gluing them back to the tree. That is not going to give them life either. They will look simply ugly; they will not be alive, they will not be green, they will not be part of the tree but glued somehow.

The psychology of the buddhas cuts the very roots of the tree, which create all kinds of neuroses, psychoses, which create the fragmentary man, the mechanical man, the robotlike man.

Psychoanalysis takes years, and still the man remains the same. It is renovating the old structure, patching up here and there, whitewashing the old house. But it is the same house, nothing has radically changed. It has not transformed the consciousness of the man.

The psychology of the buddhas does not work within the mind. It has no interest in analyzing or synthesizing. It simply helps you to get out of the mind so that you can have a look from the outside. And that very look is a transformation. The moment you can look at your mind as an object you become detached from it, you become disidentified from it; a distance is created, and roots are cut.

How are roots cut in this way?—because it is you who goes on feeding the mind. If you are identified you feed the mind; if you are not identified you stop feeding it. It drops dead on its own accord.

There is a beautiful story. I love it very much. . . .

One day Buddha is passing through a forest. It is a hot summer day and he is feeling very thirsty. He says to Ananda, his chief disciple, "Ananda, you go back. Just three or four miles back, we passed a small stream of water. You bring a little water—take my begging bowl. I am feeling very thirsty and tired." He had become old.

Ananda goes back, but by the time he reaches the stream, a few bullock carts have passed through the stream and they have made the whole stream muddy. Dead leaves, which had settled into the bed, have risen up; it is no longer possible to drink this water—it is too dirty. He comes back empty-handed, and he says, "You will have to wait a little. I will go ahead. I have heard that just two, three miles ahead there is a big river. I will bring water from there."

But Buddha insists. He says, "You go back and bring water from the same stream."

Ananda could not understand the insistence, but if the master says so, the disciple has to follow. Seeing the absurdity of it—that again he will have to walk three, four miles, and he knows that water is not worth drinking—he goes. As he is leaving, Buddha says, "And don't come back if the water is still dirty. If it is dirty, you simply sit on the bank silently. Don't do anything, don't get into the stream. Sit on the bank silently and watch. Sooner or later the water will be clear again, and then you fill the bowl and come back."

Ananda goes there. Buddha is right: The water is almost clear, the leaves have moved, the dust has settled. But it is not absolutely clear yet, so he sits on the bank just watching the river flow by. Slowly, slowly, it becomes crystal clear. Then he comes back dancing. Then he understands why Buddha was so insistent. There was a certain message in it for him, and he understood the message. He gave the water to Buddha, and he thanked Buddha, touched his feet.

Buddha says, "What are you doing? I should thank you that you have brought water for me."

Ananda says, "Now I can understand. First I was angry; I didn't show it, but I was angry because it was absurd to go back. But now I understand the message. This is what I actually needed in this moment. The same is the case with my mind—sitting on the bank of that small stream, I became aware that the same is the case with my mind. If I jump into the stream I will make it dirty again. If I jump into the mind more noise is created, more problems start coming up, surfacing. Sitting by the side I learned the technique.

"Now I will be sitting by the side of my mind too, watching it with all its dirtiness and problems and old leaves and hurts and wounds, memories, desires. Unconcerned I will sit on the bank and wait for the moment when everything is clear."

And it happens on its own accord, because the moment you sit on the bank of your mind you are no longer giving energy to it. This is real meditation. Meditation is the art of transcendence.

Freud talks about analysis, Assagioli about synthesis. Buddhas have always talked about meditation, awareness.

Meditation, awareness, watchfulness, witnessing—that is the uniqueness of the third psychology. No psychoanalyst is needed. You can do it on your own—in fact, you *have to* do it on your own. No guidelines are needed, it is such a simple process—simple if you do it. If you don't do it, it looks very complicated. Even the word *meditation* scares many people. They think it something very difficult, arduous. Yes, if you don't do it, it is difficult and arduous. It is like swimming. It is very difficult if you don't know how to swim. But if you know, you know it is so simple a process. Nothing can be more simple than swimming. It is not an art at all; it is so spontaneous and so natural.

Be more aware of your mind. And in being aware of your mind you will become aware of the fact that you are not the mind, and that is the beginning of the revolution. You have started flowing higher and higher. You are no longer tethered to the mind. Mind functions like a rock and keeps you down. It keeps you within the field of gravitation. The moment you are no longer attached to the mind, you enter the buddhafield. When gravitation loses its power over you, you enter into the buddhafield. Entering the buddhafield means entering into the world of levitation. You start floating upward. Mind goes on dragging you downward.

So it is not a question of analyzing or synthesizing. It is simply a question of becoming aware. That's why in the East we have not developed any psychotherapy like Freudian or Jungian or Adlerian—and there are so many in the market now. We have not developed a single psychotherapy because we know psychotherapies can't heal. They may help you to accept your wounds, but they can't heal. Healing comes when you are no longer attached to the mind. When you are disconnected from the mind, unidentified, absolutely untethered, when the bondage is finished, then healing happens.

Transcendence is true therapy, and it is not only psychotherapy. It is not only a phenomenon limited to your psychology, it is far more than that. It is spiritual. It heals you in your very being. Mind is only your circumference, not your center.

THERE ARE TWO TYPES OF GROWTH METHODS. YOU CAN PURSUE YOUR spiritual growth alone, or you can work through a group, through a school. Both types have always existed in the East. Sufi methods are group methods. In India also, group methods have existed, but they were never so prevalent as in Sufism.

But the West is totally group-oriented. Never before have there been so many group methods, and so many people working through them, as exist now in the West. So in a way we can say that the East has emphasized individual efforts and remained with them, and the West has moved more toward group methods. Why is this so, and what is the difference? And why this difference?

Group methods can exist only if your ego has come to a point where it is a burden to carry it. When the ego has become so burdensome that to be alone is to be in anguish, then group methods become meaningful—because in a group you can dissolve your ego.

If the ego is not very evolved, then individual methods can help you. You can move to a mountain, you can be isolated, or even living in an ashram with a master you can work alone: you do your meditation, others do their meditation. You never work together.

In India, Hindus have never prayed in groups. It was only with Mohammedans that group prayer entered India. Mohammedans pray in groups. Hindus were always praying alone; even if they went to the temple, they would go alone. It is a one-to-one relationship—you and your God.

This is possible if the ego has not been helped to grow to a point where it becomes a burden. In India, it has never been helped to grow—from the very beginning we have been against the ego. So you grow in ego but the ego remains vague, blurred; you remain humble, you are not really an egoist. It is not a peak in you, it is flat ground. You are egoistic, because everybody has to be, but not absolute egoists. You always think it is wrong, and you go on pulling yourself down. In certain situations you can be provoked and your ego becomes a peak—but ordinarily it is not a peak, it is flat ground.

In India, the ego is just like anger—if someone provokes you, you become angry; if nobody provokes you, you are not angry. In the West, the ego has become a permanent fixture. It is not like anger, it is now like breathing. There is no need to provoke it—it is there, it is a constant phenomenon.

Because of this ego, a group becomes a very helpful thing. In the group, working with a group, merging yourself into the group, you can put your ego aside easily. That's why not only in spirituality but in politics also, a few phenomena can exist only in the West: fascism could exist, for example, could become possible in Germany, which is the most egoistic country in the West. There is nothing compared to the German ego anywhere else in the world. That's why Hitler could become possible; because everyone is so egoistic, everybody is in need of merging.

Nazi rallies, millions of people marching—you can lose yourself, you yourself need not be there. You become the march, the band playing, the music, the sound, the hypnotic Hitler, a charismatic personality. Everybody looking at Hitler, the whole mass around you like an ocean, you become just a wave. You feel good, you feel fresh, you feel young, you feel happy. You forget your misery, your anguish, your loneliness, your alienation. You are not alone. Such a great mass is with you and you are with it. Your individual, private worries drop. Suddenly there is an opening—you feel light, as if you are flying.

Hitler became successful not because he had a very meaningful philosophy— his philosophy was absurd; it was childish, immature. Not because he could convince the German people that he was right—that was not the point. It is very difficult to convince German people, one of the most difficult things, because they are logicians. They have logic in their minds, rational in every way. It is difficult to convince them, and to have been convinced by Hitler would have been impossible. No, he never tried to convince them. He created a hypnotic group phenomenon. *That* convinced them.

It was not a question of what Hitler was saying; it was a question of what they were feeling when they were in the group, in the mass. It was such an unburdening experience that it was worth it to follow this man. Whatsoever he was saying—wrong or right, logical, illogical, foolish—it felt good to follow him. They were so bored with themselves, they wanted to be absorbed by the mass. That's why fascism, Nazism, and all types of group madness became possible in the West.

In the East only Japan could follow, because Japan is the counterpart of Germany in the East. Japan is the most Western country in the East. The same phenomenon existed there, so Japan could become an ally to the Hitler madness.

The same is happening in other fields also—in religion also, in psychology also. Group meditation is happening, and only group meditation will happen for a long period to come. When a hundred people are together—you will be surprised, particularly those who don't know the Western mind will be surprised—just holding hands, one hundred people sitting, just holding hands, feeling each other, and they feel elated.

No Indian will feel elated. He will say, "What nonsense! Just holding hands with a hundred people sitting in a circle, how can it be elation? How can you become ecstatic? You can feel at the most the perspiration of the other's hand."

But in the West a hundred people holding hands are elated, ecstatic. Why? Because even holding hands has become so impossible because of the ego. Even wife and husband are not together. The joint family has disappeared, it was a group phenomenon. Society has disappeared. In the West now, no society exists really. You move alone.

In America—I was reading the statistics—everybody moves within three years to another town. Now, a man in a village in India remains there—not only he, his family has remained there for hundreds of years. He is deeply rooted in that soil. He is related to everyone, he knows everybody, everybody knows him. He is not a stranger, he is not alone. He lives as part of the village, he always has. He was born there, he will die there.

In America, every three years, on average, people move. This is the most nomadic civilization that has ever existed, vagabonds—no house, no family, no town, no village, no home, really. In three years how can you get rooted? Wherever you go, you are a stranger. The mass is around you but you are not related to it. You are unrelated, the whole burden becomes individual.

Sitting in a group, in an encounter group or in a growth group, touching each other's bodies, you become part of the community. Touching each other's hands and holding each other, just lying near each other, or lying on top of each other in a pile, you feel oneness—a religious elation happens! A hundred people dancing, touching each other, moving around each other, become one. They merge, the ego is dissolved for a few moments. That merger becomes a prayerful thing.

Politicians can use it for destructive ends. Spirituality can use it very creatively—it can become a meditation.

In the East, people are in the community too much. So whenever they want to be in a spiritual space, they want to go to the Himalayas. Society is too much around. They are not fed up with themselves, they are fed up with the society! This is the difference.

In the West, you are fed up with yourself and you want some bridge, how to be communicative with the society, with others; how to create a bridge, how to move to the other so you can forget yourself. In the East, people are fed up with the society. They have lived with it so long, and the society is all around so much, that they don't feel any freedom. So whenever somebody wants to be free, to be silent, he runs to the Himalayas.

In the West, you run to the society; in the East, people run from the society. That's why individual methods have existed in the East; group methods exist in the West.

What am I doing? My method is a synthesis. In the first steps of Dynamic Meditation you are part of the group; in the last part the group disappears, you are alone. I am doing this for a particular reason, because now East and West have become irrelevant. The East is turning toward the West; the West is turning toward the East. Soon there will be no East and no West—one world.

This geographical division has existed too long; it cannot exist anymore. Technology has already dissolved it, it is already gone, but because of a habitual attitude in the mind, it continues. It continues only as a mental phenomenon, it actually exists no longer. Soon there will be no East, no West—just one world. It is already there. Those who can see, can see it is already there.

A synthesis will be needed—group and individual both. You work in a group in the beginning; in the end, you become totally yourself. Start from society and reach to yourself. Don't escape from the community—live in the world but don't be of it. Be related, but still remain alone. Love and meditate; meditate and love—but don't choose. Love plus meditation is my approach.

THE ANCIENT METHODS OF MEDITATION WERE ALL DEVELOPED IN THE East. They never considered the Western man; the Western man was excluded. I am creating techniques that are not only for the Eastern man, which are simply for every man—Eastern or Western. There is a difference between the Eastern tradition and the Western tradition—and it is the tradition that creates the mind. For example, the Eastern mind is very patient—thousands of years of teaching to remain patient, whatever the conditions may be. The Western mind is very impatient. The same methods of technique cannot be applicable to both.

The Eastern mind has been conditioned to keep a certain equilibrium in success or in failure, in richness or in poverty, in sickness or in health, in life or in death. The Western mind has no idea of such equilibrium; it gets too disturbed. With success it gets disturbed; it starts feeling at the top of the world, starts feeling a certain superiority complex. In failure it goes to the other extreme; it falls into the seventh hell. It is miserable, in deep anguish, and it feels a tremendous inferiority complex. It is torn apart.

And life consists of both. There are moments that are beautiful, and there are moments that are ugly. There are moments when you are in love, there are moments when you are in anger, in hatred. The Western mind simply goes with the situation. It is always in turmoil. The Eastern mind has learned . . . it is a conditioning, it is not a revolution, it is only a training, a discipline, it is a practice. Underneath it is the same, but a thick conditioning makes it keep a certain balance.

The Eastern mind is very slow because there is no point in being speedy; life takes its own course and everything is determined by fate, so what you get, you don't get by your speed, your hurry. What you get, you get because it is already destined. So there is no question of being in a hurry. Whenever something is going to happen, it is going to happen—neither one second before nor one second after it.

This has created a very slow flow in the East. It seems almost as if the river is not flowing; it is so slow that you cannot detect the flow. Moreover, the Eastern conditioning is that you have already lived millions of lives, and there are millions ahead to be lived, so the life span is not only seventy years; the life span is vast and enormous. There is no hurry; there is so much time available: Why should you be in a hurry? If it does not happen in this life, it may happen in some other life.

The Western mind is very speedy, fast, because the conditioning is for only one life—seventy years—and so much to do. One third of your life goes into sleep, one third of your life goes into education, training—what is left?

Much of it goes into earning your livelihood. If you count everything, you will be surprised: out of seventy years you cannot even have seven years left for something that you want to do. Naturally there is hurry, a mad rush, so mad that one forgets where one is going. All that you remember is whether you are going with speed or not. The means becomes the end.

In the same way, in different directions . . . the Eastern mind has cultivated itself differently from the Western mind. Those one hundred and twelve methods of meditation developed in the East have never taken account of the Western man; they were not developed for the Western man. The Western man was not yet available. The time that *Vigyan Bhairva Tantra* was written—in which those one hundred and twelve techniques have come to perfection—is nearabout five thousand years before us.

At that time there was no Western man, no Western society, no Western culture. The West was still barbarous, primitive, not worth taking into account. The East was the whole world, at the pinnacle of its growth, richness, civilization.

My methods of meditation have been developed out of an absolute necessity. I want the distinction between the West and the East to be dissolved.

After Shiva's *Vigyan Bhairva Tantra*, in these five thousand years, nobody has developed a single method. But I have been watching the differences between East and West: the same method cannot be applied immediately to both. First, the Eastern and the Western mind have to be brought into a similar state. Those techniques of Dynamic Meditation, Kundalini Meditation, and others, are all cathartic; their basis is catharsis.

You have to throw out all the junk that your mind is full of. Unless you are unloaded you cannot sit silently. It is just as if you tell a child to sit silently in the corner of the room. It is very difficult, he is so full of energy. You are repressing a volcano! The best way is, first tell him, "Go run outside around the house ten times; then come and sit down in the corner."

Then it is possible, you have made it possible. He himself wants to sit down now, to relax. He is tired, he is exhausted; now, sitting there, he is not repressing his energy, he has expressed his energy by running around the house ten times. Now he is more at ease.

The cathartic methods are simply to throw all your impatience, your speediness, your hurry, your repressions.

One more factor has to be remembered, that these are absolutely necessary for the Western man before he can do something like *vipassana*—just sitting silently doing nothing and the grass grows by itself. But you have to be sitting silently, doing nothing—that is a basic condition for the grass to grow by itself. If you cannot sit silently doing nothing, you are going to disturb the grass.

I have always loved gardens, and wherever I have lived I have created beautiful gardens, lawns. I used to talk to people sitting on my lawn, and I became aware that they were all pulling the grass out . . . just hectic energy. If they had nothing to do they would simply pull the grass. I had to tell them, "If you go on doing this, then you will have to sit inside the room. I cannot allow you to destroy my lawn."

They would stop themselves for a while, and as they started listening to me, again unconsciously, their hands would start pulling at the grass. So sitting silently doing nothing is not really just sitting silently and doing nothing. It is doing a big favor to the grass! Unless you are not doing anything, the grass cannot grow; you will stop it, you will pull it out, you will disturb it.

So these methods are absolutely necessary for the Western mind. But a new factor has also entered: they have become necessary for the Eastern mind too. The mind for which Shiva wrote those one hundred and twelve methods of meditation no longer exists—even in the East now. The Western influence has been tremendous. Things have changed. In Shiva's time there was no Western civilization. The East was at its peak of glory; it was called "a golden bird." It had all the luxuries and comforts: It was really affluent.

Now the situation is reversed: The East has been in slavery for two thousand years, exploited by almost everyone in the world, invaded by a dozen countries, continuously looted, raped, burned. It is now a beggar.

And three hundred years of British rule in India have destroyed India's own educational system—which was a totally different thing. They forced the Eastern mind to be educated according to Western standards. They have almost turned the Eastern intelligentsia into a second-rate Western intelligentsia. They have given their disease of speediness, of hurry, of impatience, of continuous anguish, anxiety, to the East.

If you see the temples of Khajuraho or the temples of Konarak, you can see the East in its true colors.

Just in Khajuraho there were one hundred temples; only thirty have survived, seventy have been destroyed by Mohammedans. Thousands of temples of tremendous beauty and sculpture have been destroyed by Mohammedans. These thirty survived; it was just coincidence, because they were part of a forest. Perhaps the invaders forgot about them.

But the British influence on the Indian mind was so great, that even a man like Mahatma Gandhi wanted these thirty temples to be covered with mud so nobody could see them. Just to think of the people who had created those hundred temples . . . each temple must have taken centuries to build. They are so delicate in structure, so proportionate and so beautiful, that there exists nothing parallel to them on the earth.

And you can imagine that temples don't exist alone; if there were a hundred temples, there must have been a city of thousands of people; otherwise a hundred temples are meaningless. Where are those people? With the temples those people have been massacred.

And those temples I take as an example, because their sculpture will look pornographic to the Western mind; to Mahatma Gandhi it also looked pornographic.

India owes so much to Rabindranath Tagore. He was the man who prevented Mahatma Gandhi and other politicians who were ready to cover the temples, to hide them from people's eyes. Rabindranath Tagore said, "This is absolutely stupid. They are not pornographic, they are utterly beautiful."

There is a very delicate line between pornography and beauty. A naked woman is not necessarily pornographic; a naked man is not necessarily pornographic. A beautiful man, a beautiful woman, naked, can be examples of beauty, of health, of proportion. They are the most glorious products of nature. If a deer can be naked and beautiful—and nobody thinks the deer is pornographic—then why should it be that a naked man or woman cannot be just seen as beautiful?

There were ladies in the times of Victoria in England who covered the legs of the chairs with cloth because legs should not be left naked—chairs' legs! But because they are called legs, it was thought uncivilized, uncultured, to leave them naked. There was a movement in Victoria's time that the people who take their dogs for a walk should cover them with cloth. They should not be naked . . . as if nakedness itself is pornographic. It is the pornographic mind.

I have been to Khajuraho hundreds of times, and I have not seen a single sculpture as pornographic. A naked picture or a naked statue becomes pornography if it provokes your sexuality. That's the only criterion: if it provokes your sexuality, if it is an incentive to your sexual instinct. But that is not the case with Khajuraho. In fact the temples were made for just the opposite purpose.

They were made to meditate on man and woman making love. And the stones have come alive. The people who have made them must have been the greatest artists the world has known. They were made to meditate upon, they were objects for meditation.

It is a temple, and meditators were sitting around just looking at the sculptures, and watching within themselves whether there was any sexual desire arising. This was the criterion: when they found there was no sexual desire arising, it was a certificate for them to enter the temples. All these sculptures are outside the temple, on the walls outside; inside there are no nudist statues.

But this was necessary for people to meditate, and then they were clear that there was no desire; on the contrary those statues had made their ordinary desire for sex subside. Then they were capable of entering into the temple; otherwise they should not enter the temple. That would be a profanity—having such a desire inside and entering the temple. It would be making the temple dirty—you would be insulting the temple.

The people who created these temples created a tremendous, voluminous literature also. The East never used to be repressive of sexuality. Before Buddha and Mahavira the East was never repressive of sexuality. It was with Buddha and Mahavira that for the first time celibacy became spiritual. Otherwise, before Buddha and Mahavira, all the seers of the Upanishads, of the Vedas, were married people; they were not celibate, they had children.

And they were not people who had renounced the world; they had all the luxuries and all the comforts. They lived in the forests, but they had everything presented to them by their students, by the kings, by their lovers. And their ashrams, their schools, their academies in the forest were very affluent.

With Buddha and Mahavira the East began a sick tradition of celibacy, of repression. And when Christianity came into India, there came a very strong trend of repressiveness. These three hundred years of Christianity have made the Eastern mind almost as repressive as the Western mind. So now my methods are applicable to both. I call them preliminary methods. They are to destroy everything that can prevent you from going into a silent meditation. Once Dynamic Meditation or Kundalini Meditation succeeds, you are clean. You have erased repressiveness. You have erased the speediness, the hurry, the impatience. Now it is possible for you to enter the temple.

It is for this reason that I spoke about the acceptance of sex, because without the acceptance of sex, you cannot get rid of repression. And I want you to be completely clean, natural. I want you to be in a state where those one hundred and twelve methods can be applicable to you.

This is my reason for devising these methods—these are simply cleansing methods.

I have also included the Western therapeutic methods because the Western mind, and under its influence the Eastern mind, both have become sick. It is a rare phenomenon today to find a healthy mind. Everybody is feeling a certain kind of nausea, a mental nausea, a certain emptiness, which is like a wound hurting. Everybody is having his life turned into a nightmare. Everybody is worried, too much afraid of death; not only afraid of death but also afraid of life.

People are living halfheartedly, people are living in a lukewarm way: not intensely like Zorba the Greek, not with a healthy flavor but with a sick mind. One has to live, so they are living. One has to love, so they are loving. One has to do this, to be like this, so they are following; otherwise there is no incentive coming from their own being.

They are not overflowing with energy. They are not risking anything to live totally. They are not adventurous—and without being adventurous, one is not healthy. Adventure is the criterion, inquiry into the unknown is the criterion. People are not young, from childhood they simply become old. Youth never happens.

The Western therapeutic methods cannot help you to grow spiritually, but they can prepare the ground. They cannot sow the seeds of flowers but they can prepare the ground—which is a necessity. This was one reason why I included therapies.

There is also another reason: I want a meeting of East and West.

The East has developed meditative methods; the West has not developed meditative methods, the West has developed psychotherapies. If we want the Western mind to be interested in meditation methods, if you want the Eastern mind to come closer to the Western, then there has to be something of give and take. It should not be just Eastern—something from the Western evolution should be included. And I find those therapies are immensely helpful. They can't go far, but as far as they go, it is good. Where they stop, meditations can take over.

But the Western mind should feel that something of its own development has been included in the meeting, in the merger; it should not be one-sided. And they are significant; they cannot harm, they can only help.

And I have used them with tremendous success. They have helped people to cleanse their beings, prepared them to be ready to enter into the temple of meditation. My effort is to dissolve the separation between East and West. The earth should be one, not only politically but spiritually too.

And some people think that this is a clever way of brainwashing. It is something more: It is mindwashing, not brainwashing. Brainwashing is very superficial. The brain is the mechanism that the mind uses. You can wash the brain very easily—just any mechanism can be washed and cleaned and lubricated. But if the mind that is behind the brain is polluted, is dirty, is full of repressed desires, is full of ugliness, soon the brain will be full of all those ugly things.

And I don't see that there is anything wrong in it—washing is always good. I believe in dry cleaning. I don't use old methods of washing.

And yes, people will feel cheated that their mind has been taken away, and that was the only precious thing they had. This will be only in the beginning. Once the mind is taken away, they will be surprised that behind the mind is their real treasure. And the mind was only a mirror, it was reflecting the treasure, but it had no treasure in itself. The treasure is behind the mind—that is your being.

But a mirror can deceive you. It can give you the idea that what is reflected in it is a reality. So unless the mind is taken away—and that's what meditation is, it is a state of no-mind. It is taking away the mind and giving you a chance to see not the reflection of the treasure of your being, but the treasure itself.

ZORBA THE BUDDHA:
THE WHOLE
HUMAN BEING

Take life very playfully—then you can have both the worlds together. You can have the cake and eat it too. And that is a real art! This world and that, sound and silence, love and meditation, being with people, relating, and being alone. All these things have to be lived together in a kind of simultaneity; only then will you know the uttermost depth of your being and the uttermost height of your being.

A lawyer made his way to the edge of the excavation where a gang was working and called the name of Timothy O'Toole.

"Who is wanting me?" inquired a heavy voice.

"Mr. O'Toole," the lawyer asked, "did you come from Castlebar, County Mayo?"

"I did that."

"And your mother was named Bridget and your father Michael?"

"They was."

"It is my duty then," said the lawyer, "to inform you, Mr. O'Toole, that your Aunt Mary has died in Iowa, leaving you an estate of $200,000."

There was a short silence below and then a lively commotion.

"Are you coming, Mr. O'Toole?" the lawyer called down.

"In one minute," was bellowed in answer. "I have just stopped to flatten the foreman."

It required just six months of extremely riotous living for O'Toole to expend all of the $200,000. His chief endeavor was to satisfy a huge inherited thirst. Then he went back to his job. And there, presently the lawyer sought him out again.

"It is your Uncle Patrick this time, Mr. O'Toole," the lawyer explained. "He has died in Texas and left you $400,000."

O'Toole leaned heavily on his pick and shook his head in great weariness.

"I don't think I can take it," he declared. "I am not as strong as I once was, and I misdoubt me that I could go through all that money and live."

That's what has happened in the West. Man in the West has succeeded in attaining to all the affluence that the whole of humanity has been longing for down the ages. The West has succeeded materially in becoming rich, and now it is too weary, too tired. The journey has taken all its soul. The journey has finished the Western man. Outwardly all is available, but the contact with the inner is lost. Now everything that man needs is available, but the man himself is no longer there. Possessions are there, but the master has disappeared; a great imbalance has happened. Richness is there but man is not feeling rich at all; man is feeling, on the contrary, impoverished, very poor.

Think of this paradox: When you are outwardly rich only then do you become aware of your inner poverty, in contrast. When you are outwardly poor you never become aware of your inner poverty because there is no contrast. You write with white chalk on blackboards, not on white boards. Why? Because only on blackboards will it show. The contrast is needed.

When you are outwardly rich, then suddenly a great awareness happens that "Inwardly I am poor, a beggar." And now a hopelessness comes as a shadow: "All is attained that we had thought about—all imagination and fantasies fulfilled—and nothing has happened out of it, no contentment, no bliss."

The West is bewildered. Out of this bewilderment a great desire is arising: how to have contact with one's self again.

Meditation is nothing but getting your roots again into your inner world, into your interiority. Hence the West is becoming very much interested in meditation and very much interested in the Eastern treasures.

The East was also interested in meditation when the East was rich; this has to be understood. That's why I am not against riches and I don't think that poverty has any spirituality in it. I am utterly against poverty because whenever a country becomes poor it loses contact with all meditations, all spiritual efforts. Whenever a country becomes poor outwardly, it becomes unaware of the inner poverty.

That's why on Indian faces you can see a kind of contentment that is not found in the West. It is not real contentment; it is just unawareness of the inner poverty. Indians think, "Look at the anxiety, anguish, and the tension on the Western faces. Although we are poor, we are inwardly very content." That is utter nonsense, they are not contented. I have been watching thousands of people—they are not contented. But one thing is certainly true, that they are not aware of the discontent because to be aware of the discontent, outer richness is needed. Without outer richness nobody becomes aware of their inner discontent—and there are enough proofs for it.

All the avatars of the Hindus were kings or sons of kings. All the Jaina tirthankaras, the Jaina masters, were kings; and so was Buddha. All the three great traditions of India give ample proof.

Why did Buddha become discontented, why did he start a search for meditation? Because he was rich. He lived in affluence; he lived with all the comforts, all the material gadgets. Suddenly he became aware. And he was not very old when it happened; he was only twenty-nine when he became aware that there is a dark hole inside. Light is outside; hence it shows your inner darkness. Just a little dirt on a white shirt, and it shows. That's what happened. He escaped from the palace.

That's what happened to Mahavira; he also escaped from a palace. It was not happening to a beggar. There were beggars also in Buddha's time. In fact, the story is that Buddha renounced the world when he saw a beggar for the first time, and an old man, and a dead body, and a sannyasin. Beggars were there.

Buddha was going to participate in a youth festival, he was to inaugurate it. From his golden chariot, he saw a beggar—for the first time, because his father had managed his whole life that Buddha should never see a beggar, or an ill man, or an old man, or a dead man. Because astrologers had told the father when Buddha was born, "If he ever sees these things he will immediately renounce the world, so don't allow him to see them." So wherever Buddha would go, beggars would be removed. Old people would be removed or forced to remain in their houses, not to come out. Even in Buddha's garden no dead leaf was allowed. Every dead leaf was removed during the night, so in the morning when Buddha would go to the garden he could only see youth, young leaves, young flowers. He had never seen a flower withering.

When he saw a beggar for the first time . . . And the parable is beautiful; it says the gods became worried: "The father is succeeding too much. Twenty-nine years have passed and Buddha has the capacity to become one of the most awakened persons in the world." The gods became worried: "The management of the father is such that he may never come across a beggar or an old man; he may miss." So they pretended—one god walked like a beggar, another like an old man, another became like a dead man, another like a sannyasin.

So in Buddha's time, beggars were there—but they didn't renounce. They had nothing to renounce; they were contented. Buddha became discontented.

When India was rich, many more people were interested in meditation; in fact, all the people were interested in meditation. Sooner or later they were bound to start thinking of the moon, of the beyond, of the inner. Now the country is poor, so poor that there is no contrast of the inner and the outer. The inner is poor, the outer is poor. The inner and the outer are in perfect harmony—both are poor! That's why you see a kind of contentment on Indian faces, that is not true contentment. And because of this, people have become accustomed to thinking that poverty has something spiritual in it.

Poverty is worshiped in India. That is one of the reasons why I am condemned continually, because I am not in favor of any kind of poverty. Poverty is not spirituality, poverty is the cause of the disappearance of spirituality.

I would like the whole world to become as affluent as possible. The more people are affluent, the more they will become spiritual. They will have to, they will not be able to avoid it. And only then does real contentment arise.

When you can create inner richness, and the moment comes when again a harmony happens—outer richness meeting inner richness—then there is real contentment. When outer poverty meets inner poverty, then there is false contentment. Harmony is possible in these two ways. The outer and inner in harmony, and one feels contented. India looks contented because there is poverty on both sides of the fence. There is perfect harmony, the outer and inner are in tune; but this is ugly contentment, this is really lack of life, lack of vitality. This is a stupid kind of contentment, dull, insipid.

The West is bound to become interested in meditation, there is no way to avoid it. That's why Christianity is losing its hold on the Western mind, because Christianity has not developed the science of meditation in any way. It has remained a very mediocre religion; so is Judaism.

The West was poor when these religions were born, that is the reason. Up to now the West has lived in poverty. When the East was rich, the West was poor. Judaism, Christianity, and Mohammedanism—all the three non-Indian religions, were born in poverty. They could not develop meditation techniques, there was no need. They have remained the religions of the poor.

Now the West has become rich and there is a disparity.

The Western religions were born in poverty; they have nothing to give to the rich man. For the rich man they look childish, they don't satisfy. They *cannot* satisfy. The Eastern religions were born in richness; that's why the Western mind is becoming more and more interested in Eastern religions. Yes, the religion of Buddha is having great impact; Zen is spreading like wildfire. Why? It was born out of richness.

There is a tremendous similarity between the Western psychology of the contemporary man and the psychology of Buddhism. The West is in the same state as Buddha was when he became interested in meditation. It was a rich man's search. And so is the case with Hinduism, so is the case with Jainism. These three great Indian religions were born out of affluence; hence the West is bound to be attracted to these Eastern religions.

The East is losing contact with its own religions. India cannot afford to understand Buddha—it is a poor country. In fact, poor Indians are being converted to Christianity. Rich Americans are being converted to Buddhism, Hinduism, Vedanta—and the untouchables, the poorest of the poor in India, are becoming Christians. Do you see the point? These religions have a certain appeal for the poor. But they don't have any future, because sooner or later the whole world is going to become rich.

I don't praise poverty, I have no respect for poverty. Man has to be given both kinds of richness. Why not both? Science has developed the technology to make you outwardly rich. Religion has developed the technology to make you inwardly rich: that is Yoga, Tantra, Taoism, Sufism, Hassidism—these are the technologies of the inner.

A story:

The central figure of this story is one of those persons who accepts everything that happens as manifestation of a divine power.

Not for him, he said, to question the workings of a divine providence.

All his life misfortune had been his, yet never once did he complain. He married, and his wife ran away with the hired man. He had a daughter, and the daughter was deceived by a villian. He had a son, and the son was lynched. A fire burned down his barn, a cyclone blew away his home, a hailstorm destroyed his crops, and the banker foreclosed on his mortgage, taking his farm. Yet at each stroke of misfortune he knelt and gave thanks to "God Almighty for his interminable mercy."

After a time, penniless but still submissive to the decrees from on high, he landed in the country poorhouse. One day the overseer sent him out to plow a potato field. A thunderstorm came up but was passing over when, without warning, a bolt of lightning descended from the sky. It melted the plowshare, stripped most of his clothing from him, singed off his beard, branded his naked back with the initials of a neighboring cowman, and hurled him through a barbed-wire fence.

When he recovered consciousness he got slowly to his knees, clasped his hands and raised his eyes toward heaven. Then, for the first time, he asserted himself:

"Lord," he said, "this is getting to be plumb ridiculous!"

This is the situation of the East: "This is getting to be plumb ridiculous!" But the East goes on thanking God, goes on feeling grateful. There is nothing to feel grateful for anymore! The East is utterly poor, ill, starved; there is nothing to be grateful for. But the East has forgotten how to assert, the East has forgotten how to do anything about its condition.

So the East cannot meditate. The East is living almost in a kind of unconsciousness. It is too hungry to meditate, too poor to pray. Its only interest is in bread, shelter, clothing; so when the Christian missionary comes and opens a hospital or opens a school, the Indians are very much impressed—this is spirituality. When I start teaching about meditation they are not interested—not only not interested, they are against it: "What kind of spirituality is this?" And I understand—they need bread, they need shelter, they need clothes. But it is because of their mind that they are suffering. On the one hand they need bread, shelter, clothes, better houses, better roads; and on the other hand they go on worshiping poverty. They are in a double bind.

The East cannot yet meditate. First it needs scientific technology to make it a little physically better. Just as the West needs religious technology, the East needs scientific technology.

And I am all for one world, where the West can fulfill the needs of the East and the East can fulfill the needs of the West. The East and the West have lived apart too long; there is no need anymore. The East should not be the East anymore and the West should not be the West anymore. We have come to that critical moment where this whole earth can become one—should become one—because it can survive only if it becomes one.

The days of the nations are over, the days of divisions are over, the days of the politicians are over. We are moving in a tremendously new world, a new phase of humanity—and the phase is that there can be only one world now, only one single humanity. And then there will be a tremendous release of energies.

The East has treasures, the religious technologies, and the West has treasures, the scientific technologies. And if they can meet, this very world can become a paradise. Now there is no need to ask for another world; we are capable of creating the paradise here on this earth, for the first time. And if we don't create it then except for us, nobody else is responsible.

I am for one world, one humanity, and ultimately one science that will take care of both—a meeting of religion and science—one science that will take care of the inner and the outer, both.

That's what I am trying to do here. It is a meeting place of East and West; it is a womb where the new humanity can be conceived, can be born.

THESE ARE POLARITIES IN LIFE, MEDITATION AND LOVE—THIS IS THE ultimate polarity.

The whole of life consists of polarities: the positive and the negative, birth and death, man and woman, day and night, summer and winter. The whole of life consists of polar opposites. But those polar opposites are not only polar opposites, they are also complementaries. They are helping each other, they are supporting each other.

They are like the bricks of an arch. In an arch the bricks have to be arranged against each other. They appear to be against each other, but it is through their opposition that the arch is built, remains standing. The strength of the arch is dependent on the polarity of the bricks arranged opposite each other.

This is the ultimate polarity: meditation means the art of being alone, and love means the art of being together. The whole person is one who knows both and who is capable of moving from one to the other as easily as possible. It is just like breathing in and breathing out—there is no difficulty. They are opposite—when you breathe in there is one process, and when you breathe out the process is just the opposite. But breathing in and breathing out make one full breath.

In meditation you breathe in, in love you breathe out. And with love and meditation together your breath is complete, entire, is whole.

For centuries religions have tried to attain one pole to the exclusion of the other. There are religions of meditation, for example, Jainism, Buddhism—they are meditative religions, they are rooted in meditation. And there are *bhakti* religions, religions of devotion: Sufism, Hassidism—they are rooted in love. A religion rooted in love needs God as the "other" to love, to pray to. Without a God the religion of love cannot exist, it is inconceivable—you need an object of love. But a religion of meditation can exist without the concept of God; the hypothesis can be discarded. Hence Buddhism and Jainism don't believe in any God. There is no need of the other. You just have to know how to be alone, how to be silent, how to be still, how to be utterly calm and quiet within yourself. The other has to be completely dropped, forgotten. Hence these are godless religions.

When for the first time Western theologians came across Buddhist and Jaina literature they were very puzzled: how to call these godless philosophies religions? They could be called philosophies, but how to call them religions? It was inconceivable to them because the Judaic and Christian tradition thinks that to be religious God is the most essential hypothesis. The religious person is one who is God-fearing and these people say there is no God, hence there is no question of fearing God.

In the West for thousands of years it has been thought that the person who does not believe in God is an atheist, he is not a religious person. But Buddha is atheistic *and* religious. It was very strange for Westerners because they were not at all aware that there are religions that are rooted in meditation.

And the same is true about the followers of Buddha and Mahavira. They laugh at the stupidity of other religions that believe in God, because the whole idea is absurd. It is just fantasy, imagination, nothing else; it is a projection. But to me, both are true together.

My understanding is not rooted in one pole; my understanding is fluid. I have tasted truth from both sides: I have loved totally and I have meditated totally. And this is my experience: that a person is whole only when he has known both. Otherwise he remains half, something remains missing in him.

Buddha is half—so is Jesus. Jesus knows what love is, Buddha knows what meditation is, but if they meet, it will be impossible for them to communicate with each other. They will not understand each other's language. Jesus will talk about the kingdom of God and Buddha will start laughing: "What nonsense are you talking? The kingdom of God?" Buddha will say just, "Cessation of the self, disappearance of the self." And Jesus will say, "Disappearance of the self? Cessation of the self? That is committing suicide, the ultimate suicide. What kind of religion is this? Talk about the supreme self!"

They will not understand each other's words. If they ever meet they will need a man like me to interpret; otherwise there can be no communication between them. And I will have to interpret in such a way that I will be untrue to both! Jesus will say "kingdom of God" and I will translate it as nirvana—then Buddha will understand. Buddha will say "nirvana" and to Jesus I will say "kingdom of God"—then he will understand.

Humanity needs a total vision now. We have lived with half visions for too long. It was a necessity of the past but now man has come of age. My sann-yasins have to prove that they can meditate and pray together, that they can meditate and love together, that they can be as silent as possible and they can be as dancing and celebrating as possible. Their silence has to become their cele-bration, and their celebration has to become their silence. I am giving them the hardest task ever given to any disciples, because this is the meeting of the opposites.

And in this meeting all other opposites will melt and become one: East and West, man and woman, matter and consciousness, this world and that world, life and death. All opposites will meet and merge through this one meeting, because this is the ultimate polarity; it contains all the polarities.

This meeting will create a new human being—Zorba the Buddha. That's my name for the new man. And each of my sannyasins has to make all the efforts possible to become such a liquidity, a flow, so that both poles belong to you.

Then you will have the taste of wholeness. And to know wholeness is the only way to know what is holy. There is no other way.

MY MESSAGE IS SIMPLE. MY MESSAGE IS A NEW MAN, *HOMO NOVUS.* The old concept of man was of either/or, materialist or spiritualist, moral or immoral, sinner or saint. It was based on division, split. It created a schizophrenic humanity. The whole past of humanity has been sick, unhealthy, insane. In three thousand years, five thousand wars have been fought. This is just utterly mad; it is unbelievable. It is stupid, unintelligent, inhuman.

Once you divide man in two, you create misery and hell for him. He can never be healthy and can never be whole; the other half that has been denied will go on taking revenge. It will go on finding ways and means to overcome the part that you have imposed upon yourself. You will become a battleground, a civil war. That's what has been the case in the past.

In the past we were not able to create real human beings, but only humanoids. A humanoid is one who looks like a human being but is utterly crippled, paralyzed. He has not been allowed to bloom in his totality. He is half, and because he is half he is always in anguish and tension; he cannot celebrate. Only a whole man can celebrate. Celebration is the fragrance of being whole.

Only a tree that has lived wholly will flower. Man has not flowered yet.

The past has been very dark and dismal. It has been a dark night of the soul. And because it was repressive, it was bound to become aggressive. If something is repressed, man becomes aggressive, he loses all soft qualities. It was always so up to now. We have come to a point where the old has to be dropped and the new has to be heralded.

The new man will not be either/or—he will be both/and. The new man will be earthy and divine, worldly and otherworldly. The new man will accept his totality and he will live it without any inner division, he will not be split. His god will not be opposed to the devil, his morality will not be opposed to immorality; he will know no opposition. He will transcend duality, he will not be schizophrenic. With the new man there will come a new world, because the new man will perceive in a qualitatively different way. He will live a totally different life, which has not been lived yet. He will be a mystic, a poet, a scientist, all together. He will not choose: He will be choicelessly himself.

That's what I teach: *Homo novus*, a new man, not a humanoid. The humanoid is not a natural phenomenon. The humanoid is created by the society—by the priest, the politician, the pedagogue. The humanoid is created, it is manufactured. Each child comes as a human being—total, whole, alive, without any split. Immediately the society starts suffocating him, stifling him, cutting him into fragments. Telling him what to do and what not to do, what to be and what not to be. His wholeness is soon lost. He becomes guilty about his whole being. He denies much that is natural, and in that very denial he becomes uncreative. Now he will be only a fragment, and a fragment cannot dance, a fragment cannot sing. And a fragment is always suicidal because the fragment cannot know what life is. The humanoid cannot decide on his own. Others have been deciding for him—his parents, the teachers, the leaders, the priests; they have taken all his decisiveness. They decide, they order; he simply follows. The humanoid is a slave.

I teach freedom. Now man has to destroy all kinds of bondages and he has to come out of all prisons—no more slavery. Man has to become individual. He has to become rebellious. And whenever a man has become rebellious . . . Once in a while a few people have escaped from the tyranny of the past, but only once in a while—a Jesus here and there, a Buddha here and there. They are exceptions. And even these people, Buddha and Jesus, could not live totally. They tried, but the whole society was against it.

My concept of the new man is that he will be Zorba the Greek and he will also be Gautam the Buddha. The new man will be Zorba the Buddha. He will be sensuous and spiritual—physical, utterly physical, in the body, in the senses, enjoying the body and all that the body makes possible, and still a great consciousness, a great witnessing will be there. He will be Christ and Epicurus together.

The old man's ideal was renunciation, the new man's ideal will be rejoicing. And this new man is coming every day, he is arriving every day. People have not yet become aware of him. In fact he has already dawned. The old is dying, the old is on its deathbed. I don't mourn for it and I say it is good that it dies, because out of its death the new will assert itself. The death of the old will be the beginning of the new. The new can come only when the old has died utterly.

Help the old to die and help the new to be born—and remember, the old has all the respectability, the whole past will be in his favor and the new will be a very strange phenomenon. The new will be so new that he will not be respected. Every effort will be made to destroy the new. The new cannot be respectable, but with the new is the future of the whole of humanity. The new has to be brought in.

My work consists in creating a buddhafield, an energy field, where the new can be born. I am only a midwife helping the new to come into a world that will not be accepting of it. The new will need much support from those who understand, from those who want some revolution to happen. And the time is ripe, it has never been so ripe. The time is right, it has never been so right. The new can assert itself, the breakthrough has become possible.

The old is so rotten that even with all the support it cannot survive; it is doomed! We can delay, we can go on worshiping the old; that will be just delaying the process. The new is on its way. At the most we can help it to come sooner, or we can hinder it and delay its coming. It is good to help it. If it comes sooner, humanity can still have a future, and a great future—a future of freedom, a future of love, a future of joy.

I teach a new religion. This religion will not be Christianity and will not be Judaism and will not be Hinduism. This religion will not have any adjective to it. This religion will be purely a religious quality of being whole.

My people have to become the first rays of the sun that is going to come on the horizon. It is a tremendous task, it is an almost impossible task, but because it is impossible it is going to seduce all those who have any soul left in them. It is going to create a great longing in all those people who have some adventure hidden in their beings, who are courageous, brave, because it is really going to create a brave new world.

I talk of Buddha, I talk of Christ, I talk of Krishna, I talk of Zarathustra, so that all that is best and all that is good in the past can be preserved. But these are only a few exceptions. The whole humanity has lived in great slavery, chained, split, insane.

My message is simple but it will be very hard, difficult, to make it happen. But the harder it is, the more impossible it is, the greater is the challenge. And the time is right because religion has failed, science has failed. The time is right because the East has failed, the West has failed. Something of a higher synthesis is needed, in which East and West can have a meeting, in which religion and science can have a meeting.

Religion failed because it was otherworldly and it neglected this world. And you cannot neglect this world; to neglect this world is to neglect your own roots. Science has failed because it neglected the other world, the inner, and you cannot neglect the flowers. Once you neglect the flowers, the innermost core of being, life loses all meaning. The tree needs roots, so man needs roots, and the roots can only be in the earth. The tree needs an open sky to grow, to come to great foliage and to have thousands of flowers. Then only is the tree fulfilled, then only does the tree feel the significance and meaning and life becomes relevant.

Man is a tree. Religion has failed because it is talking only of the flowers. Those flowers remain philosophical, abstract; they never materialize. They could not materialize because they were not supported by the earth. And science has failed because it cares only about the roots. The roots are ugly and there seems to be no flowering.

The West is suffering from too much science; the East has suffered from too much religion. Now we need a new humanity in which religion and science become two aspects of one human being. And the bridge is going to be art. That's why I say that the new man will be a mystic; a poet and a scientist.

Between science and religion, only art can be the bridge—poetry, music, sculpture. Once we have brought this new man into existence, the earth can become for the first time what it is meant to become. It can become a paradise: this very body the buddha, this very earth the paradise.

Highlights of Osho's Life and Work

⤫

I am the center of the cyclone, so whatever happens around me makes no difference to me. It may be turmoil or it may be the beautiful sound of running water; I am just a witness to both, and that witnessing remains the same. As far as my innermost being is concerned, in every situation I am just the same. This is my whole teaching: that things may change, but your consciousness should remain absolutely unchanging.

Things are going to change—that is their nature. One day you succeed, one day you fail; one day you are at the top, another day you are at the bottom. But something in you is always exactly the same, and that something is your reality. I live in my reality, not in all the dreams and nightmares that surround reality.

DECEMBER 11, 1931

Osho is born in Kuchwada, the village where his maternal grandparents live, in the central Indian state of Madhya Pradesh.

1932–1939: KUCHWADA

Following the death of his paternal grandmother, the care of her youngest children and of the family business falls to Osho's young parents. Osho goes to live with his maternal grandparents, who provide for him an extraordinary atmosphere of freedom and respect. According to his own accounts, and the accounts of others who knew him during his childhood, he was a daredevil and mischief-maker, never missing an opportunity to test his own physical limits and to challenge self-importance or hypocrisy wherever he found it.

1938–1951: GADARWADA

After the death of his maternal grandfather, Osho and his grandmother both move to Kuchwada, the town where his parents live. There he is enrolled in school for the first time. When he is not creating mischief and challenging his teachers, Osho continues the adventurous and often solitary approach to life that characterized his first years with his grandparents. In 1945, at the age of fourteen, he undertakes a seven-day experiment in waiting for death, provoked in part by an unusual prediction by an astrologer who was commissioned to calculate his birth chart. (See pages 55–57.)

MARCH 21, 1953: ENLIGHTENMENT

1951–1956: UNIVERSITY STUDENT

Osho majors in philosophy and wins numerous awards in debating competitions. He graduates with honors from Jain College and is invited by Professor S. S. Roy to do his postgraduate study at Sagar University.

1957–1970: PROFESSOR AND PUBLIC SPEAKER

Osho accepts a position first at Sanskrit College in Raipur and later at the University of Jabalpur, where he teaches philosophy. His unorthodox and challenging approach to teaching draws many students to his classes, regardless of whether they have actually enrolled for credit. As the years pass he begins to spend more and more time away from his teaching duties and begins traveling to public speaking engagements throughout India.

1962: THE FIRST MEDITATION CENTERS
During his travels and speaking engagements, Osho often conducts guided meditations at the end of his talks. The first meditation centers to emerge around his teachings are known as Jivan Jagruti Kendras (Life Awakening Centers), and his movement is called Jivan Jagruti Andolan (Life Awakening Movement).

With the help of meditation temples or centers, I would like to, in a scientific way, introduce the modern man to meditation—not only in an intellectual way but to introduce him to meditation in an experiential way. There are certain things that we can know of only by doing them.

The meditation centers are scientific places where a modern man can understand meditation through modern language and symbols. Not only that, he can actually meditate and get introduced to it. There are one hundred and twelve such methods in the world. I would like to give a detailed scientific basis for these methods in the meditation centers. So that not only can you understand, but also do them.

1962–1974: MEDITATION CAMPS
In addition to his speaking engagements, Osho begins to hold 3- to 10-day "meditation camps" in the countryside, where he gives daily talks and personally guides the participants in meditation.

I used to talk to crowds of fifty thousand people or one hundred thousand people, and I knew that everything was going over their heads; they were just sitting there. These people loved me, not because they understood what I was saying but just because of the way I was saying it. They loved my presence—but they were not seekers.

Seeing the situation, that it is almost futile to talk to the crowd, I started gathering a few people. The only way was to drop speaking to the crowds. I would go to a mountain and I would inform people that whoever wanted to come to the mountain for ten days, or seven days, could come and be with me. Naturally, if somebody takes ten days out of his work, he has some interest; it cannot just be curiosity. If he leaves his wife and children and job for ten days, at least he shows a sign that he is not only curious but he really wants to know. That's how the meditation camps began.

JUNE 1964: RANAKPUR MEDITATION CAMP

Ranakpur Meditation Camp became a landmark in Osho's work because for the first time his discourses and meditations were recorded and published in a book, Path to Self-Realization, *which was widely acclaimed in India. Osho later said that this book contains his whole teaching, which has never altered. The book is now in print under the title* The Perfect Way *(Rebel Publishing House, India). At the beginning of the camp, he gives three guidelines for participating:*

The first maxim is: live in the present. Only the present is real and alive. And if the truth is to be known it can be known only through the present.

The second maxim is: live naturally. Just as actors in a play remove their costumes and makeup and put them aside after the performance, in these five days [of the Ranakpur Meditation Camp], you must remove your false masks and set them aside. Let that which is fundamental and natural in you come out—and live in it.

The third maxim is: live alone. Inside, do not allow things to crowd in on you. And the same is true for the outside—live by yourself as if you are all alone at this camp. You don't have to maintain relations with anyone else.

JUNE 1966: *JYOTI SIKHA* (LIFE AWAKENING) MAGAZINE

A quarterly magazine in Hindi is published by Jivan Jagruti Kendra of Bombay, which also becomes the official publisher of books transcribed from Osho's talks. By this time, he is widely known as "Acharya Rajneesh."

1968: FROM SEX TO SUPERCONSCIOUSNESS

Osho is invited to Bombay to give a series of five talks on "love," in the prestigious Bharatiya Vidya Bhavan Auditorium. In the first discourse on August 28, Osho explains that love and meditation arise as a transformation of sexual energy, and that if sex is suppressed it cannot be transformed. Many people are outraged that he has talked about sex, and the owners of the auditorium cancel the series.

On September 28, Osho returns to Bombay to complete the talks to a very large audience at the Gwalia Tank Maidan. The series is published under the title From Sex to Superconsciousness, *which becomes his most read book. The Indian press begins to refer to him as "the sex guru."*

If you want to know the elemental truth about love, the first requisite is to accept the sacredness of sex, to accept the divinity of sex in the same way you accept God's existence—with an open heart. And the more fully you accept sex with an open heart and mind, the freer you will be of it. But the more you suppress it the more you will become bound to it. . . .

When I ended my talk that day, I was surprised to see that all the officials who had been on the platform, the friends who had organized the meeting, had vanished into thin air. I did not see one of them when I walked down the aisle to leave. . . .

Not even the main organizer was present to thank me. Whatsoever white caps there were [Gandhians, many of whom had till now been supporters of Osho], whatsoever khadi-clad people there were, were not on the dais; they had already fled long before the completion of the talk. Leaders are a very weak species indeed. And swift too! They run away before their followers do.

1970-1974: BOMBAY

On June 27, 1970, a send-off celebration is held for Osho in Jabalpur, where he has been a professor and lived for many years. On July 1, Osho moves to Bombay and begins to give regular evening discourses to about fifty people, sometimes concluding with a meditation or singing and dancing. He travels only to fulfill outstanding speaking engagements, and by December these are completed.

I will slowly confine myself to a room: I will stop coming and going. Now I will work on those who are in my mind. I will prepare them and send them out. The moving from place to place, which I cannot do myself, I will be able to do by sending out ten thousand people.

For me, religion is also a scientific process, so I have in my mind a complete scientific technique for it. As people become ready, the scientific technique will be passed on to them. With the help of that technique, they will work upon thousands of people. My presence is not needed for that. I was required only to find such people who could carry out that purpose.

1970: DYNAMIC MEDITATION INTRODUCED

In April 1970, Osho introduces a revolutionary cathartic meditation technique, which he calls Dynamic Meditation. In May at the Nargol Meditation Camp, he leads experiments in this meditation, which he continues to fine-tune over the next three years. Dynamic Meditation becomes his most famous and widely practiced meditation technique.

A friend has asked, "In your earlier teaching of meditation you always asked us to be relaxed, still, silent, and aware. And now in the course of intense breathing and asking 'Who am I?' you exhort us to bring all our efforts into it. So which of the two techniques would be good?"

There is no question of good and bad here. I understand your point but it is not a question of good and bad. You have only to find out which of the techniques gives you more peace and adds to the momentum of your meditation. It cannot be the same for everybody; they will experience it differently. There are people who attain relaxation only after they have run themselves into the ground. And there are others who can go into relaxation instantly; but they are few and far between. It is difficult to move straight into silence; only a handful of people can do it. For the majority of people it is necessary to go through a lot of exertion and tension before they can relax. But the purpose in both cases is the same, the final objective is the same. It is relaxation.

1970: A NEW DEFINITION OF SANNYAS

From September 26 to October 5, 1970, Osho holds a meditation camp in Kulu Manali, in the foothills of the Himalayas. On September 26, he initiates his first group of disciples, which he calls "neo-sannyasins." His version of this ancient Hindu institution is radically different from tradition, where the seeker renounces all possessions and relationships, is celibate, and lives on what he or she is given by those who remain engaged in society. As Osho begins to define "neo-sannyas," his challenge to the tradition becomes increasingly clear.

I am going to separate the sannyas of the future from the sannyas of the past. And I think that the institution of sannyas, as it has been up to now, is on its deathbed; it is as good as dead. It has no future whatsoever. But sannyas in its essence has to be preserved. It is such a precious attainment of mankind that we cannot afford to lose it. Sannyas is that rarest of flowers that blooms once in a great while. But it is likely that it will wither away for want of proper caring—and it will certainly die if it remains tied to its old patterns.

THE ANCIENT MEANING OF SANNYAS IS RENOUNCING THE WORLD. I am against it.

But I have still used the word *sannyas* because I can see another meaning far more significant than the old one. I mean renouncing all the conditions that the world has given to you—your religion, your caste, your Brahminism, your Jainism, your Christianity, your God, your holy book.

To me, sannyas means a commitment that "I am going to clean myself completely of all those things that have been imposed upon me, and I will start living on my own—fresh, young, pure, unpolluted." So sannyas is an initiation into your innocence.

BEGINNING IN 1970 AND CONTINUING TILL 1985, OSHO'S SANNYASINS are asked to wear shades of red and orange. They also receive a necklace from Osho, known as a mala, *which consists of one hundred and eight beads plus a locket with Osho's picture. In addition, Osho gives each sannyasin a new name. The new name includes a prefix common to all—the prefix "swami" for men and "ma" for women.*

The path of the masculine is that of awareness, and awareness brings you to a point where you become master of your own being. That is the meaning of *swami*. The feminine path is that of love, and love brings you to an ultimate point where you can mother the whole existence. And that is the meaning of *ma*. A woman in her ultimate flowering becomes a mothering energy . . . she can mother the whole existence. She feels blessed, and she can bless the whole existence. When a man arrives at the ultimate point he does not become a father, he does not become a mother, he simply becomes a master: master of his own being.

Love and awareness—these are two paths. And when I say masculine I don't mean that all males are masculine, and when I say feminine I don't mean that all females are feminine. There are women who will have to pass through the path of awareness—I would like to call them swamis too, but that would be a little more confusing. As it is, it is already too crazy . . . so I resist that temptation. But sometimes it comes to me that I see a woman taking sannyas and I feel like calling her swami, not ma. And then sometimes a man comes, very effeminate, and looks more feminine than any woman.

LATER, IN 1985, OSHO SAYS:

Slowly, slowly I started sorting out my people, and just to sort them out I started initiating them into sannyas so that I could recognize them and know who my people are. I started giving them names so I could remember, because it is difficult for me to remember all kinds of strange names from around the world. The real reason was simply to have names that I could remember; otherwise it would be impossible for me. Now there are people from almost all the countries, of all languages: it is impossible to remember their names.

But when I give you a name it is a totally different matter. When I give you a name, I give you a name for certain reasons, for certain qualities that I see in you, for certain possibilities that I see in you, for certain characteristics that are already there—and all these become associated.

The name that I give is known to me, its meaning is known to me. Its meaning and your lifestyle, pattern, potentiality, all become associated. It becomes easier for me to remember you; otherwise it is very difficult, almost impossible.

I have given you the red clothes for the simple reason so that I can recognize you; all other excuses are just hogwash. Just to give you good reasons because people will be asking you and you will have to give good reasons to them—I have been trying to make a philosophy out of nothing. But the truth is simply this, nothing more than this.

AND IN 1986, HE EMPHASIZES AGAIN THAT THE OUTER SYMBOLS OF sannyas are unimportant:

Man's mind is a very immature mind. It starts clinging with outer symbols. That has happened to all the religions of the world. They all started well, but they all went astray. And the reason was that the outer was emphasized so much that people completely forgot the inner. To fulfill the outer was such life-absorbing task that there was no space left even to remember your inward journey, which is basically the meaning of religiousness.

I want my people to understand it clearly. Neither your clothes nor your outer disciplines nor anything that has been given to you by tradition and you have accepted it just on belief is going to help. The only thing that can create a revolution in you is going beyond the mind into the world of consciousness. Except that, nothing is religious.

To begin with, and with a world that is too much obsessed with outer things, I had to start sannyas also with outer things—change your clothes to orange, wear a *mala,* meditate—but the emphasis was only on meditation. But I found that people can change their clothes very easily, but they cannot change their minds. They can wear the *mala,* but they cannot move into their consciousness. And because they are in orange clothes, wearing a *mala,* having a new name, they start believing that they have become a sannyasin.

Sannyas is not so cheap. Hence it is time and you are mature enough that beginning phase is over. If you like the orange color, the red color, perfectly good—it cannot do any harm, but it is not a help either. If you love the *mala,* if you love the locket with my picture on it, it is simply your ornament, but it has nothing to do with religion. So now I reduce religion to its absolute essentiality. And that is meditation.

THE DAY I STARTED INITIATING PEOPLE, MY ONLY FEAR WAS, "WILL I be able to someday change my followers into my friends?" The night before, I could not sleep. Again and again I thought, "How am I going to manage it? A follower is not supposed to be a friend." I said to myself that night in Kulu Manali in the Himalayas, "Don't be serious. You can manage anything, although you don't know the ABC of managerial science."

I recall a book by Bern, *The Managerial Revolution.* I read it not because the title contained the word *revolution,* but because the title contained the word *managerial.* Although I loved the book, naturally I was disappointed because it was not what I was looking for. I was never able to manage anything. So that night in Kulu Manali I laughed.

THE WOODLANDS

Osho moves to a large apartment in the Woodlands complex in Bombay, where he lives until March 1974. Now that Osho is settled, he is able to work more closely with individuals. He meets people individually or in small groups, and gives regular talks, including his talks on the one hundred and twelve meditation techniques of the Vigyan Bhairav Tantra, which he calls "The Book of Secrets." Sannyasins and other seekers meet every morning on a nearby beach to do Dynamic Meditation together. In addition, Osho still occasionally hosts meditation camps in the countryside. More and more Westerners begin to arrive to meet him, and many are initiated into sannyas.

I am more emphatically interested in meditation than in discussions. These discussions are just to give you a push, to satisfy you in an intellectual way, just to give you a feeling that whatsoever you are doing is very intellectual, rational. It is not.

So whatsoever I have been saying is in a way quite the opposite of what I have been trying to pull you into. My approach, as far as these discussions are concerned, is rational, just to satisfy you, just to give you some toys to play with so that you can be persuaded into something else. That something else is not rational; that is irrational.

Our meditation is just a jump into irrational existence. And existence *is* irrational—it is mystic, it is a mystery. So please don't cling to what I have said to you; rather, cling to whatsoever I have persuaded you to do. Do it, and someday you will realize that whatsoever I have said is meaningful. But if you go on clinging to what I have said, it may give you knowledge, it may make you more knowledgeable, but you will not attain to knowing. And whatsoever I have said may even become a hindrance.

1971: FROM ACHARYA TO *BHAGWAN*

In May 1971, Osho changes his name from Acharya Shree Rajneesh to Bhagwan Shree Rajneesh and for the first time publicly acknowledges that he is enlightened.

Many people have asked me why I kept silent about the fact I became enlightened in 1953. For almost twenty years I never said anything about it to anybody, unless somebody suspected it himself, unless somebody said to me on his own, "We feel that something has happened to you. We don't know what it is, but one thing is certain: that something has happened and you are no more the same as we are—and you are hiding it."

In those years not more than ten people asked me, and even then I avoided them as much as I could unless I felt that their desire was genuine. I told them only when they had promised to keep it a secret. And they all fulfilled their promise. Now they are all sannyasins, but they all kept it a secret. I said, "You wait. Wait for the right moment. Only then will I declare it."

I have learned much from the past buddhas. If Jesus had kept a little quieter about being the Son of God it would have been far more beneficial to humanity. I had made it a point that until I stopped traveling in the country I was not going to declare it; otherwise I would have been killed—I would not be here.

Once I had finished with traveling, mixing with the masses, moving from one town to another . . . and there was not a single bodyguard. It would have been no problem to kill me, it would have been so simple. But for almost twenty years I kept absolutely silent about it. I declared it only when I saw that now I had gathered enough people who could understand it. I declared it only when I knew that now I could create my own small world and I was no longer concerned with the crowds and the masses and the stupid mob.

1973–1975: ACTIVE MEDITATIONS AND MUSIC

Osho brings a five-piece conga drum band to a July 1973 meditation camp, and when he finally settles in Pune he works with disciples to compose music to accompany each of the active meditations he has developed.

Your mind is in chaos. That chaos has to be brought out, acted out. Chaotic music can be helpful, so if you are meditating and chaotic music is played, it will help to bring out your chaos. You will flow in it, you will become unafraid of expression. And this chaotic music will hit your chaotic mind within and will bring it out. It helps.

Rock, jazz, or other music that is chaotic in a way also helps something to come out, and that something is repressed sexuality. I am concerned with all your repressions. Modern music is more concerned just with your repressed sex, but there is a similarity. However, I am not concerned only with your repressed sex; I am concerned with all your repressions, sexual or not sexual. . . .

This state of mind is neurotic. The whole society is ill. That is why I so much insist on chaotic meditation. Relieve yourself, act out whatsoever society has forced on you, whatsoever situations have forced on you. Act them out, relieve yourself of them, go through a catharsis. The music helps.

1974–1981: "PUNE ONE"

On March 21, 1974, exactly twenty-one years after his enlightenment, Osho moves to Koregaon Park in Pune, where two residences in adjoining properties of six acres have been purchased. He holds interviews on the lawn only with sannyasins arriving or leaving and no longer meets with individuals seeking advice or private interviews.

It is very deliberately that I have become inaccessible. I was very accessible, but then by and by I began to feel that I couldn't help; it became almost impossible to help. For example, if I give you one hour, you talk rubbish. If I give you one minute you say exactly the thing that is needed—that's how mind functions.

If I am available to you the whole day, I am not available at all. If you have to wait eight days or ten days, that waiting is needed for a certain tuning in yourself, for certain significant problems to arise.

Sometimes I see that if you have a problem and you can come immediately, you will bring me trivia. During the day there are a thousand and one problems arising—they are not significant, but in the moment they appear significant. If you have to wait just one hour, the problem changes—then you bring another problem. If you are allowed to bring all your problems you will be in a mess, because you yourself will not be able to know what is needed, what is significant. So this is part of the whole process.

THE WAY OF THE WHITE CLOUDS
In May 1974, Osho gives a series of discourses in English, in which he explains his approach, his view of the master-disciple relationship, and his vision for the development of his work in Pune. The discourses are published under the title My Way: The Way of the White Clouds *and attract many seekers from the West.*

A white cloud drifts wherever the wind leads—it doesn't resist, it doesn't fight. A white cloud is not a conqueror, and still it hovers over everything. You cannot conquer it, you cannot defeat it. It has no mind to conquer—that's why you cannot defeat it.

Once you are fixed to a goal, purpose, destiny, meaning, once you have got that madness of reaching somewhere, then problems will arise. And

233

you will be defeated, that is certain. Your defeat is in the very nature of existence itself.

A white cloud has nowhere to go. It moves, it moves everywhere. All dimensions belong to it, all directions belong to it. Nothing is rejected. Everything is, exists, in a total acceptability. Hence I call my way "the way of the white clouds." The white cloud's way is a pathless path, a wayless way. Moving, but not with a fixed mind—moving without a mind . . .

So I am the white cloud, and the whole effort is to make you also white clouds drifting in the sky. Nowhere to go, coming from nowhere, just being there this very moment—perfect.

I don't teach you any ideals, I don't teach you any oughts. I don't say to you be this, become that. My whole teaching is simply this: Whatsoever you are, accept it so totally that nothing is left to be achieved, and you will become a white cloud.

"A NEW PHASE"

In June 1974, Osho introduces the first meditation camp in Pune with the announcement that a new phase of his work will begin. From now on he will work only with authentic seekers. And for the first time, Osho does not lead the meditations in person. Instead, his empty chair is brought into the meditation hall.

This camp is going to be different in many ways. This night I start a completely new phase of my work. You are fortunate to be here because you will be witnesses to a new type of inner work. I must explain it to you because tomorrow morning the journey starts.

. . . Another new thing, I will not be there; only my empty chair will be there. But don't miss me, because in a sense I will be there, and in a sense there has always been an empty chair before you. Right now the chair is empty because there is no one sitting in it. I am talking to you but there is no one who is talking to you. It is difficult to understand, but when the ego disappears, processes can continue. Talking can continue, sitting and walking and eating can continue, but the doer has disappeared. Even now, the chair is empty. But I was always with you up till now in all the camps because you were not ready. Now I feel you are ready. And you must be helped to get more ready to work in my absence, because knowing that I am physically present you may feel a certain enthusiasm that is false. Just knowing that I am present you may do things that you never wanted to do; just to impress me you may exert yourself more. That is not of much help, because only that can be helpful which comes out of your being. My chair will be there, I will be watching you, but you feel completely free. And don't think that I am not there, because that may depress you, and then that depression will disturb your meditation.

And this too has to be remembered: I cannot always be in this physical body with you; one day or another the physical vehicle has to be dropped. My work is complete as far as I am concerned. If I am carrying this physical vehicle, it is just for you; someday, it has to be dropped. Before it happens you must be ready to work in my absence, or in my nonphysical presence, which means the same. And once you can feel me in my absence you are free of me, and then even if I am not here in this body the contact will not be lost.

It always happens when a buddha is there: His physical presence becomes so meaningful, and then he dies and everything is shattered.

My chair can be empty; you can feel my absence. And remember, only when you can feel my absence can you feel my presence. If you cannot see me while my physical vehicle is not there, you have not seen me at all.

This is my promise: I will be there in the empty chair, the empty chair will not really be empty. So behave! The chair will not be empty, but it is better that you learn to be in contact with my nonphysical being. That is a deeper, more intimate touch and contact.

That is why I say a new phase of my work starts with this camp—and I am calling it a *samadhi sadhana shibir*. It is not only meditation, it is absolute ecstasy that I am going to teach to you. It is not only the first step, it is the last.

COMMENTARIES AND RESPONSES TO QUESTIONS

From July 1974, Osho continues to give discourses every morning until 1981, speaking alternate months in Hindi or English. He comments on the teachings of enlightened mystics in many spiritual traditions: Tao, Zen, Christianity, Hassidism, Sufism, the Bauls, Hindu mystics, Tibetan Buddhism, Tantra, etc. On alternate days he answers questions submitted to him by his audience. Each series of ten days is published as one book—over two hundred and forty books in seven years.

You have to search for your own path; each one has to search for his own path. I will make all the paths available to you, so you can see and feel. And when the right path happens you will immediately see great joy arising in you.

That is indicative; that shows that your climate has arrived, that this was the time you were waiting for, that this is your spring.

I AM PROCLAIMING A NEW RELIGION—THE ESSENTIAL RELIGION. In Islam it is known as Sufism, in Buddhism it is known as Zen, in Judaism it is known as Hassidism—the essential core. But I speak your language, I speak the way you understand, the way you can understand. I speak a very religionless language. I speak as if I am not religious at all. That's what is needed in this world. This twentieth century needs a religion completely free from all kinds of superstitions, utterly nude, naked.

DARSHAN

Osho meets with groups of seekers in a small auditorium adjoining his residence at seven P.M. each evening for one or two hours. In these darshans he initiates new sannyasins from all over the world, greets people who are arriving or leaving, answers questions, and advises on problems. Groups of ashram workers and participants in ashram programs attend these meetings on a rotating schedule. Recordings are made of these intimate, face-to-face meetings between Osho and his guests and are published as "Darshan Diaries."

One has to learn by and by to be on one's own and one has to trust oneself more and more. My help should not become a dependence. It should help you to become really more alert, more trusting of your own life, of your own heart's voice.

So when you come to me and ask, it is not that I answer. I have to search into your heart to see what really would have been your decision if your own heart were functioning. I never give any decision on my own because that would be destructive. It would be something from the outside. So when you ask, I look into you; I don't decide. I look into you, I feel you, I see your own heart that you cannot see, and I let that heart decide. So at the most I interpret your heart to you. I am a midwife.

So if you can decide, good. By and by you will start listening to your own inner core and what it is saying. And that trust has to arise. Otherwise trusting in me can become dangerous to you, because then you're always depending on some outside agent. It can become a habit, so that when you are alone or when you have gone far away from me you will be at a loss as to what to do.

So even while you are here, whatsoever you can decide, decide. When you feel that it is almost impossible for you to come to a decision, the pros and cons are almost balancing, you are divided half and half, only then come to me. And then too, I can only help you; I don't impose anything on you. At the most I become a bridge between you and yourself. That's my function.

So by and by you can see the bridge, and you can go on moving from yourself to your real self; the need for me is less and less. One day there is nothing that you cannot decide. Then you have come of age. You become mature and ripe.

Whenever you see some problem has arisen, it is a good opportunity, a challenge, a critical moment. Use it creatively, find out ways and means. Listen silently to your own heart and if a certainty arises from there, good; you have taken my help already. But only in rare moments when you cannot decide, when the darkness is too much and you are absolutely confused—if you decide this and the mind says that, if you decide that and the mind says this, and you go on hanging between the two; you cannot even see that one voice is the voice of your major being, you are divided fifty/fifty—then only come to me. Then too, remember always that it is not my advice that I am giving to you. It is your innermost heart that I am handing over to you. Soon you will start seeing it.

SHARING THE VISION

Many Western sannyasins spend a few months in Pune and then return to their native countries. During their "leaving darshan" they often ask how they can continue their meditations at home and what they can do to share Osho's vision and unique meditation techniques with their friends and families. Although he often suggests that people can start meditation centers in the West, Osho repeatedly emphasizes that he is not interested in proselytizing or converting people to sannyas, but only that his work be made available to those who are interested.

When I say don't be a missionary, I mean don't impose yourself upon others. Share, but don't impose. Sharing is totally different, it is very respectful toward the other person. Sharing is not violent, imposing is. You are not respectful toward the other person, you are simply using the other person as a means; you are interested only in converting him. That is wrong. Never use a person as a means to anything, because each person is an end unto himself.

The missionary is very disrespectful toward the person. His whole idea is how to convert him, how to make one more person part of his sect. He is not really interested in sharing. Sharing is totally different: you share because you have experienced something, because you have seen something. You share unconditionally. If the person becomes converted that is just a by-product but that is not the motive of it. If he does not become part of it, you are perfectly happy—happy because you shared. Your work is finished. You are not looking for any result.

It is good to be conscious about all the possibilities, otherwise one tends to become a missionary. Just share and forget about it. Sow the seeds and go on moving and don't look back to see what is happening to those seeds. In their time, when the spring comes, something will happen.

THERAPY AS A PREPARATION FOR MEDITATION

Throughout 1975, Osho guides an expansion of programs and workshops that revolutionize Western methods of therapy with Eastern techniques of meditation. In August 1975, the first therapy groups begin. Included in all group processes are daily Dynamic and Kundalini Meditations, Osho's morning discourse, and participation in a ten-day meditation camp before or after the group. In darshan, Osho suggests groups to new arrivals, advises group leaders, and meets with group participants. By the end of 1977, there are fifty different group offerings, and the ashram is known as the largest and most innovative growth center in the world.

The growth group is needed because you have a tremendous need to relate, to love, to communicate. In the West the basic problem is how to communicate, how to relate. Many Westerners are here. When they come to me in darshan their problems are a hundred percent relationship problems—how to relate.

Not even a single Indian has come who has said, "How to relate?" That is not a problem at all. He says, "How to be silent? How to be into one's own being?"

That's why I do not suggest that Easterners participate in groups, except Japanese. I have suggested therapy groups to a few Japanese because Japan is the most Western part of the East. I have sent Indians only once or twice—and these were Indians only in name. They have been born in the East but their mind has not been influenced by the Eastern concept, their mind is Western.

They have been taught by Christian missionaries in Christian schools. Their whole education and upbringing is Western.

It depends on the person, on what he needs. To a few Westerners also I don't suggest groups. When I see some Westerner who has no need to relate, then I don't suggest groups; then I say there is no need. But at least five thousand years of different psychological conditioning exists. That has to be taken note of.

MY THERAPISTS ARE THE BEST IN THE WORLD, FOR THE SIMPLE REASON that other therapists are only therapists, they are not meditators. My therapists are meditators too.

Therapy is a superficial thing. It can help to clean the ground, but just to have a clean ground is not to have a garden.

You will need something more. Therapy is negative; it simply takes away the weeds from the ground, removes the stones from the ground, prepares the soil for the garden. But there its work ends.

Western therapy is still in its very primitive stage. It has to go a long way. And unless it becomes associated with meditation, it may help a little bit superficially but it cannot really help the person to grow.

So when I say my therapists are the best in the world, I simply mean that my therapists are not only therapists, they are meditators too. Other therapists are only therapists.

PUSHING THE ENVELOPE:
ENCOUNTER AND PRIMAL THERAPY

Although only a small percentage of therapy groups in the Pune ashram during the 1970s involve cathartic processes or nudity, it is these groups that attract the most media attention. A German film company is allowed to film a (staged) encounter group session, and their resulting documentary, Ashram, *provokes worldwide controversy and outrage. The movie continues to be shown well into the 1980s and is used by anticult groups to support their claim that Osho's work is dangerous and should be opposed.*

In this commune, I have arranged for many psychotherapies. They will be misunderstood by the masses, *bound* to be misunderstood—because in a psychotherapeutic situation you have to bring all the denied parts to the surface. If somebody has been denying his anger, it has to be allowed in a psychotherapeutic situation. Only then can psychotherapy be of any help, can it be thera-peutic, can it heal you. It has to open all your wounds.

Much pus starts flowing. If you watch the encounter group you will feel sick. You will feel sick because you will see such animality coming out; you could never have imagined that human beings can be such animals. But that animality is within you too, just repressed. By repression you cannot dissolve it.

In the encounter group—that is the meaning of the word *encounter*—you have to encounter yourself in your totality. You have to bring out all that is repressed—you have to bring out *all*, without any evaluation about what is good, what is bad. And suddenly you see great animals roaring inside you. They are violent, and you have been taught to be nonviolent. Your nonvio-lence has repressed your violence. Great rage, for *no* reason at all, will arise. You will start beating the wall; you may start beating yourself. And you will say, "What am I doing? I have never done it before. From where is it com-ing?" But it is coming in great surges, in great waves. And the whole process is to let it be.

When all the parts have been expressed—your sex, your anger, your greed, your jealousy, your rage—when all parts have been expressed, a great calmness arises, the silence that follows the storm.

This cannot be understood by the masses. In fact they are very much on their guard. They don't want to understand either, because to under-stand means they will have to look within, and they will find the same things inside themselves.

IN PUNE THERE WERE A FEW GROUPS, AND I WAS DECIDING WHICH group people should participate in, and in what sequence. These groups were therapies; so first silent therapies were given, meditative therapies were given. To those who could not succeed in them, then more active therapies were given. If even that was not enough, then therapies were given to them in which they can beat pillows, shout, scream . . . but not to touch anybody. Mostly this was enough.

Rarely there was a person who still needed something more, was yet not cleansed. Then for these there were therapies where they were allowed to have physical encounters. But there was a therapist to take care that nothing harms anybody. And these people were required to sign a form that they were accepting a certain therapy on their own—if they don't want to participate, they need not. It was their individual choice.

These therapies helped these people immensely. And during all these therapies whatever they were doing, they had constantly to remember witnessing—that was the part that has not been known to the world—that even if they were hitting somebody, inside there was a watcher. And after hitting each other they would hug each other and cry and weep, and great compassion would come out.

In sexual therapies, I asked the men and the women about their experience: "What is your experience? What you have gained out of it?" And it was again surprising. One woman told me that she had always dreamt that she was being raped, and she woke up in the middle of the night afraid, trembling, perspiring. It was a constantly recurring dream. But after this therapy the dream disappeared and her sleep has become silent and quiet.

She was not raped in the group, but in a sexual therapy she was a participant. It was all playful, nobody was being raped. Nobody was forced against his or her will. And if anybody wanted to get out of it at any moment, he was free to get out of it.

REMEMBER, THESE GROUPS ARE NOT THE END, THEY ONLY PREPARE you for meditation. They are not the goal; they are just simple means to undo the wrong of the past. Once you have thrown out of your system all that you have been repressing all along, I have to lead you into watchfulness. Now it will be easier to watch.

But you are not to become a group-addicted person, you are not to become a groupie. There are people now in the world who are group addicted; they go from one group to another. One encounter finishes, then another marathon, then gestalt, then this and that. . . . After just a few days the itch arises—because where to express? In the normal society they cannot express, they have to repress. So the group becomes just an outlet. The normal society forces you to repress, the group helps you to express but you are not *really* growing. Again you will be back in the normal society, again repressing.

That's where this commune is different from institutes like Esalen. They end with groups—we begin with groups. Where they end, that's exactly the point from where we begin.

And it is not a coincidence that thousands of therapists have become interested in my work. Among my sannyasins, the greatest group from any profession is that of psychotherapists. A great need is felt now all over the world: encounter, primal therapy, gestalt, can help a little bit to unburden people, but they cannot help to make them buddhas. They cannot help them to become awakened.

ASHRAM EXPANSION

In March 1976, renovation and remodeling of many newly acquired buildings have been completed. Osho names the buildings after enlightened mystics: Francis, Jesus, Eckhart, and Krishna. For his daily morning talks he appears in Chuang Tzu Auditorium, where mosquito netting encloses a large circular veranda adjoining his residence. By March 1977, construction of Buddha Hall is completed, where Osho's English-language discourses can accommodate more people. Ashram work departments include publishing, a press office, crafts, a music department, silk screen facilities, a clothing boutique, and a carpentry shop that also makes musical instruments. And by August 1977, there is a bakery and studios for the creation of jewelry, pottery, and weaving.

This place is a marketplace. Can you find any other place that is more like the market? I could have made the ashram somewhere in the Himalayas. I love the Himalayas, for me it is a great sacrifice not to be in the Himalayas. But for a certain purpose I have not made my ashram in the Himalayas.

I want to remain part of the marketplace. And this ashram is run almost as part of the marketplace. That's why Indians are very annoyed—they cannot understand. They have known ashrams for centuries, but this ashram is beyond their comprehension. They cannot think that you have to pay to listen to a religious discourse. They have always listened free of charge—not only free of charge, but after the discourse the ashram distributes *prasad*, food and sweets, too. Many go to listen to the discourses not because of the discourse but for the *prasad.*

Here you have to pay. What am I doing? I want it to be absolutely a part of the marketplace because I want my sannyasins not to move into the monasteries. They have to remain in the world. Their meditation should grow in the world, their meditation should not become escapist. So whatsoever peace you are finding here, you will be able to retain anywhere you go. There will be no problem, not at all. I have been managing things in such a way that all that can disturb you anywhere else is present here!

My whole effort here is to create a miniature world where money is absolutely accepted, where women and men live together in joy, in celebration, without fear, where all that goes on in the world also continues and, alongside, the meditation grows. It becomes stronger and stronger because all the challenges are there.

You can go anywhere you like. Nobody can take your peace away. Your silence is yours! It is not because of me. You have earned it, you have gained it.

HARASSMENT

With growing numbers of visitors from the West, incidents of harassment of foreigners, particularly women, increase. Public displays of affection between men and women, and even the wearing of sleeveless clothing, is seen as provocative in the context of the sexually inhibited Indian culture. And Osho's frequent critiques of Indian politics and corruption rankle government officials at all levels. They begin to initiate a range of repressive measures against the ashram, including restrictions on new construction and denial of tourist visas to foreigners who name the ashram as their destination.

I cannot be supported by the society. It is a sheer miracle that I am existing, it is very illogical. I should not be here at all. The society does not support me, it *cannot* support me. In every possible way it will create—it *is* creating—hindrances for my work.

Just the other day I was reading in the newspapers, one man has suggested to the government that I should be expelled from India. He must be a very religious man, because he says I am destroying religion. And he is not satisfied with just my expulsion—he then suggests my tongue should be cut out, so that I cannot speak; and my hands should also be cut off, so that I cannot write. And he thinks he is a religious man!

WHAT IS WRONG IN HUGGING A PERSON YOU LOVE, IN KISSING A person you love? Don't enforce your hug on anybody, that's true; then it is ugly—and that's what the Indians go on doing. And my women sannyasins are aware of it. If you are there in the marketplace, then Indians behave really in an ugly way. They will pinch your bottoms. Now, that is ugly. They will rub their bodies against your body—that is ugly. They will look at you as if they would like to eat you—that is ugly. But that behavior is accepted by them, that is perfectly good.

If you love a person and you hold hands and you hug each other and you kiss each other, it should be nobody's business. Why should others feel offended? If they feel offended, then something is wrong with them. Maybe they are feeling jealous, but they cannot show their jealousy, so they become angry. Maybe they would also like to hug somebody but they don't have the courage; they are afraid of the society. Hence they feel very angry with you. What they cannot do, they would not like anybody else to do either.

THE VISION OF A NEW COMMUNE

In his discourses, Osho begins to talk about finding an isolated place where his work can take place without harassment and interference. A search is initiated for a large place in the Indian countryside, where a "new commune" can be built and the spiritual dimensions of the work can go deeper.

Gurdjieff lived a life that was very mysterious; it was not public. His school was a hidden school. What was happening there, people were simply guessing.

And that's what is going to happen in the new phase of my work. My commune will become hidden, underground. It will have a facade on the outside: the weavers and the carpenters and the potters . . . that will be the facade. People who will come as visitors, we will have a beautiful showroom for them; they can purchase things. They can see the creativity of the sannyasins—paintings, books, woodworking. They can be shown around—a beautiful lake, swimming pools, a five-star hotel for them—but they will not know what is really happening. That which will be happening will be almost all underground. It has to be underground, otherwise it cannot happen.

I have a few secrets to impart to you, and I would not like to die before I have imparted them—because I don't know anybody else now alive in the world who can do that work. I have secrets from Taoism, secrets from Tantra, secrets from Yoga, secrets from Sufis, secrets from Zen people. I have lived in almost all the traditions of the world; I have been a wanderer in many lives. I have gathered much honey from many flowers. And the time, sooner or later, will come when I will have to depart—and I will not be able to enter again in the body. This is going to be my last life. All the honey that I have gathered I would like to share with you, so that you can share it with others, so that it does not disappear from the earth.

This is going to be a very secret work; hence I cannot speak about it. I think I have already spoken too much! I should not have said even this. The work will be only for those who are utterly devoted.

Right now, we have a big press office to make as many people as possible aware of the phenomenon that is happening here. But in the new commune the real work will simply disappear from the world's eyes. The press office will function—it will function for other purposes. People will go on coming, because from the visitors we have to choose; we have to invite people who can be participants, who can dissolve in the commune. But the real work is going to be absolutely secret. It is going to be only between me and you.

And there will not be much talk between me and you either. More and more I will become silent, because the real communion is through energy, not through words. As you get ready to receive the energy in silence, I will become more and more silent. But I am keeping a great treasure for you. Be receptive. . . .

All that is beautiful and all that is great in human history has happened only through a few people who put their energies together for the inner exploration. My commune is going to be a mystery school for inner exploration. It is the greatest adventure there is, and the greatest dance too.

SILENT *SATSANGS* AND COMMENTARIES ON BUDDHA'S *DHAMMAPADA*

In June 1979, Osho conducts a ten-day experiment in silent communion, or satsang. He appears in Buddha Hall and sits with the assembly for an hour of music and silent meditation in place of discourse. On June 21, Osho introduces his twelve-part series of commentaries on Gautam Buddha's Dhammapada.

Words are becoming more and more difficult for me. They are becoming more and more of an effort. I have to say something so I go on saying something to you. But I would like you to get ready as soon as possible so that we can simply sit in silence . . . listening to the birds and their songs . . . or listening just to your own heartbeat . . . just being here, doing nothing. . . .

Get ready as soon as possible, because I may stop speaking any day. And let the news be spread to all the nooks and corners of the world: those who want to understand me only through the words, they should come soon, because I may stop speaking *any* day. Unpredictably, any day, it may happen—it may happen even in the middle of a sentence. Then I am not going to complete the sentence! Then it will hang forever and forever . . . incomplete.

But this time you have pulled me back.

These sayings of Buddha are called the *Dhammapada*. . . .

ASSASSINATION ATTEMPT

On May 22, 1980, Vilas Tupe, a member of a fundamentalist Hindu group, throws a knife at Osho during his morning discourse. The local police have been tipped off and are present in the hall when the incident occurs. After the police remove Tupe and take him into custody, Osho continues his talk. Because of subsequent manipulations of the legal proceedings by police officials and members of Vilas Tupe's group, the case is dropped and Tupe is released without being convicted of any crime. A few weeks later, Osho explains what has happened.

The Pune magistrate has given his judgment concerning the case of one madman who had thrown a dagger at me, obviously intending to kill me. He has freed him, and the reason that he has freed him—the most basic reason that he has given—is really worth consideration. I laughed at it, I enjoyed it! The reason that he has freed him is that if it was an attempt to murder me, then I would not have continued my discourse! Who can continue talking when somebody is trying to murder you? But he does not know me. I would have continued even if I had died—I would not have finished before ten!

But he cannot understand—and I can understand that he cannot understand. When somebody is trying to kill you, can you go on speaking the same way? His argument seems to be very valid. So what to say about the ordinary masses? Even an educated magistrate thinks in the same way.

WORLDWIDE EXPANSION

In late 1980 and early 1981, a center is set up in the United States to distribute Osho's books, audio tapes, and videotapes. Sannyasins overseas are encouraged to support their local meditation centers and communes. There are programs to train new group leaders. In London in the spring of 1981, a two-day sampling of Osho's meditations and group workshops called The March Event is organized and draws about five hundred participants through advertising that includes signs on London buses and underground trains. This is followed by similar events in other capitals in the world.

My effort is not only to create a buddhafield here, but to create small oases all over the world. I would not like to confine this tremendous possibility only to this small commune. This commune will be the source, but it will have branches all over the world. It will be the root, but it is going to become a big tree. It is going to reach every country, it is going to reach every potential person. We will create small communes, centers, all over the world.

Be in the world, but don't be of it. Live in the world, but don't allow the world to live in you. That's my message.

There is a Zen saying: "The wild geese do not intend to cast their reflections. The water has no mind to receive their image."

The wild goose has no desire to cast its reflection in the water, and the water has no desire or no mind to receive its image—although it happens! When the wild goose flies, the water reflects it. The reflection is there, the image is there, but the water has no mind to reflect and the wild geese do not hanker to be reflected either.

This should be the way of my sannyasins. Be in the world, live in the world, live totally, without ambitions, without desires—because all desires distract you from living, all ambitions sacrifice your present. Don't be greedy, because greed takes you into the future; don't be possessive, because possessiveness keeps you clinging to the past. A man who wants to live in the present has to be free of greed, of possessiveness, of ambitions, of desires.

And that's what I call the whole art of meditation. Be aware, be alert, so all these thieves have no possibility to enter and contaminate you. Be meditative, but be in the world. And this is my experience: that the world helps *immensely*— it helps immensely to make you meditative. It gives you all the opportunities to be distracted, but if you don't get distracted then each success becomes a tremendous joy. You remain centered, you become the center of the cyclone. The cyclone goes on roaring around you, but your center remains unaffected.

That's the way of a true sannyasin: being in the world but remaining untouched, unaffected by it.

IN SILENCE

On April 10, 1981, Osho sends a message that he is entering the ultimate stage of his work, and that from this date he will speak only through silence. He continues to meet with his secretary but does not appear until three weeks later when the satsangs are resumed and Osho appears in the meditation hall to sit silently with his disciples and visitors. An ancient Buddhist chant is sung at the beginning of the meetings, and they end with music, singing, and dancing.

Meanwhile, Osho's health has become more and more fragile. In addition to his allergies, he now has severe back pains, and doctors are concerned that he might need surgery at some point. Their concern is heightened when a dangerous crisis arises related to a prolapsed disk and the potential for nerve damage if it is aggravated. The assistant to

Osho's personal secretary, Ma Anand Sheela, arranges for him to go to the United States where he can be treated should another crisis arise. On June 1, 1981, he flies from Bombay to New York with his household and medical staff.

1981–1985: THE BIG MUDDY RANCH

A few weeks after Osho's arrival in the United States, Sheela finalizes the purchase of a one hundred and twenty-six-square-mile former cattle ranch in the high desert of eastern Oregon. Twenty miles away from the nearest town of Antelope, the Big Muddy Ranch, as it is called, is a severely overgrazed parcel fronting the John Day River and straddling two Oregon counties. It contains only a small farmhouse and a few outbuildings in a valley at the end of a steep and dusty unpaved road. By the end of August, a number of prefabricated houses have been installed on the land, including one for Osho's residence. He and his household staff are taken to the Ranch on August 29.

Buddha committed mistakes, Mahavira committed mistakes; and I am sitting before you—in coming to Oregon, do you think I have not committed a mistake? I am proof enough that being enlightened does not mean you are infallible. You can fall into the Big Muddy Ranch! And now it is so difficult to get out of it. The more you try to get out of it, the more you are going into the mud.

This is so clear that there is no need for me to quote what mistakes Buddha committed, what mistakes Mahavira committed: I have committed mistakes, and I go on committing them; but that does not endanger my enlightenment. It has nothing to do with it.

I make the best possible use of my mistakes. That's what we are doing in the Big Muddy Ranch—trying—that's why I say, trying, in an enlightened way, to make something good out of it. If we have fallen into it, it may be our mistake—but it is fortunate for the Big Muddy Ranch, so let's make the best of it. And we are trying hard to make the best of it.

But all these other people have been claiming infallibility. I am, in many ways, a crackpot. I should not be saying such things, that I commit mistakes. This is not in tune with my profession; it is against it. That's why people of my profession hate me, because they say, "These things you should not say. Even if you come to know that you have committed a mistake, try to cover it. Try to make it appear as if it is not a mistake." That's what they have been doing for centuries. But I cannot do it. I am simply helpless, I cannot deceive.

RAJNEESHPURAM: THE ILLEGAL CITY

Within a few months it becomes clear that Osho's sannyasins are hoping to create a self-sufficient community with facilities for housing up to five thousand residents, hosting large festivals four times a year, and publishing Osho's books. The population grows quickly over the spring and summer and, while housing themselves in tents, the newcomers create a huge truck farm and dairy operation, begin to lay pipes and wiring for infrastructure, set about improving roads, restoring creekbeds, and revegetating barren hillsides. Local hostility toward the settlement quickly grows vocal and aggressive. Construction permits are denied, threats of violence against Osho and members of the community are made, and a hotel purchased by sannyasins in Portland is bombed. The governor of Oregon states that in his opinion, if the newcomers are not welcome by the surrounding community they should leave.

In 1982, residents of the ranch vote to incorporate themselves as the City of Rajneeshpuram in Wasco County. This incorporation is approved by county commissioners, only to be challenged in court by a land-use watchdog group calling itself "1000 Friends of Oregon." The state's attorney general later challenges the incorporation of the city on constitutional grounds, claiming that it violates the separation of church and state. Fundamentalist Christian preachers suggest that Osho is the antichrist, and local ranchers use directional signs to Rajneeshpuram for target practice. T-shirts and baseball caps featuring the crosshairs of a rifle scope overlaid on Osho's image are sold at "anti-Rajneesh" rallies.

Osho applies for a residency permit as a religious teacher, but it is denied on the grounds that he is in silence and therefore cannot be a teacher—a decision later overturned on appeal. By 1984, the city's legal department has a staff of more than two hundred people and is engaged in dozens of court cases. Documents obtained under the Freedom of Information Act reveal that the highest levels of the Reagan administration are involved in pressuring federal and state agencies to find a way to dismantle the community and expel Osho from the country.

They want this city to be demolished because of their land-use laws. And none of those idiots has come to see how we are using the land. Can they use it more creatively than we are using it? And for fifty years nobody was using the land; they were happy, that was good use. Now we are creating out of it. We are a self-sufficient commune. We are producing our food, our vegetables, our fruits; we are making every effort to make it self-sufficient.

This desert . . . somehow it seems to be a destiny of people like me. Moses ended up in a desert. I have ended up in a desert and we are trying to make it green. We have made it green. If you go around my house you cannot think it is Oregon; you will think it is Kashmir. There was not a single tree when I arrived. There was no greenery. I was simply shocked when Sheela brought me here; the house was standing naked. And I have always lived in beautiful gardens; wherever I have lived, I have created a beautiful garden.

We have turned the place, with great effort, toward fertility. Our people are working twelve, fourteen hours a day; and they don't come to see what has happened here. Just sitting in the capitol they decide that it is against land-use laws. If this is against land-use laws, then your land-use laws are bogus and should be burned. But first come and see, and prove that this is against land-use laws. But they are afraid to come here.

I have always respected America as a country of democracy. I have always appreciated the respect for the individual, for freedom, freedom of expression. I have always loved the American Constitution. And now I feel it would have been better if I had not come here, because now I am feeling absolutely disappointed. That Constitution is bogus. These words—*individual, freedom, capitalism, freedom of expression*—are all just words. Behind the screen it is the same politician, the same ugly face, the same mean mind—because in my opinion only the meanest people in the world are attracted to politics. The meanest, the lowest, because they know they can do something only if they have power. You need power only to do something harmful; otherwise love is enough, compassion is enough.

YOUR CITY IS REALLY UNIQUE IN THE WHOLE HISTORY OF HUMANity. There have been cities and there have been no cities; but an illegal city? Never heard before. It is a city, but illegal. It is not recognized that you are. Ignored, you don't exist.

I am here, and I am going to be here. There is no way to send me back . . . because I have my own arrangements. I persuaded the Indian government to reject me, so where are you going to send me? You can deport me only to India. India I persuaded beforehand; they are not going to accept me at all. Now I am stuck here in the Big Muddy Ranch. There is no way, no crane to get me out.

But these fools are in power. They have removed even the name of Rajneeshpuram from the Wasco County master plan. In the Wasco County files, Rajneeshpuram does not exist. If five thousand people suddenly disappear, the Oregon government will not be able even to say that they have disappeared, because then they would have to first accept that we were here—and we are not here!

But in a way it is perfectly good. If we are not in Oregon, then of course we are not in America. This seems to be the new birth of a new nation. Soon we will have to make our own constitution and declare our own independence. What else to do?

CHURCH AND STATE

Just the other day some information came to me: The attorney general of Oregon has declared Rajneeshpuram illegal. The reason that he has given is that here in Rajneeshpuram, religion and state are mixed.

Now, in the first place, our religion has nothing to do with any religion that has ever existed on the earth. It is just a legal necessity that we have to declare that we are a religion; otherwise, you cannot find such an irreligious commune in the whole world. What religion is there? No God, no Holy Ghost, no Jesus Christ, no pope, no prayer, nobody concerned at all about death. Everybody is so much involved with life, who has time?

In fact, even if death comes to my people, she will have to wait. My people are so involved in living that even death will have to consider . . . She can take people easily who have been dead for thirty, forty, or fifty years. It is not a problem for death, there is no need to be concerned; they just have to be carried away. They have lived posthumous lives long enough.

Perhaps death is too busy—must be. This planet and fifty thousand other planets have life; and no religion has said that there are even associates, deputies, of death. Death is alone. Poor death needs a great bureaucracy, and she is doing the whole job all alone. So of course many people die when they are near about thirty years of age, and then they have to wait for forty, fifty years, or sixty years, when their number comes up. What can death do? She has not yet cleaned out the old pending files, and you go on dying.

But with my people death will be surprised.

These are living people, so involved in life that they have not even bothered about death. She will have second thoughts before she can take you. She may think, "It is better to let me first finish the pending job, which is unending. These people can be taken later on; let them live a little more."

What kind of religion is this? I have called it a religionless religion. I have called it religiousness.

Here there is no sermon. Certainly my talks cannot be called sermons. You can call them antisermons. What religion do they think is here, which is interfering with the state? And what state is there? In the first place we are not a religion defined by any dictionary in the whole world. We will have to create our own dictionary, our own definitions.

And what state is there? Just a city council, which has to take care of the roads, of cleanliness, of the houses, of the hospital. How is religion going to interfere with the roads? I have tried hard but cannot figure it out: how to mix religion with roads? How to mix religion with houses? How to mix religion with hospitals, with medicines, with injections? They should give us some clue as to how they do it. Because here, no religious priest even goes to our hospital to bore the patients.

Those people write on their dollar, "We trust in God." On the dollar! Who is mixing religion with state? You are mixing religion even with the dirty dollar! In front of the Supreme Court it is written, "We trust in God." If someday I happen to be in the Supreme Court—it is very possible, I may manage it—then I am going to ask them, "Where is God? And on what authority have you written this? And if at the very gate there is a lie, you cannot ask me to take the oath for the truth. Rather, ask me to take the oath to only speak lies and not truth"—because the greatest lie is there, just at the gate of the Supreme Court. On every dollar bill is the great lie: We trust in God.

These people go on mixing religion in every way, but they are legal. I don't have any way to mix my religion with anything, it is so unmixable. This is the only legal city in the whole world. If mixing religion makes a city illegal, then all the cities of the world are illegal because everywhere religion is mixed. This is the only place where religion is not mixed at all.

Religion, in fact, does not exist here at all.

AFTER SEVERAL APPEALS, THE LEGALITY OF THE CITY OF RAJNEESHPU-ram was finally upheld by the U.S. Supreme Court in May 1988, after Osho had been back in India for almost two years.

1983: CITYWIDE AIDS TESTING

Osho is still in silence and seclusion, but when his doctor informs him about the development of the AIDS epidemic, he suggests that the City of Rajneeshpuram initiate universal testing for all residents and visitors. He further recommends that people take precautions to avoid infection with the virus, including use of condoms, using latex gloves in foreplay that involves contact with body fluids, and avoidance of kissing. At the time, these measures are considered to be extreme and even absurd, and provoke ridicule by the media. Members of the community who are found to be HIV positive are secluded in separate housing and provided with work to do, entertainment, and medical care.

Perhaps this is the only place in the world where every precaution has been taken against AIDS. Six thousand people have gone through tests—no other place has guts enough to put the whole city through tests. They are afraid that they may find people who have AIDS. And the people who feel perhaps they may have it are not going through the test, for the simple reason that if they are found positive, then even their wives, their children, their parents, will reject them. They will have no place in their own home. They will not be allowed in any restaurant. Their own friends will become their enemies.

So they don't want to be tested; the government does not want it, the hospitals do not want it. And the fire is spreading; nobody wants to recognize it, to see it. This is not intelligence. Just closing your eyes does not mean that the enemy has disappeared.

We have found a few people with AIDS, two persons. We have made a beautiful isolation place for them; the best that we could afford has been given to them. They have all our respect and love.

1984: A TASTE OF FASCISM

In October 1984, Osho decides to end his period of silence and seclusion and resume his daily talks. Curiously, his secretary Sheela is opposed to this decision and tries to persuade him not to speak, citing concerns about his health. It is finally arranged that he will begin by speaking to small groups of people in the living room of his home.

At first, videotapes of his talks are shown to the whole community on the following day, in the large meditation hall. When Sheela proposes that these showings should be suspended because there is too much work to be done, the community revolts and a compromise is worked out so that the videos can be shown late at night, after the day's work is complete.

Finally, on September 14, 1985, Sheela and a close-knit group of her supporters pack up and leave with all their possessions and go to Germany. As soon as she is gone, an avalanche of evidence emerges about criminal activities some of her followers had been engaged in, including attempted murder by poisoning of Osho's physician and caretaker, firebombing of a county planning office, and wiretapping of Osho's room and of phones and offices within the community.

Osho makes public all the information he has received and offers his full cooperation to state and federal investigators. Members of the press arrive in droves to interview Osho and question him about how such events could have taken place.

Q: IN MY MEETING SHEELA, CERTAINLY ONE COULD SEE HER INTELLIGENCE, at least in very practical matters, in her cleverness about things, but you could also see the very oppressive side, the very mean-spirited side as well. You must have seen that being in contact with her every day?

A: I know! But it was needed for all those mean politicians all around. I could not put the commune in the hands of some innocent people—the politicians would have destroyed it.

Q: But you didn't see what she was doing on the ranch itself?

A: No, because I was never coming out and never meeting anybody. . . .

Q: But if you're creating such a big experiment [as the commune in Oregon], don't you think it would have been helpful to have had at least one other person coming to talk to you?

A: No. The experiment means nothing compared to my silence. I am teaching everybody to be an individual and depend on his own insight. And if he feels that he is being forced to do something that he does not want to do, he is perfectly capable of revolting against it. There is no need to submit—and many people left.

Now there will be a totally different atmosphere—but looking at the world, whatever happened, although it was not good, only bad people could have managed it. Good people could not.

Q: Over the last year I thought to myself, When is he either going to get rid of Sheela or turn things around? And it felt like maybe you were just letting her go and do things.

A: I will do something only when I feel it is time. When I saw that the point had come to do something, I did it.

Q: How did you know the point had come to do something?

A: When her group poisoned my physician. That was the point when I started asking my physician and my caretaker about things, and I declared that I was going to speak and meet with people. Then information started coming by and by, and I started exposing Sheela and her group. Then I informed the government, the police, the FBI—they are all here, but they are doing almost nothing. We have given them every proof—and they go on saying, "We don't have any solid proof." I don't understand what solid proof they want—do they want the person, caught red-handed?

Q: *Why did you wait nine months or so?*

A: It was needed, because she was fighting so many legal cases—I did not want to disturb things in the middle. I wanted things to come to a conclusion from where a new group could start. And this was the time, when many cases are finished and the new cases will start almost eight months later, so these new people within eight months will be perfectly prepared to take over. And they will be able to fight—there is no problem.

Q: *You play a very risky game.*

A: Certainly! I am a risky person. And it is a game—I know the right timings. I am just a referee, nothing more.

•from an interview with James Gordon,
The New Yorker

GROWING REVELATIONS ABOUT THE CRIMINAL ACTIVITIES OF SHEELA'S group create a state of shock and disarray within the community, and waves of hindsight arise about the underlying strategy behind previously inexplicable situations and events. As people begin to struggle with the issues of personal responsibility and accountability, Osho addresses these questions with increasing sharpness in his daily discourses.

We are trying to live a different kind of life than in the outside world. So there are only two ways: either the way of Sheela or my way. I had chosen Sheela to be my secretary to give you a little taste of what fascism means. Now, live my way. Be responsible, so that there is no need for anybody to dictate to you. . . .

If you want Sheela back, I can call her and her whole gang, and give the commune to her. If you don't want anybody to be dictatorial to you, then take responsibility.

And you are a group of very intelligent people, but this is the trouble with intelligent people. They always try to misuse freedom.

I would like to remind you that Germany is one of the most intellectual countries in the world. It has given to the world people like Kant, Hegel, Feuerbach, Karl Marx, Sigmund Freud, Martin Heidegger—great philosophers, great psychologists. And still a third-class crackpot, Adolf Hitler, managed to get all the intelligentsia of the country to follow him.

And I don't think humanity has learned anything out of it. If you don't learn, then history repeats. If you learn, then you can stop history from repeating again.

Martin Heidegger was perhaps one of the most significant philosophers of the century, and he was a contemporary of Adolf Hitler. He supported Adolf Hitler—inconceivable! The whole youth, which is the cream of the society, its intelligence, all the universities' vice-chancellors, professors—they all supported Adolf Hitler, a man who was uneducated, a man who was refused from the school of art, who was refused from the school of architecture because he had no intelligence. This man became the leader of the most intelligent country in the world, and he created the most fascist regime. He killed almost ten million people, and still people were supporting him.

It has to be psychoanalyzed. What was the reason? The reason was, Germany was defeated in the First World War. And the intellectuals tend to fight among themselves. They argue, rationalize, philosophize; they are not physically active people. And they are egoists. They think they have found the secret of life, every one of them.

After its defeat in the First World War, Germany was in a chaos. The chaos created Adolf Hitler, because he promised, and he fulfilled the promise, "I can make this country again united, again strong, so strong that it can rule over the whole world."

It was something that was immensely needed. People were not working, people were not being creative. Somebody was needed to make the country again creative, disciplined, and Adolf Hitler filled the gap. Within ten years Germany was again a world power.

Strange—if you give people freedom, they become lazy, they don't want to work. But if you give them a fascist order, they work to their very potential; they create, they are united, they become strong. Germany went on winning for five years. That proved that the people of Germany had chosen the right person—the whole world on one side, and he alone was enough.

He gave the intelligentsia their ego as nobody had given them before. He said to them that the Nordic German race is the purest Aryan race, and it is its destiny to rule over the world because all others are subhuman. It was tremendously gratifying. The intellectual ego was very much fulfilled, and even a man like Martin Heidegger fell into the trap.

Only after Hitler was defeated and Germany was almost destroyed, then people started looking back at what they had done, what kind of man they were supporting: a monster, a murderer who has killed millions of people—perhaps the greatest murderer in the whole of history.

So remember one thing: freedom is not license. Freedom is responsibility. And if you cannot take your responsibility yourself, then somebody is going to take the responsibility on your behalf. And then you are enslaved.

People have been asking me how it happened that five thousand people, almost all university graduates, having the best qualifications from the best universities of the world, could not see for four years what was happening.

The reason is that Sheela was not only doing something ugly and fascist, she was also creating the commune. She was also making the desert into an oasis. She was making the commune comfortable in every way. Every coin has two sides, so you looked at the light side. And you were surrounded—which Sheela and her group created—with hostility in Oregon. That is a simple political strategy.

Adolf Hitler, in his autobiography, *Mein Kampf*, says that if you want a nation to be strong, create enemies all around it; otherwise, people relax. Keep them continuously in paranoia, fearing that there is danger all around. And Sheela created that. She created the hostility of the Oregon government. She created the hostility of Americans in general. That made you come close to each other, become strong: "Be ready so that nobody can harm you."

So if you don't take the responsibility, something like that is bound to happen again. History certainly repeats, because man does not learn.

ARREST
Osho has promised to cooperate with law enforcement agencies to fully investigate Sheela's crimes, but investigators turn most of their attention toward finding reasons to

indict Osho and the remaining residents of the city instead. There are persistent rumors of a grand jury indictment to come, charging Osho and several sannyasins with immigration violations. But attempts by Osho's attorneys to negotiate a peaceful surrender are rebuked by U.S. Attorney Charles Turner, on the grounds that it is "premature" to have such a discussion.

Meantime the National Guard has been mobilized into position to stage an invasion of Rajneeshpuram. Amid concerns that they intend to conduct an armed and aggressive raid on the community, a decision is made to fly Osho across the country to Charlotte, North Carolina. There, it is reasoned, he can be out of harm's way while his attorneys continue to try and clarify the situation. When Osho and his staff land in Charlotte they are met by heavily armed Customs agents and U.S. marshals, who have been told to expect dangerous terrorists. Having no warrant, the officers read out a list of suspects that has been faxed to them from Oregon. None of these people are on the plane; nevertheless all are arrested, along with Osho, and taken to prisoner holding cells in Charlotte's federal building.

In a hearing that begins three days later, the sannyasins accompanying Osho are released, but the judge orders that Osho be returned to Oregon for a separate bail hearing. Authorities insist that he be taken on a prisoner transport plane rather than flown in a commercial airline or private jet. The prisoner transport plane takes six days to complete the journey across the country, and for one of those days the government refuses to reveal Osho's whereabouts even to his own attorneys. It is eventually learned that during this time he was being held in a federal penitentiary in Oklahoma, under a false name, allegedly for his own protection.

Osho is finally released on bail in Oregon, charged with a string of immigration violations alleging that he participated in arranging marriages among his disciples and that he misstated his intent on his original tourist visa application. After negotiations with Oregon officials, Osho's lawyers remain very concerned for his safety should the case proceed. Reluctantly, Osho agrees to plead "no contest" to two of the thirty-four charges against him and to leave the country.

His health declines dramatically as a result of his imprisonment, although it will be more than two years before his doctors begin to suspect that Osho was poisoned while he was in government custody.

WHEN THEY DEPORTED ME, [U.S. ATTORNEY CHARLES TURNER] ADMITted in a press conference that I had not committed any crime. The reason he gave for deporting me was: "We wanted to destroy the commune. That was our priority." And without deporting me, it was impossible to destroy the commune.

They arrested me without any arrest warrant and without showing me any reason for arresting me. Just a piece of paper on which there were a few names—"We have been ordered that these people should be immediately arrested."

I said, "But you should look at our passports! My name is not on this paper; neither are the names of the six people who are with me on this paper. You are absolutely absurd. Just look at our passports and compare with your names; you are arresting the wrong people." Still, we were arrested.

In fact, they had no evidence at all to arrest me. But they did not give me bail for twelve days. They arrested me in North Carolina, and the flight from North Carolina to Oregon, where the commune was located, was only five hours. It took twelve days for me to reach Portland, and they dragged me from jail to jail; in twelve days I was dragged to six jails.

Only later on I became aware of it, when the British experts in poisoning looked into my symptoms and gave the verdict, that I was given a certain poison, thallium. It is not detectable either from blood or from urine; it simply disappears. I had all the symptoms—when the poison disappears, it leaves certain kinds of sicknesses in the body. This poison has been used against political prisoners. But if you give it in a bigger dose, the person dies immediately. That's why they wanted twelve days, to give it to me in small doses so I would not die in their jails—they would be condemned by the whole world.

And when they released me, I was ordered to leave America immediately, within fifteen minutes. My car was in front of the courthouse and my jet plane was kept with its engine running at the airport; I should leave immediately. They were afraid that if I stayed one day more, I might appeal to the Supreme Court. And there was every reason for me to win the case, because none of their charges . . . thirty-four charges against a man who was in silence, had never moved out of his house. How can he commit thirty-four crimes? And they had no evidence of any crime.

When I saw democracy American-style at work . . . it was absolute nonsense to talk about democracy. Their Constitution is just a showpiece for the world. The country consists of criminals talking about freedom.

1985-1986: THE "WORLD TOUR"

KULU MANALI

On November 14, 1985, immediately after his trial, Osho leaves from the Portland airport and flies to Delhi via Cyprus. He lands in Delhi on November 17 and is greeted by thousands of Indian sannyasins. There he gives a press conference and continues on to Kulu Manali, where he schedules regular press interviews beginning November 19. His sannyasins meantime begin a search to find a place where he can settle again and resume his work. The Indian government refuses to extend visas for his caretaker, physician, and other household staff, and threatens to confiscate Osho's passport unless he stops giving press interviews and meeting with his disciples. On January 3, 1986, he flies to Kathmandu in Nepal.

The king of Nepal was ready for me to have my residence and commune there, but the condition was that I should not speak against Hinduism. Nepal is a Hindu kingdom, the only Hindu kingdom in the world.

I refused. I said, "I never plan what to speak and what not to speak. I cannot promise. And if I see anything wrong, then it does not matter whether it is Hinduism or Christianity or Mohammedanism, I am going to speak against it."

On January 21, Osho makes an announcement:

I am going on a world tour—because I don't believe in political boundaries, and I conceive of the whole earth as mine. And I have my people all around the world, many of whom I have not seen for years—my people who have already taken the first step; they have already separated themselves from the crowd. They are no longer Christians, no longer Jews, no longer Hindus. They have done a great job, something rare, something unique never done by such a vast number of people before.

Now there are only two ways: either they should come to me . . . which the vested interests are going to make more and more difficult. They would like to isolate me from my people—they have already started doing that. I have my own way to respond to their fascist strategy. Rather than calling people to me, I will be going to my people.

Three governments have invited me, knowing perfectly well that America is against me and is pressuring governments that I should not be allowed to go anywhere. Three governments have been courageous enough—and those countries are not rich, they are poor countries, South American countries. But they want to show America: "You don't have the monopoly over the world."

So going around the world will help us to find who is a friend and who is not. And my own experience is that one of our friends is equal to one hundred enemies . . . because *they* don't have anything, just old, rotten ideas that are out of date. Just a little push and they will fall apart.

They are fighting for the dead.

We are fighting for the unborn.

And the decision of existence is always for life.

CRETE

On February 16, Osho flies to Greece with a four-week tourist visa and stays in a villa on the island of Crete. Three days later he begins giving talks outdoors on the grounds of the villa, under a huge spreading tree. Within days, many of his sannyasins begin to arrive from nearby European countries. The local Greek Orthodox bishop speaks against Osho in his sermons to his congregation, distributes a pamphlet in which he accuses Osho of corrupting the morals of young people, and threatens to bring a protest march to the villa. On March 5, the police arrive while Osho is taking his afternoon nap, to arrest and deport him. When Osho's legal secretary asks them to show a warrant, the police arrest her and proceed to break down doors and windows to enter the house and take Osho into custody.

ON THE ROAD TO URUGUAY, SWITZERLAND, SWEDEN, LONDON, IRELAND, SPAIN, SENEGAL

From Greece we moved to Geneva, just for an overnight rest, and the moment they came to know my name they said, "No way! We cannot allow him into our country."

I was not even allowed to get out of the plane.

We moved to Sweden, thinking that people go on saying that Sweden is far more progressive than any country in Europe or in the world, that Sweden has been giving refuge to many terrorists, revolutionaries, expelled politicians, that it is very generous.

We reached Sweden. We wanted to stay overnight because the pilots were running out of time. They could not go on anymore; otherwise it would become illegal. And we were happy because we had asked only for an overnight stay, but the man at the airport gave seven-day visas to everybody. But immediately the police came and canceled the visas and told us to leave: "This man we cannot allow in our country."

They can allow terrorists, they can allow murderers, they can allow Mafia people and they can give them refuge—but they cannot allow me. And I was not asking for refuge or permanent residence, just an overnight stay.

We turned to London, because it was simply a question of our basic right. And we made it twice-legal—we purchased first-class tickets for the next day. Our own jet was there, but still we purchased the tickets in case they started saying, "You don't have tickets for tomorrow, so we won't allow you to stay in the first-class lounge."

We purchased tickets for everybody just so that we could stay in the lounge, and we told them, "We have our own jet, and we also have tickets." But they came upon a bylaw of the airport that nobody can interfere with: "It is our discretion—and this man we won't allow in the lounge."

I wondered: "How can I destroy their morality, their religion, by staying in the lounge? In the first place I will be sleeping, and by the morning we will be gone." But no, these so-called civilized countries are as primitive and barbarous as you can conceive. They said, "All that we can do is, we can put you in jail for the night."

IN IRELAND, WE SIMPLY WANTED ONE DAY'S STAY TO GIVE A REST TO the pilots—the man at the airport gave us seven days. He did not bother who we were, what the purpose was. He must have been really drunk! We reached a hotel, and in the morning the police came, asked for the passports, and canceled those seven days.

We said, "You have given us seven days and now you have canceled them without giving any reason. None of our people has gone out of the hotel; they have not committed any crime. You cannot do this."

They were caught in a dilemma. They had given seven days; now they had canceled them and they didn't have any reason to show why. So they said, "You can stay as long as you want, but don't go outside the hotel."

We remained there for fifteen days because we needed some time. Our people were working in Spain, and the Spanish government was willing to give me permanent residence. So we just wanted time: if Spain was ready we could move from Ireland to Spain. We stayed in Ireland for fifteen days without any visa.

And the day we left Ireland, a minister informed the members of the parliament that we had never *been* in Ireland. Cultured people, educated people— and flatly lying, saying I had never been in Ireland! And he knew, his government knew, the chief of police knew.

I am thinking that once I get settled somewhere then I will start . . . one by one each country had to be dragged into court for their lies, for calling me "dangerous," for saying yes and then refusing after one hour. I am going to expose it to the world for the simple understanding that there is no democracy anywhere.

ON MARCH 14, OSHO AND HIS PARTY ARE PROMISED VISAS TO SPAIN, but three days later they are refused on the basis of dossiers supplied by the American and German governments. On March 18, Osho's jet lands in Madrid and is surrounded by Guardia Civil while the Uruguayan consul stamps Uruguayan visas in the passports of Osho and his attendants. The next stop is in Dacca, Senegal, for an overnight stay in a hotel before traveling on to Uruguay. On the same day, the European Parliament discusses a motion to prevent Osho from entering any European Commonwealth country.

You will be surprised: I am being discussed in parliaments of countries where I have never been, even in countries where not a single sannyasin exists, as if I am the biggest world problem to them. They are facing a nuclear third world war, but their worry is about me!

It is significant that they have recognized that if I am allowed to go on teaching, their rotten societies will start collapsing. And I am going to continue no matter what; they cannot prevent me. I will find my ways. And now more than ever I am going to sharpen every argument against them and expose every government that has been preventing me from reaching my own people.

URUGUAY

On April 12, Osho settles into a large house near the sea in Punta del Este, Uruguay. There he resumes his daily talks in an intimate setting, for a group of twenty to thirty people. At this time he begins to talk about his vision of the next phase of his work.

My new phase of work is a mystery school. You can work in the world, where roads are already there, houses are already there, you need not make them. Factories are already there . . . in thousands of years the world has created all that. So you can manage—five hours work, five days a week is enough. On the weekend you can meditate, you can go into silence or you can go to some isolated spot and just relax. And in a year you will be able to earn so much money, save so much money, that you can come here for one month, two months, three months . . . as much as you can manage.

Then being with me has no connotations of work. Then being with me is simply joy, celebration, meditation, singing, dancing. Those three months are simply holiday. You forget the world for those three months. They are pure search for the truth. And after three months, whatever you have learned, continue it at home; there you have time. Five hours you work—you have enough time; you can get at least two hours for yourself.

So each year you will be coming, then going, whatever you can manage. You will not be a burden on anybody, and there is no need for anybody to dominate you; there is no need for any strict discipline—work needs that. There is no need for coordinators, so we can avoid the power trip.

But both our communes have helped to bring us to this point where we can start a mystery school. Without those two communes it would have been impossible. This is my way of looking at things. Even failures bring you closer to success, because each failure gives you insight into what went wrong, how it went wrong. So both the experiments have been immensely significant.

Now we are in a position to create a totally different kind of place, which is simply a festival all the year round. People will be coming and going. They will take whatever they learn and they will practice it in the world, and they will come again to renew, to refresh, to go further, deeper. Only a skeleton crew will be there to take care of you.

THE URUGUAYAN GOVERNMENT HAD ORIGINALLY ISSUED A ONE-year residency permit for Osho, with the intention of extending it to three years and eventually granting him citizenship. By early June, however, the government is under pressure from the Americans not to allow Osho to settle. In mid-June the American government delivers an ultimatum to the Uruguayan president: deport Osho from the country or risk losing billions of dollars of U.S. aid. Reluctantly, he complies.

On June 19, 1986, Osho flies from Uruguay to Jamaica, where he has a two-week visa, but the following morning the police tell him to leave by that evening. On June 20, he flies to Lisbon, Portugal, where he stays quietly in a rented villa for a few weeks. Police surround his villa, and on July 30, he flies to Bombay.

The president of Uruguay said, "It is unfortunate that I have to do it. I am doing it against my own conscience."

The Americans were not even willing to concede that I should simply leave the country. My plane was waiting at the airport. . . . I said, "There is no problem; I can leave the country. I will not put your country into such jeopardy."

He said, "The American president insists that you should be deported; you should not leave the country without being deported. I am forced to commit crimes: first, to tell you for no reason to leave the country; you have done nothing. Second, to deport you. But I am absolutely helpless. Still, I want one thing: that on your passport there should be no stamp of deportation from Uruguay. We have a small airport—so move your airplane to that airport, and in the evening leave without informing us so we can say, "He left without informing us. There was no time to deport him."

But he was wrong. As my jet moved to the small airport, an American representative was there with all the stamps and the official whose business it is to deport people. I was delayed there, because they had to fill in all the forms, and as I left the country, I said, "It doesn't matter. In fact, my passport has become a historical document! I have been deported from so many countries without any reason."

When I left Uruguay the president was invited to America immediately, and Ronald Reagan gave him thirty-six million dollars as a "gesture of friendship." That was a reward because I was thrown out within thirty-six hours: exactly thirty-six million dollars, one million dollars per hour. In fact, I should start asking these governments for my percentage! You are getting billions of dollars because of me—I should get at least two percent.

1987: "PUNE TWO"

After spending five months in Bombay and resuming his daily schedule of talks in the home of one of his disciples, on December 30, 1986, Osho returns to the commune in Pune, which has been maintained by Indian sannyasins in his five-year absence. When

he first arrives, local government officials and an organization headed by the Hindu fun-
damentalist Vilas Tupe (see assassination attempt on page 246) stage a number of hos-
tile actions against Osho and the commune. After a few months, however—with the
support of Pune's Mayor Dhole Patil and with the help of friends in the Indian govern-
ment and judiciary—the commune is allowed to function more or less normally, with rel-
atively few incidents of overt harassment or interference.

Just yesterday I received another letter from the mayor of Pune:

> With my deepest love and pleasure I wish to state that Osho,
> presently residing at 17 Koregaon Park, Poona, in my home con-
> stituency, is undoubtedly an enlightened person. His authoritative
> views on religion are most needed in these turbulent times. He is one
> of the well-versed, great mystics and a spiritual master of our time.
> His conduct and loving behavior cannot and has never created any
> legal problems, nor has he ever been found guilty in any provisions of
> criminal law. In fact, his teachings are conducive to creating a very
> peaceful and tranquil atmosphere in the present circumstances when
> the country as a whole is passing through a very disturbed state.

By the end of 1987, thousands of sannyasins and visitors are coming through the com-
mune gates every day. Osho continues to suffer periods of ill health, plagued by pain in his
bones and joints, difficulties with his vision and sensitivity to light, lack of appetite, and recur-
ring ear infections. He is often unable to appear for his daily talks for days or weeks at a time.
And in his talks, he often refers to the fact that he will not be physically present forever, and
urges his listeners to make meditation their first priority. In March, he begins a "stop exer-
cise" as he enters and leaves the meditation hall, where he leads the gathering in dancing
with wild music and then suddenly stops for a few moments before resuming the dance.

I am trying to get you to come back home. You have gone far away, wandering after ephemeral things, wandering after dreams. And I want you to come back
home—because that which can give you contentment, that which can give you
fulfillment is not out there, it is in here; it is not in any other time, but now. And
the feeling of a stop—a total stop—is nothing but an experience of herenow.

I can give you only the taste, and once you have got the taste, then you will
be in search of it. Then there is no way to prevent you. The most fundamental
thing is a taste.

You have heard words, beautiful words, but they have not driven you into a mad search. I want to give not only words to you, but some content. And that is possible only by giving you some taste.

And the time is ripe. For so many of my sannyasins, the first flowers of spring have started showing. More and more flowers will be blossoming. And you have to be very impatiently patient—with a deep longing, but without any demands. Because I cannot be here forever. And I have waited long enough; now it is time that I should start giving you the taste. Words I have given you many—that was a preparation. Seeds I have sown many, and now that the spring is very close, you have to be courageous, and total, and intensively with me—in my silence, in my joy.

It is time that the duality between you and me is dropped.

Those who are intelligent should drop it immediately. Those who are a little less intelligent will take a little time. I have a little time more to linger on your shore . . . but it cannot be very long.

I CANNOT BE ALWAYS WITH YOU. I WOULD LOVE TO, BUT EXISTENCE does not allow it. Existence gives only so much rope, and it is good; otherwise you will start taking me for granted.

One day I will not be among you. It is good that once in a while I am absent, so you can start learning that what happens in my absence is your reality. When I am with you, you become overwhelmed with me. You forget yourself.

And you have not to forget yourself! You have to remember yourself, because only through remembrance will you be able to transform yourself.

It is natural that you miss my presence; hence I am not condemning it. But you are in search of something beyond—beyond the normal, the natural—something transcendental. You have to learn the way, and the way has to be traveled alone.

I cannot come with you. I can show you the way, I can show you the moon. But my fingers are not the moon, and I cannot continue to show you the moon. Sooner or later you have to forget my fingers and you have to look at the moon yourself. You have to follow the path alone.

Naturally when I was not coming daily, morning and evening, to be with you, you started feeling a kind of breakdown. It was not a breakdown; it was simply that your reality was surfacing. It had not been getting the opportunity to surface. I was so much with you that you had gone into the shadow, into the background. I had become more real to you than yourself.

When I was not coming, in my absence your reality was exposed to you. It is good, because unless you know what you are, where you are, your pilgrimage cannot begin. So those days were of great importance.

Remember: whatever you find within yourself, however much rubbish it may be, it is your reality. It can be cleaned, it can be dropped; you can move away from it. But before anything can be done about it, you have to know it. That is the first and the most significant thing.

MY APPROACH TO YOUR GROWTH IS BASICALLY TO MAKE YOU INDEpendent of me. Any kind of dependence is a slavery, and the spiritual dependence is the worst slavery of all.

I have been making every effort to make you aware of your individuality, your freedom, your absolute capacity to grow without any help from anybody. Your growth is something intrinsic to your being. It does not come from outside; it is not an imposition, it is an unfolding.

All the meditation techniques that I have given to you are not dependent on me—my presence or absence will not make any difference—they are dependent on you. It is not *my* presence, but *your* presence that is needed for them to work.

It is not *my* being here but *your* being here, your being in the present, your being alert and aware, that is going to help.

POISONED IN RONALD REAGAN'S AMERICA

After a period of seven weeks during which doctors were unable to cure Osho of an ear infection and he was very ill, he appears on November 6, 1987, to announce that his doctors believe he was poisoned with thallium during the time he was imprisoned in the United States.

My personal physician, Dr. Amrito, immediately informed all sannyasin doctors around the world and asked them to contact the best experts about poisoning, because his own analysis was that unless I have been poisoned there is no possibility to explain why my body has lost all resistance. And as this idea became stronger in his mind, step by step he started searching into the matter and he found all the symptoms that can happen only if some kind of poison has been given to me.

Since those twelve days in the American prisons, all sleep has disappeared. Many things started to happen in the body that were not happening before: disappearance of all appetite, food seeming to be absolutely without taste, a churning feeling in the stomach, nausea, a desire to vomit . . . no feeling of thirst, but a tremendous sense as if one is uprooted. Something in the nervous system also seems to have been affected. At times there has been a sensation of tingling all over the body which was very strong—particularly in both my hands—and a twitching of the eyelids.

The day I entered the jail I was one hundred and fifty pounds; today I am only one hundred and thirty pounds. And just three months ago, the bone in my right hand started hurting tremendously. These are all symptoms of certain poisons. Dr. Amrito immediately informed all the doctors who are my sannyasins to approach all the best poison experts in the world. And one of the doctors, Dr. Dhyan Yogi, immediately took my blood samples, urine samples, samples of my hair, and went to England, to Germany, to the best experts. The European experts suggest that after two years there is no poison that can be detected in the body, but all the symptoms show that a certain poison has been given.

The European experts in England and Germany have suggested thallium, which is part of a family of poisons of heavy metals. It disappears from the body in eight weeks' time but leaves its effects and destroys the body's resistance against diseases. And all the symptoms that I have told you are part of thallium poisoning.

These seven weeks you were not aware . . . you were simply thinking I was sick. Dr. Premda, my eye surgeon, had immediately rushed from Germany with the best medications, but nothing helped against the poisons except my meditations—the only medicine that can transcend all that belongs to matter. These seven weeks I have been lying in darkness almost the whole day and night, silently witnessing the body and keeping my consciousness unshadowed by anything. I was struggling with death, it was a fight between death and your love. And you should celebrate that your love has been victorious.

It would have been immensely painful for me to leave you in this beautiful state when you have started growing upward. I would like my people to transform themselves and through them I would like to bring authentic civilization and humanity to this beautiful planet.

There is only one religion, and that is the religion of love. There is only one god, and that is the god of celebration, of life, of rejoicing. This whole earth is one and the whole humanity is one. We are parts of each other.

I have no complaint against those who have poisoned me. I can forgive them easily. They certainly do not know what they go on doing.

It is said that history repeats itself. It is not history that repeats itself; it is the unconsciousness of man, the blindness of man that repeats itself. The day man will be conscious, alert, and aware there will not be any repetition anymore. Socrates will not be poisoned, Jesus will not be crucified, Al-Hillaj Mansoor will not be murdered and butchered. And these are our best flowers, they are our highest peaks. They are our destinies, they are our future. They are our intrinsic potential that has become actual.

I am sure you will not have any anger in your hearts or any hatred for anyone, but just an understanding and a loving forgiveness. That is the only authentic prayer. And only this kind of prayerfulness can raise humanity to higher levels of consciousness.

I have absolute inner certainty: They may have been able to poison my body, my nervous system, but they cannot destroy my consciousness, they cannot poison my being. And it was good that they have given me a chance to see myself beyond my body, beyond my mind.

These seven weeks have been a fire test. Without your knowing you have always, each moment of these seven weeks, been a tremendous help to me. Without your love it would not have been possible for me to overcome the poison, because without your love there would be no need for me even to struggle. I am fulfilled and absolutely contented; I have arrived home. But I see you are stumbling, groping, and it will be very heartless and uncompassionate for me to leave you in this situation. I would like in all your lives a sunrise, the birds singing and the flowers opening. Other than that, I don't have any reason to be here at all.

Remember it: I am here for you. That remembrance will help you not to go astray. That remembrance will help you to be aware of the uncivilized world in which we are living, in this madhouse that we call humanity. It will go on reminding you that we have to give birth to a new man and to a new humanity.

This is the tremendous challenge. Those who have guts and intelligence and a desire and a longing to touch the farthest stars . . . only those very few people have been able to understand me, have been able to become my fellow travelers. I don't have any followers—I have only lovers and friends and fellow travelers.

I would like you all to reach to the same beatitude, to the same blissfulness, to the same ecstasy that has become my very heartbeat. It is also the heartbeat of the whole universe.

THE WORLD ACADEMY OF SCIENCES FOR CREATIVITY

On January 17, 1988, Osho talks about a vision for the commune that involves the creation of a meeting place where people can explore both the outer science of matter and the inner science of meditation. It is a proposal he has talked about often in the past, but now he refines it even more.

I want this ashram slowly to develop into a World Academy of Sciences for Creativity. This will be perhaps the greatest synthesis ever. Your search for religious truth in no way hinders your search for the objective reality, because the areas are absolutely separate; they don't overlap.

You can be a scientist and a meditator. In fact, the more you go deeper into meditation, the more clarity, the more intelligence, the more genius you will find flowering in you, which can create a totally new science.

The old science was created as a reaction against religion. The new science I'm talking about is not a reaction against anything, but an overflowing energy, intelligence, creativity. Politics corrupted science because its own interest was only war. Religions could not accept science because they were all superstitious, and science was going to demolish all their gods and all their superstitions. Science has passed these three hundred years in a very difficult situation, fighting on the one hand with religion and on the other hand unconsciously becoming a slave to the politicians.

I want this place to grow and I am making arrangements for a world academy of sciences and arts totally devoted to life-affirmative goals.

The science that can create Hiroshima and Nagasaki and destroy thousands of people, birds, trees—without any reason, just because the politicians wanted to see whether atomic energy works or not—the same science can create more food, more life, better health, more intelligence in all fields of life. But it should be taken out of the hands of politicians and it should not bother about religions.

Nobel Prize winners, eminent scientists, artists of different dimensions will constitute the academy, and they will make efforts to change science's whole trend of being destructive.

Our sannyasins—and there are many who are scientists, artists, physicians—will help the academy. We will arrange scholarships, and people from all over the world can come and study a new way of science, a new way of art that affirms life, that creates more love in humanity, and that prepares for the ultimate revolution.

That ultimate revolution is a single world government—because while the world does not have one government, you cannot stop wars. Each nation has to have its own military, its own defenses, its own weapons, and there is competition as to who has more destructive power. But once there is one world government there is no need of any armies, air forces, or navies; all these can be transformed into services dedicated to life, to the whole of humanity.

And the World Academy of Sciences will be the first step, because if we can take scientists from all over the world slowly out of the grip of the politicians, all the power of the politicians will be finished. They are not powerful; the scientist is the power behind them. And the scientist is in a difficulty, because there is no institute in the world that will give the scientist enough of the resources that he needs to work with.

The days are long gone when Galileo could make a small lab in his own house, and scientists could work independently without any support from outside. Now science is so complex and has grown so many branches—and each branch has become a science in itself—that unless he is supported by a government or a very powerful institution that has money, that has intelligence, that has dedicated students, the scientist cannot work.

It seems existence is arranging for the money that we will need to create the academy. Another very important man in Japan, who holds many foundations for humanitarian services, is also coming to see whether it is possible to bring money from those many foundations to create this world institute. And it will have support from all over the world, from all the scientists without exception, because now everybody is seeing that they are serving death, not life.

We can have the greatest library for scientific research and we can have sannyasins working, studying. The synthesis will be that everybody who is working in the institute will also be meditating, because unless meditation goes deep in you, your love sources remain dormant. Your blissfulness, your joy remain unblossomed.

Man is not for science, science is for man.

But scientists are in a difficulty. They cannot work individually; they have to work under a government. The government's interest is war, and no religion is going to support them because their findings go on destroying religious superstitions.

There is an immense vacuum that I want to fill by creating a world academy absolutely devoted to life, love, laughter—absolutely devoted to creating a better humanity, a better and more pure, healthy atmosphere, to restoring the disturbed ecology.

We are finding sources of money to purchase the whole of Koregaon Park. And one thing is good about India: things are cheaper, and people can come from every country, be here for three or four months, and then in eight months back in their country they can earn enough and come back. There is no need for them to work here. Here is their temple of meditation. And I want all the dimensions— the best musicians to teach you music, the best artists to teach you painting, the best poets to teach you the experience of poetry and the expression of it.

I am an incurable dreamer.

But I can say to you that whatever I have dreamed in my life, I have managed it, without doing anything. Just a proposal to existence . . .

YAA-HOO! THE MYSTIC ROSE
Beginning March 19, 1988, Osho starts a series of talks that will turn out to be the last series devoted only to responses to questions. During these talks he begins to develop a "let-go" meditation, which he personally leads. He also introduces what he calls a "mantra salute"—based on a joke that he has told during one of the talks—that involves raising both arms in the air and shouting "Yaa-Hoo!"

On April 30, Osho announces that he has developed a new process that he calls a "meditative therapy." The process is refined, after the first experiments, to take place three hours a day over a period of three weeks: one week of laughter, one week of tears, and one week of silent witnessing. There is no interaction among the participants and no "therapist" but only a facilitator who has been trained in conducting the process. It is called "The Mystic Rose."

No meditation can give you so much as this small strategy. This is my experience of many meditations, that what has to be done is to break two layers in you. Your laughter has been repressed; you have been told, "Don't laugh, it is a serious matter." You are not allowed to laugh in church, or in a university class. . . .

So the first layer is of laughter, but once laughter is over you will suddenly find yourself flooded with tears, agony. But that too will be a great unburdening phenomenon. Many lives of pain and suffering will disappear. If you can get rid of these two layers you have found yourself.

I have invented many meditations, but perhaps this will be the most essential and fundamental one.

IN THE WEEKS TO COME, OSHO ADDS TWO MORE MEDITATIVE THERA-pies: "No-Mind" is a structure that involves gibberish followed by silent watching, and "Born Again" allows participants the freedom to play as if they were children. He also suggests that therapists who are skilled in guided meditations and hypnosis revive an ancient Tibetan technique of body-mind healing, which he names "Reminding Yourself of the Forgotten Language of Talking to the Body."

THE ZEN DISCOURSES

After completing the Mystic Rose series, Osho begins to speak on Zen stories and haikus. As part of the Zen talks he answers questions from his editor about the meaning of the stories or haikus and often comments on current world affairs and social concerns. But he never again answers questions about people's relationships or other personal prob-lems. He often dedicates his talks to the trees surrounding the meditation hall, to the birds, to the clouds or rains, and other elements of nature.

It is one of the most fundamental things to be remembered by all of you that a religion is living only when there is no organized doctrine, no system of beliefs, no dogma, no theology. When there is just this silence and the trees enjoying the dance in the breeze, in your heart something grows. It is your own, it does not come from any scripture; nobody can give it to you because it is not knowledge.

That is the greatest difference between all the religions on one side and Zen on the other side. All religions except Zen are dead. They have become fossilized theologies, systems of philosophies, doctrines, but they have forgotten the language of the trees. They have forgotten the silence in which even trees can be heard and understood. They have forgotten the joy that has to be natu-ral and spontaneous to the heart of every living being.

The moment the experience becomes an explanation, an expression, it breathes no more; it is dead—and all over the world people are carrying dead doctrines.

I call Zen the only living religion because it is not a religion but only a religiousness. It has no dogma, it does not depend on any founder. It has no past; in fact it has nothing to teach you. It is the strangest thing that has happened in the whole history of mankind—strangest because it enjoys in emptiness, it blossoms in nothingness. It is fulfilled in innocence, in not knowing. It does not discriminate between the mundane and the sacred. For Zen, all that is, is sacred.

THE GUIDED MEDITATIONS AT THE END OF THE ZEN TALKS GROW longer, and Osho adds a stage of gibberish. This is followed by silent sitting, a "let-go" (relaxing the body and falling to the floor), coming back to a sitting position for more silence, and finally celebration as Osho leaves the hall. Osho guides the assembly through the silent stages, and each stage is announced by a drumbeat.

Be silent. Close your eyes, feel your body to be completely frozen.

Now look inward, gathering all your consciousness—almost like an arrow, forcing toward the center.

At the center you are the buddha. On the circumference you may be anybody, Tom, Dick, Harry; on the circumference you are all different, but at the center your essential nature is that of a buddha, the man of Tao.

Deeper and deeper—because the deeper you go, the more will be your experience of your eternal reality. Flowers will start showering on you, the whole existence will rejoice your silence.

Just be a witness, from the center, and you have arrived home.

To make it clear . . .

(Drumbeat)

Relax. Just remember that you are only a witness. The body is not you, the mind is not you. You are just a mirror. And as you settle down into a mirrorlike witnessing, the whole existence takes on a tremendously beautiful form. Everything becomes divine.

This evening was beautiful on its own, but Joshu's lion's roar has made it tremendously beautiful.

This very moment you are a buddha.

When you come back, bring the buddha with you. You have to live out the buddha in your day-to-day life. I am against renouncing the world—I am for re-creating the world. The more buddhas there are, the world will have new skies, new dimensions, new doors opening . . . new mysteries, new miracles.

Collect as much fragrance and flowers as you can.

(Drumbeat)

Come back, but come back as a buddha—peacefully, gracefully. Sit for a few moments just to recollect your experience of the space that you have visited and the splendor that you have experienced.

Every day you have to go deeper and deeper. So always remember how far you have gone: Tomorrow you have to go a little more. It may take two, or five, or twenty, or thirty years—but you are to become a buddha. As far as I am concerned you are right now a buddha, you have only to gain courage. In those thirty years you will not be changing into a buddha—you are a buddha already. Those thirty years are just to drop the doubt, the doubt that you—how can you be a buddha? Even if I say it, even if all the buddhas try to convince you, deep down is the doubt: "My god, me? And a buddha?" But one day you will become convinced by your own experience. There is no real conversion without your own experience.

THE END OF "BHAGWAN"

In December 1988, Osho is again gravely ill, requiring the attendance of his personal physician twenty-four hours a day. When he returns to the meditation hall after a three-week absence, he makes a startling announcement. A Japanese seeress has sent a message that she believes Gautam Buddha is using Osho as a vehicle. He confirms that this is true and announces that he is dropping the name Bhagwan. *He also removes the sunglasses that he has been wearing for several months because the video lights had disturbed his eyes and gives them to one of his disciples. His new name goes through several variations over the next few days, and one comes about in response to a question from a UPI reporter:*

Gautam the Buddha has taken shelter in me. I am the host, he is the guest. There is no question of any conversion [to Buddhism]. I am a buddha in my own right, and that is the reason he has felt to use my vehicle for his remaining work. He has been waiting, a wandering cloud for twenty-five centuries, for a right vehicle.

I am not a Buddhist. Neither is Gautam the Buddha's intention to create

Buddhists, or to create an organized religion. Even twenty-five centuries before, he never created an organized religion. The moment truth is organized it becomes a lie. An organized religion is nothing but a hidden politics, a deep exploitation by the priesthood. They may be *shankaracharyas,* imams, rabbis, or popes—it makes no difference.

Gautam Buddha did not leave behind him any successor. His last words were, "Don't make my statues, don't collect my words. I don't want to become a symbol that has to be worshiped. My deepest longing is that you will not be imitators. You don't have to be Buddhists because your own potential is to be a buddha."

I would like to say: I don't teach Buddhism, or any 'ism,' for that matter. I teach the buddha himself. The people who are with me are not part of any organized religion. They are independent, individual seekers. My relationship with them is that of a fellow traveler.

By the way, I have to remind you of Gautam Buddha's prophecy twenty-five centuries ago: "When I come again I will not be able to be born through a woman's womb. I will have to take shelter in a man of similar consciousness and the same height and the same open sky. I will be called 'The Friend.' "

A tremendous freedom is implied in the word. He does not want to be anybody's guru, he simply wants to be a friend. He has something to share, with no conditions attached to the sharing.

This also will help you, because a few sannyasins have been confused how they will make the difference between the ancient Gautam Buddha and me. Gautam Buddha's prophecy helps to clarify the confusion.

Although he has taken shelter in me, I will not be called Gautam the Buddha. I will love to be called according to his prophecy: Maitreya the Buddha. *Maitreya* means "the friend." That will keep the distinction. There will not be any confusion.

ON THE FIFTH NIGHT OF THE UNUSUAL VISIT, OSHO COMES TO THE meditation hall with another announcement. Gautam Buddha has left, because of certain incompatibilities in the respective lifestyles of guest and host.

These four days have been of immense difficulty to me. I had thought that Gautam Buddha would be understanding of the change of times, but it was impossible. I tried my hardest, but he is so much disciplined in his own way—twenty-five centuries back—he has become a hard bone.

Small things became difficult.

He used to sleep only on the right side. He did not use a pillow; he used his hand as a pillow. The pillow was, for him, a luxury.

I told him, "The poor pillow is not a luxury, and it is sheer torture to keep your hand the whole night under your head. And do you think to lie down on the right side is right, and the left is wrong? As far as I am concerned, this is my basic fundamental, that I synthesize both the sides."

He was eating only one time per day, and he wanted, without saying a word, that I should do it also. He used to beg his food. He asked me, "Where is my begging bowl?"

This evening exactly at six o'clock when I was taking my Jacuzzi, he became very much disturbed—"Jacuzzi?" Taking a bath twice a day was again a luxury.

I said, "You have fulfilled your prophecy that you will be coming back. Four days are enough—I say good-bye to you! And now you need not wander around the earth; you just disappear in the ultimate blue sky.

"You have seen for four days that I am doing the work that you wanted to do, and I am doing it according to the times and the needs. I am not in any way ready to be dictated to. I am a free individual. Out of my freedom and love I have received you as a guest, but don't try to become a host."

These four days I have had a headache. I had not known it for thirty years, I had completely forgotten what it means to have a headache. Everything was impossible. He is so accustomed to his way, and that way is no longer relevant.

So now I make a far greater historical statement, that I am just myself.

You can continue to call me the buddha, but it has nothing to do with Gautam the Buddha or Maitreya the Buddha. I am a buddha in my own right. The word *buddha* simply means "the awakened one." Now I declare that my name should be Shree Rajneesh Zorba the Buddha.

SHREE RAJNEESH ZORBA THE BUDDHA SOON DROPS ALL HIS NAMES *and says that he will simply remain nameless. His sannyasins, however, are at a loss without a name to use in addressing him and suggest "Osho," which has appeared often in the Zen stories as a term of respect and honor. Osho agrees and adds his own meaning to the word, relating it to William James's term* oceanic. *Later he says it is not his name at all but just a healing sound.*

THE ZEN MANIFESTO: FREEDOM FROM ONESELF

In the weeks following the "visitation" by Gautam Buddha, Osho seems to tap into new reservoirs of strength and energy. His talks grow longer—on a couple of occasions he speaks for nearly four hours without a break—and his speaking is noticeably more fiery and energetic. In different series of talks, he relates Zen to the work of Friedrich Nietzsche and Walt Whitman, compares it with Christianity, and recommends it to Gorbachev as a path to ease the transition from communism to capitalism. But in February 1989, two days into a new series of talks entitled "The Zen Manifesto," Osho is taken ill again and does not appear in the meditation hall until the beginning of April. "The Zen Manifesto" will prove to be his last series of talks.

The Zen manifesto is absolutely needed, because all old religions are falling apart. And before they fall apart and humanity goes completely bananas, Zen has to be spread wide around the whole earth. Before the old house falls down, you have to create a new house.

And this time don't commit the same mistake. You have been living in a house that was not there; hence you were suffering rain, winter, sun, because the house was only an imagination. This time really enter into your original home, not into any man-made temple, any man-made religion. Enter into your own existence. Why be continuously a carbon copy?

This time is very valuable. You are born in a very fortunate moment, when the old has lost its validity, its proof, when the old is simply hanging around you because you are not courageous enough to get out of the prison. Otherwise the doors are open—in fact, there have never been any doors, because the house you are living in is completely imaginary. Your gods are imaginary, your priests are imaginary, your holy scriptures are imaginary.

This time don't commit the same mistake. This time humanity has to take a quantum leap from the old rotten lies to the fresh, eternally fresh truth.

This is the manifesto of Zen.

OSHO'S LAST WORDS SPOKEN IN PUBLIC ARE AT THE END OF THE meditation for the evening of April 10, 1989:

This moment you are the most blessed people on the earth. Remembering yourself as a buddha is the most precious experience, because it is your eternity, it is your immortality.

It is not you, it is your very existence. You are one with the stars and the trees and the sky and the ocean. You are no longer separate.

The last word of Buddha was *sammasati*.

Remember that you are a buddha—*sammasati*.

THE INNER CIRCLE

On April 6, Osho sets up what he calls an "Inner Circle" of twenty-one disciples who will take care of the practical administration of the commune. He does not discuss it in public, but later he makes it clear in guidelines to the group that their purpose is not to provide spiritual direction but to take care of the practical aspects of making his work available. Members of the Inner Circle who die or for some other reason decide to leave will be replaced by unanimous decision of the remaining members, and all decisions reached by the group will be through consensus.

You cannot avoid a tradition; it is beyond your hands. Once you are dead, what people will be doing you cannot prevent. Rather than leaving it in the hands of the ignorant, it is better you should give the right guidelines.

PREPARING FOR DEPARTURE

APRIL 10, 1989: *Osho tells his secretary that as he finished the discourse, his energy completely changed. He explains that in the same way one enters the world through nine months in the womb, nine months before dying the energy again enters an incubatory period for death. This evening's discourse was to have been the beginning of a new series titled "Awakening of the Buddha."*

MAY 19: *In a general meeting in the meditation hall, it is announced that Osho will not speak publicly again.*

MAY 23: *It is announced that Osho will come to the meditation hall in the evenings. When he arrives, music will be playing so that everyone can celebrate with him, and this will be followed by a period of silent meditation, after which Osho will leave. A video of one of his talks will be shown after he has left the hall.*

JUNE–JULY: *Osho Multiversity is formed, with different "faculties" to look after the various workshops and programs offered by the commune. These include the Center for Transformation, Mystery School, School of Creative Arts, and School of Martial Arts.*

People are asked to wear white robes for the evening meetings, and this change is instituted during a traditional Indian festival honoring enlightened masters during the full moon of July, which has long been celebrated by the commune.

AUGUST 25: *Osho suggests that arrangements be made so maroon robes are worn during all daytime activities within the commune.*

AUGUST 31: *A new bedroom for Osho is completed in the former Chuang Tzu Auditorium adjoining his residence. He has been directly involved in the design of the new room, which is lined with marble and lit by a large chandelier, with floor-to-ceiling windows overlooking the surrounding jungle garden.*

SEPTEMBER 14: *Osho moves back to his former bedroom, and the new room is used for Mystic Rose and No-Mind meditative therapies. A new enclosed and air-conditioned glass walkway, which has been built for Osho to take walks in the garden, will be used for vipassana, zazen, and other silent meditation groups.*

NOVEMBER 17: *Osho gives instructions about what should happen when he leaves his body. He also asks for a group to be formed to translate his Hindi books into English and gives further instructions on how the Inner Circle will function.*

DECEMBER 24: *The* Sunday Mail, *UK, prints an article about the Vatican being partly responsible for Osho's expulsion from the United States.*

JANUARY 17, 1990: *Osho's physician announces that he will not be able to sit in the meditation hall during the evening meditation from now on but will appear briefly to greet the assembly and leave immediately afterward. When Osho appears in the hall, it is obvious that he is very fragile and unsteady on his feet.*

JANUARY 18: *Osho remains in his room during the evening meeting but sends a message that his presence will be felt as if he were there.*

JANUARY 19, 1990: *Osho leaves his body at five P.M., refusing extraordinary treatment suggested by his doctor with the the words "existence decides its timing" and peacefully closing his eyes and slipping away. His doctor makes the announcement at seven P.M., when people have gathered in the meditation hall for the usual evening meeting. After a brief inter-*

val to allow friends to inform those who might not be present in the hall but want to come, Osho's body is brought into the hall for a ten-minute celebration, then carried in procession to the nearby burning ghats where his send-off celebration continues throughout the night.

Two days later, Osho's ashes are brought to Chuang Tzu Auditorium—the room that had been renovated as a new "bedroom"—where he had given talks and met with sannyasins and seekers for many years. The ashes are placed, according to Osho's instructions, "under the bed"—a marble slab at the center of one end of the room that had indeed been designed as a bed platform—and covered by a plaque on which are inscribed the words he had dictated some months before:

OSHO
NEVER BORN
NEVER DIED
ONLY VISITED THIS PLANET EARTH BETWEEN
1931–1990

EPILOGUE: 1990-PRESENT

Osho Commune International in Pune continues to thrive and has expanded into a luxury resort for meditation and self-discovery according to the vision Osho laid out in the months before his death. He was personally involved in much of the design of the expanded facilities—including pyramid-shaped buildings for meditations and workshops, a spa, recreation and sports complex, and a new pyramid-shaped meditation hall that is scheduled to be completed by January 2001.

My trust in existence is absolute. If there is any truth in what I am saying, it will survive. The people who remain interested in my work will be simply carrying the torch but not imposing anything on anyone.

I will remain a source of inspiration to my people. And that's what most sannyasins will feel. I want them to grow on their own—qualities like love, around which no church can be created, like awareness, which is nobody's monopoly; like celebration, rejoicing, and maintaining fresh, childlike eyes . . .

I want my people to know themselves, not to be according to someone else.

And the way is in.

REFERENCES

⁓

PREFACE

The Rebel, #27

PART ONE
JUST AN ORDINARY HUMAN BEING:
THE HISTORY BEHIND THE LEGEND

The Last Testament (press interviews), Vol. 1, #14

GLIMPSES OF A GOLDEN CHILDHOOD
I have never been spiritual . . . *Transmission of the Lamp* (talks in Uruguay), #10
I am reminded of . . . *Glimpses of a Golden Childhood,* #1
In the past there were . . . *Sat Chit Anand,* #15
I was brought up by . . . *From Darkness to Light* (talks in America), #2
My grandfather . . . *Glimpses of a Golden Childhood,* #2
I can understand . . . *Glimpses of a Golden Childhood,* #5
Jainism is the most . . . *Glimpses of a Golden Childhood,* #7
I don't remember . . . *Glimpses of a Golden Childhood,* #8
Nana was not . . . *From Personality to Individuality* (talks in America), #27
Separation has its own . . . *Glimpses of a Golden Childhood,* #6

THE REBELLIOUS SPIRIT
As far back as . . . *The Last Testament,* Vol. 1, #13

My grandfather's death . . . *Glimpses of a Golden Childhood*, #13

That was my first . . . *Glimpses of a Golden Childhood*, #12

The first seven years . . . *From Misery to Enlightenment* (talks in America), #1

I said to my father . . . *Glimpses of a Golden Childhood*, #20

The first thing . . . *The Dhammapada: The Way of the Buddha*, Vol. 5, #3

In my town . . . *From Misery to Enlightenment*, #15

In my village . . . *The Sword and the Lotus*, #4

My father's father . . . *From Ignorance to Innocence* (talks in America), #13

My grandfather was not . . . *From Ignorance to Innocence*, #16

When I passed . . . *From Death to Deathlessness* (talks in America), #27

IN SEARCH OF THE DEATHLESS

You know that . . . *The Last Testament* (press interviews), Vol. 3, #12

In the East we have been watching . . . *Nirvana: The Last Nightmare*, #9

It was one of my pastimes . . . *From Personality to Individuality*, #12

My mother's father . . . *The Book of Secrets*, #24

ENLIGHTENMENT: A DISCONTINUITY WITH THE PAST

There is a beautiful . . . *Tao: The Pathless Path*, Vol. 2, #9

I was from my very childhood . . . *The Great Zen Master Ta Hui*, #28

My first experience out of the body . . . *The Miracle*, #3

I have been looking for the door . . . *The Last Testament*, Vol. 1, #20

I was taken to a Vaidya . . . *Tao: The Three Treasures* Vol. 2, #9

When you first enter . . . *Tao: The Pathless Path*, Vol. 2, #9

You ask me: What happened . . . *Theologia Mystica*, #9

For many lives I had been working . . . *The Discipline of Transcendence*, Vol. 2, #11

Enlightenment is a very individual . . . *The Last Testament*, Vol. 3, #29

SHARPENING THE SWORD

From my very childhood . . . *The Rebel*, #2

The scholars are so clever . . . *Tao: The Golden Gate*, #6

After receiving my B.A . . . *From Darkness to Light*, #6

The first day I joined his class . . . *From Unconsciousness to Consciousness* (talks in America), #3

I used to walk in an Indian sandal . . . *From Ignorance to Innocence*, #21

When on the first day I entered . . . *From Misery to Enlightenment*, #1

I am reminded of . . . *From Bondage to Freedom* (talks in America), #38

I enjoyed my student life immensely . . . *Transmission of the Lamp*, #7

In India, Muhammadans have a certain dress . . . *From Misery to Enlightenment*, #26

When I became a teacher . . . *The Last Testament*, Vol. 2, #8

I was called to a seminar . . . *The Search*, #2

ON THE ROAD

Just think of me . . . *From the False to the Truth* (talks in America), #24

The situation of the world has changed . . . *Transmission of the Lamp*, #37

The awakened man . . . *The Dhammapada: The Way of the Buddha*, Vol. 11, #9

I would have loved . . . *From Personality to Individuality*, #14

It happened once that I was speaking . . . *Socrates Poisoned Again After 25 Centuries* (talks in Greece), #27

If I see people silently sitting . . . *The Book of Wisdom*, #6

EXPRESSING THE INEXPRESSIBLE:
THE SILENCES BETWEEN WORDS

For thirty-five years I have been . . . *From Ignorance to Innocence*, #23

You don't know about thousands of . . . *The Path of the Mystic* (talks in Uruguay), #14

The question arises for almost everyone . . . *The Invitation*, #14

PART TWO
REFLECTIONS IN AN EMPTY MIRROR:
THE MANY FACES OF A MAN WHO NEVER WAS

Come Follow to Yourself, Vol. 2, #4

SEX GURU

It has been written, and people . . . *The Last Testament*, Vol. 1, #1

I have written one book . . . *The Secret of Secrets*, Vol. 2, #10

Sexual orgasm, according to me . . . *I Celebrate Myself: God is Nowhere, Life is Now Here*, #1

I have been telling you it is possible . . . *Walking in Zen, Sitting in Zen*, #4

I have never taught "free sex" . . . *The Last Testament*, Vol. 4, #14

CULT LEADER

What has grown around you . . . *The Last Testament*, Vol. 4, #3
You are certainly brainwashed . . . *The Osho Upanishad*, #23
My effort is to take away . . . *The Last Testament*, Vol. 6, #14

CON MAN

I have to work on two levels . . . *Beyond Enlightenment*, #6
I am reminded of a story . . . *The Razor's Edge*, #15

"SELF-APPOINTED" *BHAGWAN*

The critics who have been . . . *Light on the Path* (talks in the Himalayas), #4
I am very strange in a way . . . *From Unconsciousness to Consciousness*, #3
"Bhagwan" is a noncomparative term . . . *The Discipline of Transcendence*, Vol. 2, #4
By the way, I have been calling myself . . . *No-Mind: The Flowers of Eternity*, #1

THE RICH MAN'S GURU

I always spend before I get . . . *The Last Testament*, Vol. 3, #25
You ask, "Are you not a . . ." *The Discipline of Transcendence*, Vol. 3, #10

THE JOKER

Who is the better showman . . . *The Last Testament*, Vol. 1, #3
In one press conference, you . . . *The Last Testament*, Vol. 1. #17
I have to tell jokes because . . . *A Sudden Clash of Thunder*, #9
And I have to tell jokes because . . . *The Discipline of Transcendence*, Vol. 3, #2

THE ROLLS-ROYCE GURU

I would like the whole world to live . . . *The Last Testament*, Vol. 2, #3
Just a few days ago I told my secretary . . . *The Secret of Secrets*, Vol. 2, #4
The Americans think they are . . . *Om Mani Padme Hum*, #18
People are sad, jealous . . . *Socrates Poisoned Again After 25 Centuries*, #15

THE MASTER

One beautiful morning . . . *The Last Testament*, Vol. 3, #23
Masters do not tell the truth . . . *Ah, This!*, #1
The Master is a physician . . . *The Osho Upanishad*, #2

The wise man wants you only . . . *The Dhammapada: The Way of the Buddha,* Vol. 5, #7

From your very childhood you have . . . *The Last Testament,* Vol. 1, #6

The sannyas movement is not mine . . . *The Last Testament,* Vol. 6, #14

PART THREE
THE LEGACY

I may be gone, but . . . *The Shadow of the Whip* (unpublished darshan diary), #18

RELIGIONLESS RELIGION
I have been constantly inconsistent . . . *From Personality to Individuality,* #8

Christianity, Hinduism . . . *Going All the Way* (unpublished darshan diary), #22

Science is the search for truth . . . *The Last Testament,* Vol. 5, #4

The credit of bringing a quantum leap . . . *The Last Testament,* Vol. 5, #16

MEDITATION FOR THE TWENTY-FIRST CENTURY
I was working for ten years . . . *The Ultimate Alchemy,* Vol. 1, #7

One of my colleagues . . . *The Path of the Mystic,* #15

You cannot do meditation, you can only . . . *The White Lotus,* #3

It happens many times: an atheist comes . . . *The Guest,* #5

There are one hundred and twelve methods . . . *From Bondage to Freedom* #26

For sixty minutes every day . . . *Take It Easy,* Vol. 1, #11

The morning meditation is . . . unpublished translation from the Hindi

My understanding is that sooner or later . . . *In Search of the Miraculous,* Vol. 1, #11

When a person meditates . . . *The Discipline of Transcendence,* Vol. 2, #5

Meditation is not . . . *Yoga: The Alpha and the Omega,* Vol. 3, #4

THE THIRD PSYCHOLOGY:
THE PSYCHOLOGY OF THE BUDDHAS
In the commune I had . . . *The Rebellious Spirit,* #6

Sigmund Freud introduced . . . *The Dhammapada: The Way of the Buddha,* Vol. 10, #4

There are two types of growth methods . . . *My Way: The Way of the White Clouds,* #14

The ancient methods of meditation . . . *Light on the Path,* #15

ZORBA THE BUDDHA: THE WHOLE HUMAN BEING

Take life very playfully . . . *The Dhammapada: The Way of the Buddha*, Vol. 2, #2

A lawyer made his way . . . *The Secret*, #8

These are polarities in life . . . *The Imprisoned Splendor* (unpublished darshan diary), #23

My message is simple . . . *Zorba the Buddha* (unpublished darshan diary), #8

APPENDIX
HIGHLIGHTS OF OSHO'S LIFE AND WORK

I am the center of the cyclone . . . *The Last Testament*, Vol. 4, #23

1957–1970: PROFESSOR AND PUBLIC SPEAKER

With the help of meditation temples . . . unpublished translation from the Hindi

I used to talk to crowds . . . *Hyakujo: The Everest of Zen*, #8

The first maxim is . . . *The Perfect Way*, #1

If you want to know . . . *From Sex to Superconsciousness*, #1

When I ended my talk . . . *From Sex to Superconsciousness*, #5

1970–1974: BOMBAY

I will slowly confine myself to a room . . . *Dimensions Beyond the Known*, #4

A friend has asked . . . *In Search of the Miraculous*, Vol. 1, #9

I am going to separate the . . . *Krishna: The Man and His Philosophy*, #22

The ancient meaning of sannyas . . . *The Last Testament*, Vol. 4, #17

The path of the masculine . . . *The Divine Melody*, #6

Slowly, slowly I started . . . *From Misery to Enlightenment*, #21

Man's mind is a very immature mind . . . *The Last Testament*, Vol. 6, #13

The day I started initiating people . . . *Glimpses of a Golden Childhood*, #23

I am more emphatically interested in . . . *That Art Thou*, #17

Many people have asked me . . . *The Dhammapada: The Way of the Buddha*, Vol. 11, #2

Your mind is in chaos . . . *The Book of Secrets*, #28

1974–1981: "PUNE ONE"

It is very deliberately . . . *Above All, Don't Wobble* (unpublished darshan diary), #4

References

A white cloud drifts . . . *My Way: The Way of the White Clouds,* #1

This camp is going to be . . . *A Bird on the Wing,* #1

You have to search . . . *Take it Easy,* Vol. 2, #8

I am proclaiming . . . *Sufis: The People of the Path,* Vol. 1, #10

One has to learn . . . *A Rose is a Rose is Rose,* #26

When I say don't be a missionary . . . *Believing the Impossible Before Breakfast,* #21

The growth group is needed because . . . *Tao: The Three Treasures,* Vol. 2, #14

My therapists are the best . . . *Light on the Path,* #16

In this commune, I have . . . *Philosophia Perennis* (talks on Pythagoras), Vol. 1, #10

In Pune there were a few groups . . . *The Last Testament,* Vol. 4, #21

Remember, these groups are . . . *The Dhammapada: The Way of the Buddha,* Vol. 1, #5

This place is a marketplace . . . *The Secret of Secrets,* Vol. 1, #4

I cannot be supported by the . . . *Unio Mystica,* Vol. 2, #2

What is wrong in hugging a person . . . *The Secret,* #16

Gurdjieff lived a life . . . *The Dhammapada: The Way of the Buddha,* Vol. 2, #2

Words are becoming more and more difficult . . . *The Dhammapada: The Way of the Buddha,* Vol. 1, #1

The Pune magistrate has given . . . *I Am That,* #8

My effort is not only to create a buddhafield . . . *The Wild Geese and the Water,* #1

1981–1985: THE BIG MUDDY RANCH

Buddha committed mistakes . . . *From Personality to Individuality,* #24

They want this city to be demolished . . . *From Unconsciousness to Consciousness,* #7

Your city is really unique . . . *From Personality to Individuality,* #16

Just the other day some information came . . . *From Personality to Individuality,* #28

Perhaps this is the only place . . . *From Bondage to Freedom,* #16

In my meeting Sheela . . . *The Last Testament,* Vol. 3, #16

We are trying to live a different . . . *From Bondage to Freedom,* #4

When they deported me . . . *Communism and Zen Fire, Zen Wind,* #1

1985–1986: THE "WORLD TOUR"

The king of Nepal was ready . . . *Socrates Poisoned Again After 25 Centuries*, #5

I am going on a world tour . . . *Light on the Path*, #20

From Greece we moved to Geneva . . . *Beyond Psychology* (talks in Uruguay), #6

In Ireland, we simply wanted . . . *The Path of the Mystic*, #39

You will be surprised . . . *The Path of the Mystic*, #6

My new phase of work is a . . . *Beyond Psychology*, #38

The president of Uruguay said . . . *The Rebellious Spirit*, #25

1987: "PUNE TWO"

Just yesterday I received . . . *The Messiah* (on Kahlil Gibran), Vol. 1, #17

I am trying to get you to . . . *The Razor's Edge*, #1

I cannot always be with you . . . *The Great Pilgrimage: From Here to Here*, #26

My own approach to your growth . . . *Beyond Enlightenment*, #11

My personal physician, Dr. Amrito . . . *Jesus Crucified Again, This Time in Ronald Reagan's America*, #1

I want this ashram slowly to develop . . . *Om Mani Padme Hum*, #30

No meditation can give you so much . . . *Yaa-Hoo! The Mystic Rose*, #30

It is one of the most fundamental . . . *Live Zen*, #1

Be silent. Close your eyes . . . *Joshu: The Lion's Roar*, #4

Gautam the Buddha has taken shelter . . . *No-Mind: The Flowers of Eternity*, #3

These four days have been . . . *No-Mind: The Flowers of Eternity*, #5

The Zen Manifesto is absolutely needed . . . *The Zen Manifesto: Freedom from Oneself*, #1

This moment you are the most blessed . . . *The Zen Manifesto: Freedom from Oneself*, #11

You cannot avoid a tradition . . . *Hari Om Tat Sat*, #30

EPILOGUE: 1990–PRESENT

Dictated response to a question submitted by an Italian journalist, November 1989

FURTHER READING

Anumber of books of interest to those who want to know more about specific events mentioned in this autobiography have been published by Rebel Publishing, India. These include accounts written by eyewitnesses to events in Rajneeshpuram and during Osho's "world tour," and a detailed presentation of the evidence that led doctors to believe that Osho might have been poisoned while in custody of the U.S. government.

A Passage to America, by investigative journalist Max Brecher (published by Book Quest in India), outlines the events leading up to Osho's arrest in Charlotte, North Carolina, and his subsequent incarceration. It includes a number of fascinating and revealing interviews with government and law enforcement officials at all levels, who were involved in the affair.

"Glimpses of a Golden Childhood" is Osho's own dictation of significant events and escapades in his childhood and student days, and contains far more detail about his early years than has been possible to include in this autobiography.

Excerpts from these works and ordering information, where applicable, can be found on the World Wide Web at www.osho.com/autobio.

MEDITATION RESORT

Osho Commune International

Osho Commune International, the meditation resort that Osho established in India as an oasis where his teachings could be put into practice, continues to attract thousands of visitors per year from more than one hundred different countries around the world. Located about one hundred miles southeast of Bombay in Pune, India, the facilities cover thirty-two acres in a tree-lined suburb known as Koregaon Park. Although the resort itself does not provide accommodation for guests, there is a plentiful variety of nearby hotels.

The resort meditation programs are based in Osho's vision of a qualitatively new kind of human being who is able both to participate joyously in everyday life and to relax into silence. Most programs take place in modern, air-conditioned facilities and include everything from short to extended meditation courses, creative arts, holistic health treatments, personal growth, and the "Zen" approach to sports and recreation. Programs are offered throughout the year, alongside a full daily schedule of Osho's active meditations.

Outdoor cafes and restaurants within the resort grounds serve both traditional Indian fare and a variety of international dishes, all made with organically grown vegetables from the commune's own farm. The campus has its own private supply of safe, filtered water.

For booking information call (323) 563-6075 in the USA or check osho.com for the Pune Information Center nearest you.

For more information: www.osho.com

A comprehensive Web site in different languages, featuring an online tour of the meditation resort, information about books and tapes, Osho information centers worldwide, and selections from Osho's talks.

Osho International
570 Lexington Avenue
New York, NY 10022
Telephone: (212) 588-9888
Fax: (212) 588-1977
email: osho-int@osho.com

INDEX

From Rebecca Mercuri
14 June 2012